# How to Run
# a Catering Business
# from Home

# HOW TO RUN
# A CATERING BUSINESS
# FROM HOME

## Christopher Egerton-Thomas

**John Wiley & Sons, Inc.**

New York   Chichester   Brisbane   Toronto   Singapore   Weinheim

Copyright © 1996 by John Wiley & Sons, Inc.

**Library of Congress Cataloging in Publication Data:**

Egerton-Thomas, Christopher.
   How to run a catering business from home / Christopher Egerton-Thomas.
      p.      cm.
   Includes bibliographical references.
   ISBN 0–471–14106–2 (paper : alk. paper)
      1. Caterers and catering.    I. Title.
TX921.E34    1996
642'.4—dc20                                              96–18264

Printed in the United States of America

10 9 8 7 6 5 4 3 2 1

*To super editor Claire Thompson,*
*with thanks*

# CONTENTS

# Preface

The dream of gainful self-employment is a common one. Running a catering business from home is one of the most realistic and easy ways of making that dream come true. For some, the idea of escape into self-employment is an elusive ambition. But for an increasing number of people, self-employment is the only option.

A new monster has loomed in American life. "*Unemployment*" was an academic word for about three generations of Americans. For decades, if you wanted a job in America, you simply went out and got one.

It might not be the exact job you wanted. You might have to settle for something less congenial for a time, at least until you made your required connection, but the prospect of not getting a job was something safely consigned to history.

Suddenly things changed. Job-destroying technology went on the rampage. An increasing number of people are going to have to earn their living in new and different ways, without resorting to the job market. Many of us are going to have to wear more than one hat.

Catering is so elegant a business that it ought to be the envy of the corporate world—perhaps it is. One person, working from home, can operate a well-paid business that has no serious overhead, apart from some small telephone, transportation, and stationery bills.

The answering machine is your secretary. You don't require storage space, plant, vehicles, or investment. A caterer only incurs expense when assured of income. And you only have a payroll to attend to when money is coming in because you only employ people for a specific project. There is nothing to be stored for more than a day or so and nothing to deteriorate or spoil.

The joy of catering is shared by its consumers. Your clients only employ you when they need you. Thus, you are welcomed, not resented. The constant changing of place and circumstance can be stimulating and the operations so swiftly accomplished that there is no time for so-called political situations or personality clashes to build. The working atmosphere is generally cheerful because the emphasis is on hospitality, and as a rule people do not attend functions or offer entertainment with long faces.

The required skills are little more than those required for running an ordinary home and family. A small amount of restaurant experience or work for other caterers, plus the commonsense approach of putting oneself in the clients' place and imagining what is wanted, will qualify almost anyone for the business.

And let us not forget that "from tiny acorns, mighty oaks do grow." Many a caterer, who perhaps started out baking "cheese straws" and distributing them to local bars as appetizers, has expanded to big-company size. Of course, at that point you may forego some of the delights of self-employment. But running a successful company as a full-time job is usually acceptable. After all, it's your very own baby.

You will not need to spend much time exploring your town or neighborhood before being able to assess the potential. If only all businesses were so simple, the world would be a happier place.

The advantages of running a catering business from home can be summarized as follows:

- No permanent business premises are required.
- No cash investment is required.
- The overhead is tiny—almost negligible.
- There is no payroll to meet between jobs.
- No job is too small or too big—you can expand easily.
- Personnel and equipment can be hired as required.
- If you're organized the work is simple and unstressful.
- You only work when you want to work.
- Every job you do is live advertising for your service.
- Payment is usually immediate.
- Emergencies are rare. You can plan well ahead.
- You're the boss.

# How to Run
# a Catering Business
# from Home

# Chapter One

# Who Employs Caterers, and What Do They Want?

CATERING must surely be one of the oldest professions. As soon as civilization developed to the point where people started gathering and entertaining each other, the requirement for catering services was born.

In early days, villagers would be recruited to help at the manor house or castle when guests were to be fed and watered. Nowadays a "catered affair" might be as small as a hostess hiring a bartender for the evening to handle a cocktail party or as big as the late Shah of Iran's celebration, which involved building a temporary small city with an airstrip and yacht marina. Every stage between is covered, from dinners for a thousand or more to weddings, christenings, wakes, reunions, awards functions, dances, and birthday and anniversary celebrations.

There are, of course, alternatives to employing caterers. If you want to give a party, why not simply take over a restaurant or hotel ballroom for the occasion? Many corporations, charities, and people involved in commercial, as opposed to personal and social, hospitality, do exactly that. There's nothing wrong with it. It can be efficiently done, but it is usually prohibitively expensive to the private host or hostess, and—let's call a spade a spade—it can be just a little bit plastic and impersonal.

For a commercial organization, the critical factor is the size of the event. An informal drinks-and-buffet event can be held on company premises, and it is often easier and less expensive to bring in caterers to take care of it. The fact that most of the guests are conveniently on site is an advantage here. The problem of getting the guests to the party is eliminated.

When a large number of people are to be entertained, or a lavish degree of entertainment and hospitality is envisaged, some companies will hold their events in hotels or restaurants. However, there are still opportunities for caterers—even single freelancers operating from home—to pick up business here.

## Advantages of the Small Private Caterer

In these cost-cutting times, the economies offered by a small private caterer can be attractive to the business community. While executives twist and turn to save money and stay within budget, they still need to maintain morale in a workforce where almost everyone is doing the work of one and a half, if not three, people. To promote the image of "one big happy family," companies often hold functions such as open houses and picnics provided someone can put them on at an acceptable price. Because of their huge overheads and the certainty that a big company can afford it, most hotels and restaurants tend to charge high rates. Of course, some of the expenses incurred in such entertaining may be tax deductible.

However, unlike some businesses, for example, the finely tuned Travel Industry, the caterer need not be obsessed by the need to attract corporate customers. There are charities, there are clubs, and there are private individuals who can use the caterer's services. We will explore this further in the discussion on location and elsewhere.

As a caterer, you should not mind much whether the affairs you handle are for private or commercial purposes. You should bring the same warmth and efficiency to all your events.

As in all businesses, continuity is of the essence. Whenever you do a party, no matter how big or small, you should approach it determined that your clients will call you in the future whenever they need a caterer. This is how you build regular business. Once customer confidence is established, you need not fear that you will lose business to people who charge less.

When you decide to start a catering business from home, some of the most likely people to hire you will be small businesses—a new store opening or celebrating the arrival of a new range of goods—and ordinary (but reasonably affluent) people entertaining at home.

## Why People Hire Caterers

People hire caterers for one main reason. They want to devote all their time to their guests and not be hampered by the need to ensure that everyone has a drink and a bite to eat, has been shown the cloakroom, and so on. It is (or should be) altogether more convenient—and good value for money—when a caterer (solo or with a crew) arrives, performs, cleans up, and departs leaving one's house, office, or store in pristine condition. Some caterers manage to leave places cleaner than they were when they arrived.

Of course, some people actually prefer to do all the donkey work at their own parties. Apart from the obvious economy, it eliminates the need for conversation or relating on any deep level with one's guests. Some people are much happier discussing the assembly of the barbecue grill and the ideal fuel than talking about business or life. It depends on the purpose of the event.

If the event is simply a gathering of family, friends, and neighbors, with no grand objectives or results required or anticipated, then the guests pitching in and helping each other to more white wine and slices of cheese becomes part of the fun—part of the essential theater of the occasion. There's no need for a caterer.

But if the purpose of the event is to extend social acquaintance and introduce people with things in common, or to do some romantic matchmaking or business and professional networking, then the advantage of employing caterers is overwhelmingly obvious. When a temporary catering staff is employed, critical discussions about the deals or connections one might make need not be interrupted for more than a second by trivial diversions such as "Have you got a drink?" or "Do try the smoked salmon."

## Getting Business

No businessperson can afford to dismiss any area of potential revenue. Any time you hear of someone who may be considering having a party or gathering of any kind, you should politely offer your services. The best way is to drop in briefly and leave your card. This way they see you, you can describe your available service, and they'll put you on file. Nothing works better than a personal approach.

Personal letters can be effective, as can be simple advertising. You can make a friendly call to a company—or a hundred companies—gently inquiring who would be the right person to approach on the subject of functions and entertainment. If the reply is "We have our own staff who handle all that kind of thing," you still want to know who's in charge and you should approach them, anyway. Who knows when they may find themselves short-staffed for an unusually big affair?

Your follow-up letter, ideally on paper with a business-like letterhead, which you can easily achieve on a word processor (or have the local copy shop design for you quite cheaply), might run something like this:

Dear Mrs. Smith,

This is to introduce myself as a local caterer. I have considerable experience in the field. J. P. Blodgett and A. C. Widget are among my regular clients.

I can handle any size function, given sufficient notice, from company picnics to staff parties. If you need advice or assistance on how to arrange a function of any kind, or if you require a location away from company premises, I can certainly offer a wide choice.

Yours sincerely,

Circulars sent out scattershot are the least effective means of obtaining business. A 5 percent return on inquiries would be considered excellent.

There's no reason why you shouldn't suggest to people that they do some entertaining and hire you to take care of it. Many people love to entertain but, after some experience, find they dread the preparation and cleaning up involved— especially if they have a busy professional or business life. It's up to the caterer to sell the world on the great liberating effect her services can bring.

Some catering companies sell their services by flaunting the fact that their staff are mainly gorgeous hunks and beautiful girls. Tacky though this may seem to some, it is undoubtedly an inducement to many. After all, we now live in the age of the professional "party brightener"—a person who attends parties with the sole purpose of making them go with a zing. All of this is merely a reflection of the routine theater of restaurants, where often the maitre d' is a very personable and attractive man or woman, and some of the visible staff look as though they are merely killing time while awaiting Hollywood's call. Immature and shallow maybe, but most people, especially when in celebratory mood, would rather be faced with good-looking smiling people than dour wet blankets, no matter how deeply worthy they may be underneath.

Remember, deep down the party spirit is very superficial. We are working in an area where the quip, the smile, and the glib answer are more appropriate than the deliverance of profound wisdom. This is harmless enough—most of us spend more time being serious than going to parties, anyway. But it is very important to be aware of the light and entertaining nature of most parties. That's how hosts and hostesses usually want them to be.

Even funeral wakes can be extraordinarily jolly. It's not uncommon for people to leave money in their will for a cocktail party to be held in their honor a year after their demise. Clearly they want the bereaved to have fun rather than mope about the inevitable.

## What Catering Offers

What do people want from caterers? Mainly, the certainty that their event will go smoothly and achieve its objectives, and that their guests will be well looked after. It is of paramount importance that you, the caterer, convey a responsible air of professionalism at all times, especially at the planning stage or when selling someone on the notion of hiring you. This can be achieved, quite simply, by demonstrating that you know what you're doing and bringing some flair and imagination to the situation.

Occasionally, customers will be repeating so-called set-piece events—their annual Christmas party, for instance—and will have very fixed ideas as to how they should be run. For example, "We always set up a bar in that corner and use the smaller bedroom for coats . . ."

Usually, the best thing is to go along with the preset plans. It must be admitted that repeat performances usually go smoothly—consider the big dinner at the grand hotel, where they may do one every day during festive seasons. Things go like clockwork.

If you think you can greatly improve on existing plans, you might gently suggest better ways of handling the event. But if you run into a brick wall—"This is the way we always do it"—then the best thing is to go along with your client's routine. Once in a while, you will find yourself fuming at rank inefficiency that brings clear displeasure to guests and might reflect on you, but on these occasions one can only bite the bullet and adopt a philosophical view —"Theirs not to reason why . . ."—and collect the fee.

# CHAPTER TWO

# Caterers' Qualifications and Skills

## Training

People who've been fortunate enough to be brought up in rich households where there was regular entertaining will have all the basic disciplines of catering at their fingertips. As children they helped (or hindered) the staff and parents in preparing for the arrival of guests—setting tables, rearranging furniture, and helping in the kitchen.

Alas, very few of us are privileged to have had such an upbringing. Also, we live in an informal age. It isn't even very common for families to sit down to meals regularly. How often one has been invited to suburban and country houses and told "There's plenty of beer and soda in the refrigerator, and the liquor's over there. If you feel like a sandwich there's plenty of cold cuts—and that cheesecake is out of this world." People mean well, but it can be disappointing for guests, especially if they're city-dwelling singles who don't get much family life and had perhaps hoped to sit down to roast-lamb-and-mashed-potatoes kind of meal.

Perhaps one should not grumble too much. This informal approach to life makes the caterer's job much simpler in many ways. Our grandparents would blanch at the sight of smart people, dressed to the nines, drinking out of plastic cups and eating off disposable plastic plates. But the dreaded washing up that was part of their domestic folklore has diminished in the age of disposable utensils and dishwashers.

Also, people are happy to help themselves. An advantage of this (for hosts, anyway) is quite simply that fewer personnel are needed to service a function.

At one extreme of catering is the super-formal dinner, usually for presidents and royalty, with footmen in livery standing behind each chair and waiters scurrying. At the other you have the self-service bar and buffet.

## LEARNING FROM OTHERS

When you first start catering from home, you'll find that most of the events you're hired to take care of are quite small. Sometimes you can handle them completely by yourself, acting as bartender, short-order cook, waiter, bus-boy, and cleaner all in one.

One way to learn the business is to attend a course at one of the many hotel, catering, and cooking schools that you find all over the country. But the simplest way to acquire all these skills is to work in restaurants or hotels for a while. In these trying times, such work is not as easy to find as it used to be, but if you can squeeze in at even a low level, you will be free to observe how others carry out their tasks.

Most reasonably mature and sensible people like showing others how things are done—it feels vaguely creative, perhaps. The trick is to choose your moment— that is, when people aren't terribly busy. You can get the bartender to show you how to open a bottle of wine, and maybe he'll let you open a few for practice.

Around the kitchen there's lots to learn. Restaurateurs are understandably a little nervous sometimes about allowing untrained or inexperienced people loose on their customers at the table or at the bar, and here you will usually only be allowed initially to watch and learn.

But as it becomes apparent that you have a good idea of how things should be done, workers will be only too glad to let you take care of various tasks, as long as you lessen their workload without threatening their tips.

Few things please an employer more than discovering a worker who is generally interested in the business. Interested employees are a good value because they are more committed and their acquired skills mean they can pinch hit, or take over when other workers fail to show up. Versatility can turn a part-time job into a full-time job, too.

## THE ADVANTAGES OF VERSATILITY

By standing in here and there and filling odd nooks and crannies in the work schedule, the person who's prepared to wear different hats every day can become indispensable to a hotel or restaurant and acquire a useful general overview of business. It's not uncommon in the restaurant business for a young person to come in as a busboy, start filling in as waiter, bartender, assistant chef, and maître d' and, often quite rapidly, find himself promoted to managerial status.

If you are genuinely motivated, you can learn enough to go out and sell yourself as a caterer in three months. The relevant skills are discussed in later chapters. For the moment, let us address the acquisition of skills in the most general way.

## Learning at Home

If it isn't possible for you to do hands-on work in a restaurant, club, or hotel, you can always practice at home. Invite friends over for lunch and handle it as though they were not friends but clients. This simple exercise will put you on your toes, and if they're friends, a little teasing about your super formality or efficiency will be tolerable. You may well find that you enjoy the exercise—it is, after all, creative, and people may share your enjoyment.

Some people really enjoy entertaining in this way and never turn a hair, no matter how many people are invited or how elaborate the menu. Such people make useful spouses and they are born caterers.

# The Essentials of Service

The keys to good service are preparation, planning, and anticipation. One important discipline easily acquired is putting yourself in the position of the client, guest, or customer. If this suggests a military commander trying to put himself in the enemy position to figure out his likely moves, so be it—the method works very well. The difference is that you are seeking out people's requirements and trying to make them happy, not planning to destroy them.

You must learn to be observant and to look for detail. The dessert has been placed in front of the guests. What are they going to eat it with? Have they got a spoon, a fork, or both? What happened to that guy's napkin? He didn't realize he dropped it—so give him a fresh one.

This doesn't mean that you should become a neurotic nit-picker. A common scene in the restaurant business is the arrival of the dragonlike owner or his or her spouse who approaches with beady eyes and fierce expression to say "There's a fork missing on Table Two" as though a replay of Pearl Harbor had just been announced. There are managers who know that if they look around long enough they'll find an ashtray with a butt in it, or a lemon peel that might be a millimeter off the official house specification. They exploit this sort of thing to make it look as though they're doing an efficient job, but they almost invariably turn out to be phonies.

## The Light Touch

Though an eye for detail is a strong requirement if you are to make it as a caterer, there's also a need for a light touch, especially when dealing with your help. After all, if you throw a fit of rage when a spoon is missing, you won't have much steam left for when something serious goes wrong, such as failure to arrange the ice supply or forgetting some aspect of the operation, causing stress and worrying the client.

When you go to a function or a restaurant where all the staff are scowling, what do you think the reason is? It is almost always the heavy-handed presence of a disliked manager who has been on the rampage, sometimes overdemanding, unfair in arranging the schedule, or, not uncommonly, just a general pain in the neck.

A certain mentality in some business managers amounts almost to bullying. They like to see people looking miserable. It's called "adversarial management," and it won't go away. A motto of some Roman dictators was *Oderint sed metuant*," meaning "Let them hate, as long as they fear . . ."

A hugely expensive restaurant and catering venture recently fell flat on its face. The reason? The owners had brought in a Hitlerian management team who actually had the staff lined up and inspected, military-style, for clean hands and shiny shoes. This approach is insulting to staff. Their efficiency in these regards should have been assessed when they were hired.

The prison-like atmosphere was all-pervading, and customers were not prepared to dine in a rather expensive morgue. Nor did many people want such an atmosphere for their catered parties in their own homes. The business went under in record time, and the diagnosis of the failure was, as it so often is, lousy management.

Corrections and changes should be made in a lighthearted way. A wink is as good as a nod to the wise, and as Alexander Pope had it "Man should be led as though you led him not." If personnel simply don't respond to the civilized approach, then they must be replaced.

## Knowing What's Essential

Caterers, and indeed anyone in the service sector, can make life easier and more pleasant for themselves and their clients by becoming so steeped in the job that everything happens efficiently and automatically, without stress. It is important to understand the needs of people with tastes and preferences totally alien to your own.

You may not be a coffee drinker. But an awful lot of people are, and they drink their coffee in different ways. Take a look at one of the new ubiquitous coffee bars, and you will see what a huge range of tastes exists within this one consumer item. People's brand loyalties and tastes must be catered to if you are to get and keep their business.

Consider the minutiae of a light breakfast tray delivered to an upscale hotel room. It all looks so efficiently prepared, but when you look for the sugar it isn't there. That may well be because the person who assembled the tray was not a tea drinker, but a plain black coffee drinker, and so there is no automatic or instinctive sense of what goes on a tray when tea is served. Thus, the guest has to call room service one more time, and the waiter has to make one more trip. There is irritation all around. Time is wasted, and time is money.

## Planning for Customer Satisfaction

The importance of preparation and planning—setting up—cannot be too often stressed. It is the key to success. Nor should one lose sight of the fact that tipping is an integral part of all aspects of the hospitality industry. Generally speaking, the more efficient the worker, the better the tips, or "gratuities," as some prefer to call them. After all, the very word tip is said to derive from the expression "To insure promptitude".

In a top hotel, of course, there is a payroll-swelling and thus price-increasing dispatcher in the kitchen who meticulously checks everything as it goes out. This is fine, except that it takes time, and the eggs and bacon may arrive with all the requested appurtenances but cold—a variation on the old medical adage "Operation a success—patient died." The computer may record a correctly dispatched breakfast, but in his room the customer may be fuming.

These minor but irritating—and customer confidence destroying details are almost invariably the result of employing people who only go through the motions of doing the job. If you never drink tea, a tea tray from which the lemon, sugar, milk, extra hot water, or teaspoon are missing will not stand out. If you don't drink alcohol, you may not be aware that white wine is drunk chilled and red usually at room temperature.

You may think this superficial and trivial detail. If so, the catering business is not for you. You absolutely have to learn what most people generally want and expect, even with foods and beverages that are unfamiliar to you or that you personally disdain. You may be revolted when you serve Steak Tartare (chopped raw beef), but don't let that make you forget the capers, the onions, the raw egg, the Tabasco, and the Melba toast.

One might observe, in the case of our top hotel dispatcher, that if someone bothered to train the cook or waiter, or provide them with a simple checklist, time and at least one salary could be saved. But it is a curious phenomenon of business in general that management is often reluctant to take even the briefest amount of time to train. How often one sees the portentous words "Must be computer literate" in a job advertisement, when the actual function is so simple that a person who'd never seen a computer in his or her life could learn how to cope if given ten minutes of instruction. All too often, a huge problem is made out of finding someone to spare that ten minutes.

## The Small but Important Details

An example of unimaginative hospitality sometimes occurs at the personal domestic level. Invited to dine with friends, you'll see no salt or pepper on the table. Many people have bought the anti-sodium propaganda and put no salt whatsoever in their food, and many restaurants have adopted the same policy. This way, when a customer inquires, "Is that salt-free?" the waiter can triumphantly assure the customer that it is. One less problem.

Some cranky cooks will tell you that they're offended if people add salt to food they've prepared, taking it almost as a gratuitous insult. They are even more incensed if someone sprinkles salt or pepper on food before they've tasted it. But the simple truth is that people's salt requirements vary enormously. It is an individual and personal matter. Some very active people will need four times as much as the average person. You can't survive without salt, mainly because without it the body can't retain and process water—something else you can't live without. But in any case, the rule of *de gustibus non est disputandum* ("each to his own taste"), which is really no more than simple good manners, should always be observed.

So, from a caterer's point of view, if food is served, then salt and pepper must be available. Apart from the fact that it's rude and unimaginative not to fulfill such obvious requirements at a personal domestic level, if you are selling your services and omit such basics, you may not get any repeat business. You risk losing a client, and you'll never know why.

Whether you like it or not, we are all to one extent or another Trained Consumers. This has its downside in that it sometimes stifles individuality, but on the whole it makes life easier for the simple reason that, in almost every business, one has a good idea of what the customer expects and requires.

There is little excuse for not acquiring the disciplines of service, because nobody performs better in this sector than Americans. Start taking an interest in what goes on, and how things are laid out, whenever you go to a restaurant, bar, or coffee shop, and you'll swiftly and instinctively see how it's handled. At the humble level of the coffee shop, for example, when did you ever have to ask for sugar, sugar substitute, salt, pepper, napkins, cutlery, or ketchup? They're all there on the table when you sit down. They are part of the setup, which anticipates the customers' most likely requirements.

## Difficult Guests

Just in case you thought this discussion was rather simple, remember that there are exceptions that prove the rules. At some point you have to draw the line as to how accommodating you can be when you're catering a function. If a guest requests something that stretches your resources too much, you must pleasantly, politely, and firmly tell them so. The best way for softening such a confrontation is to eagerly offer alternatives.

GUEST: Oh no—you haven't any Old Bayou Bourbon?

SERVER: I'm sorry—but there's a nice scotch if you like . . .

Some guests, fortunately only a few and rarely, will snarl and sulk at the most minor deprivation, even though this is clearly bad manners at a friend's party. That's their problem, not yours. You simply must not jeopardize the smooth running and general gratification of the majority of guests at a function by wallowing in the petty demands of some quirky, strange, or overdemanding guest.

Many people are strangers to hospitality. They're rarely invited anywhere and rarely go out. Some quirk of fate may bring them to the party you're running. "May I get you a drink?" you, or your bartender, will ask, leading to the following exchange:

GUEST: Well, I don't really drink a lot . . .

SERVER: A glass of white wine perhaps?

GUEST: How about a, uhm, Piña Colada?

SERVER: Sorry, no can do. May I offer you a . . . ?

## The Host Who Wants Everything

Some hosts may take a fierce view of what to offer. "I want my guests to have anything they want," they insist when you're planning the event. You must then gently and politely point out that while your bartender is scurrying around trying to make some obscure cocktail for one guest, ten guests are without refreshment. If the host still insists on an all-embracing service, then you hire more staff, bring in more equipment and stick it on the bill.

Again, there are exceptions within exceptions. Once in a while a host will instruct you something like this: "See the guy with the white hair? He's the real reason for this party. I'm hoping to do business with him. Make sure he has a good time. He only drinks Ohio Sparkling Water, but he drinks gallons of it and he likes it really chilled, with a big chunk of completely squeezed lime. Keep him supplied at all costs."

Trivial stuff, is it not? But both God and the devil are in the details. Though it's always wise to contemplate the worst-case scenario, the good news is that confrontations and problems are actually very unusual in the catering business. Part of the reason for this is that the air at parties is full of goodwill. The host wants to give a nice party, and the guests want to enjoy themselves. People are on their best behavior and will not generally assert themselves in petty ways, as they may do in the more impersonal arena of the restaurant—where some customers occasionally engage in a kind of reverse Dale Carnegie course as they interrogate waiters and send food back. If you, the caterer, do your bit by setting up well and anticipating requirements, it can be a very genial business, indeed.

## Chapter Three

# Employing Others

DELIGHTFUL though it is to be a "one-person band," handling small parties easily and pocketing the entire fee, if your reputation grows it won't be long before you find yourself being asked to cater parties that are simply too big for one person to handle. A cocktail party for up to 40 people, with simple canapés such as nuts, cheese, and crackers with dip, can be competently handled by one bartender, provided that he or she is experienced, well setup, well supplied, and not required to provide exotic space- and time-consuming cocktails such as Brandy Alexanders, Piña Coladas, and Frozen Daiquiris.

Such requests are unlikely these days, but you'll do well to be aware that once in a while you may have to go into apologetic mode for the general good of the assembly. If 40 people sound daunting, remember that they don't all arrive at once (although there will inevitably be a peak hour of maximum activity).

Furthermore, once a guest has a drink in his or her hand, there will be no more demands for a while. Indeed, this is a golden rule of entertaining—give guests something to hold, eat, or drink as soon as they arrive. Then they won't feel neglected; they'll feel comforted and begin to relax.

## Hiring Staff

If the cocktail party for 40, with drinks and simple canapés, escalates to drinks and elaborate hot appetizers, then you will almost certainly require one assistant. Many hosts make a thing of this—hot shrimps, curry sauce, prunes wrapped in bacon, and so on. Someone has to be dedicated to the task of preparing and serving them.

This is where you have to cast about and find assistance. Often a friend or relative will help. Mother-daughter teams are common in the business and usually work very well.

It's important not to be too casual in making your arrangements. The assistants must absolutely understand where and when to turn up, what to wear, what their general tasks are to be, and what time they're likely to finish. The amount they'll be paid should be stated, too, and if you're unable to pay them on the spot you should make sure they understand and accept that.

It's sometimes difficult to get across to people that although the party you are catering is often, though not always, entirely recreational, it simply won't work properly unless someone behind the scenes is seriously addressing themselves to its organization. The casual approach will usually lead to disaster. The host won't be able to relax and get on with networking and socializing, and the guests will go hungry and thirsty.

## Getting Firm Commitments

When you start phoning around to friends and acquaintances you must be very businesslike in your approach. Responses such as "I might be able to do it," or "I'll let you know," won't do. You need a firm promise to appear and perform. Nor should you accept a late arrival, unless of course it's a tried and trusted person who you know will not let you down. "I should be able to make it by six" may put you into stress mode at 5:45 if not earlier. It is precisely the business-like and professional approach that makes catering operations delightfully easy.

Finding people at short notice is always a nightmare, and the earlier you can book people the better. While it's true that catering is a fairly low-stress business, mainly because it's so finite and you can plan in advance, the one area that can generate some headaches is the help. Sensible employees understand this and cultivate their image of reliability. Apart from anything else, they get more work that way.

## The Right Attitude

When talking to potential assistants or employees, it's very important to assess attitude. Many employers are so lacking in general experience, or so dumb, that they will only assess people on their degree of technical knowledge and are so intimidated by the threat to their own organizational and teaching abilities that they pass up excellent candidates.

Thus, sometimes the frowning, uncharming applicant for the bartender's job who knows how to make a Bronx Fizz (or some other drink that hasn't been requested in forty years) will be hired, while the friendly, willing, and generally competent woman who knows more about baseball than Yogi Berra does will be turned down because she's never served champagne before. The two minutes necessary to show her how will be begrudged.

The specific attitude you must try to assess is the one that potential assistants or employees display toward customers, clients, and their guests. They must learn that when they're on duty the customer is king or queen and the guests all members of the royal family.

An endearing facet of all service industries is the way in which workers team up and become friends—it can work in everyone's favor. But the spirit of "us against the world" must be avoided. How often does one enter a restaurant or find oneself among the early arrivals at a party, only to be made to feel guilty as the staff rise, reluctantly abandon their amusing gossip, and scatter, stubbing out their cigarettes, collecting dirty plates, glasses, and newspapers, as they hastily move to their action stations.

## Building a Reliable Crew

As you gain confidence you'll be happy to take on bigger and better-paying assignments. At that point you cannot avoid the inevitable need for more help. Cheer up, it's what's known as success. At the point where you run out of friends, and this can happen quickly, you need to look for help more formally. You'll need a list of available people far longer than the list of people you normally reckon to use for an engagement.

The simple reason for this is that not everyone will be available all the time or at the drop of a hat. Events can be scheduled for any time from breakfast to after theater. Therefore, even at the still easily manageable stage where you and an assistant can handle parties without problems, there will come a time when that usually reliable person can't make it.

You need a reliable group of experienced catering personnel. You should review it regularly. We live in a peripatetic society and people move a lot. What most caterers do, is assemble a list of people in descending order of likelihood of availability. Of course, this list is subject to discreet editing because, for instance, your most personable bartender or efficient waitress may be in constant demand elsewhere. The more notice you give your employees, the more likely you are to field your best team.

**Job Preferences and Limitations**    Although there are few prima donnas in the catering field, you will occasionally come across people with strong preferences for the job they do. Some bartenders prefer not to work as waiters, for instance, and chefs often restrict themselves to cooking. There's no point in asking them if they'll run a bar or work as a waiter because they'll turn up their noses in disdain. However, the more flexible a person is, the more work he or she will get.

Similarly, you should note minor but important physical limitations. Some people, for instance, can't or won't work where there are stairs; others won't work certain hours. (The latter is an unfortunate limitation because the catering industry requires all participants to regularly work what are sometimes called "unsociable hours.") Some won't travel beyond a short distance. In general, anyone seeking work in the hospitality industry will do well to have as few quirks as possible, or they may miss opportunities.

Make a note of these preferences and limitations to save wasted calls when you have to fill a spot on short notice. The caterer has quite enough to do without having to peruse a list of workers thus: "Let's see, I'll give Joe a call but, uh-oh, it's a long way uptown for him, hmmm, maybe Suzie . . . but she doesn't do stairs"—and so on.

# Where to Find Help

With luck the majority of your available work force will be versatile. A job is a job, it isn't forever, and the pay is useful.

Once you decide to go ahead and do catering, spread the word to anyone who will lend you their ear for ten seconds. You are probably reasonably gregarious and fond of people if you want to do catering, so it's likely that you have a wide neighborhood acquaintance and probably a restaurant and bar or two where they know your face and sometimes your name.

## Restaurant Employees

Local restaurant workers (or co-workers, if you're already employed in a restaurant, hotel, or catering company) may be happy to give you their names and home telephone numbers, and willing to volunteer for an occasional event. It's as well to be formal in your conversations; otherwise, especially (though not exclusively in these liberated times) if you're talking to a member of the opposite sex, he or she may dismiss your overtures as just one more tactic in a pick up repertoire. The best way to show you're on the level is to hand out a business card.

Remember, they'll need lots of notice if they already have a regular job. But if they can't make it, they may know someone who can.

## Retirees and Students

Retirees can be an excellent source of help, as long as they're still in good shape and can react promptly. Old hands can be a treasure trove. One caterer used to hire the ex-maitre d' of a famous cruise liner's restaurant. The man had plenty of money after decades of generous tips, but simply liked to get out and about once in a while because he found retirement boring. Naturally he could handle and charm a party of 50 people standing on his head, sometimes taking care of the cooking and cloakroom, too. He was an excellent value—he'd seen every scenario imaginable and was acquainted with world cuisine. Working a party with him was a pleasant and amusing learning experience.

If there's a college or university in your neighborhood, you may be sure that there's a supply of willing hands. Often, there's a telephone number dedicated to providing casual workers. If it isn't in the phone book, call the main switchboard and inquire.

## Advertising

There's no reason why you shouldn't advertise for assistants, either in the local press or on local bulletin boards, especially those in big company offices and places like the local delicatessen, supermarket, and liquor store. Press advertising is not terribly expensive, though it does vary from paper to paper and from magazine to magazine. You should make it clear that you are offering occasional part-time work and not a career. At a certain point, you might also consider advertising your service by placing either a simple one-line entry or small box ad in the Yellow Pages. Of course, simply advertising your service, without reference to your need for personnel, will usually generate some inquiries from people who are seeking work. Thus, you may find yourself killing two birds with one stone.

## Catering Companies and Temp Agencies

It may sound odd, but there's no reason why you shouldn't call a bigger catering company and hire help through them. This is also a way of discovering the going rate for employing catering staff. If they've been in business some time, they'll probably have built up a long list of workers in all capacities—bartenders, waiters, busboys, chefs, coat-room attendants, car valets, and so on.

However, be careful with this method—treat it as a last resort, as you may dilute your profits. The agency may provide people at, say, $17 an hour, of which they will pay the worker $10. To make any profit on the labor you're providing, you will have to charge your customer more than the $17-per-hour rate, and she may not like it.

Do remember that many of your part-time staff will be registered with several other agencies and possibly have full time jobs as well. At peak periods of the year, they will be very much in demand. Given the choice between working as a waiter at a banquet and playing the role of butler or bartender at a smaller party in someone's house, they will invariably choose the latter because it is not only easier but more fun, and the chance of a generous tip is high. If you find a client offers you a general tip for yourself and the whole crew, be sure to make some kind of gesture in the right direction by sharing it in order to promote staff loyalty. Cash works wonders.

## Working for a Catering Company Yourself

Incidentally, once you've learned the ropes, and if you're still essentially working from home, there's no reason why you shouldn't register yourself with every caterer in town as being available for work. The more exposure and the more work you get, the better.

In this regard, a common situation occurs when you're working for another agency. A client or host likes the way you work and asks how to get hold of you for future occasions. Almost invariably the client will be interested in obtaining your good services, not in merely seeking a reduced fee. Now, ethically you may feel that you owe your position to the agency and that it's naughty to eliminate them from the business. However, the prospect of pocketing (say) $18 an hour for yourself and not surrendering $8 of this to the agency may be tempting. (That would be a typical cut, by the way.)

It is of course every agent's fear that a potential employee will discover a vacancy for herself and approach the employer directly, thus saving herself the agency placement fee. The employer will be delighted to save himself the placement fee too—yes, many agents charge both parties. That's why agents keep their cards close to their vests and never divulge the location and name of the job until the seeker is all signed up and has perhaps paid a deposit—also not an uncommon requirement. Agencies supplying temporary office workers usually have the most elaborate rules and regulations about their temps accepting regular employment, and sometimes require a finder's fee when this occurs.

It is entirely a matter of conscience—Solomon in all his glory would find this a tough one to decide. By accepting a direct invitation to work for someone you wouldn't be breaking the law, and an agent who decided to put this to the test might find himself spending a lot of money to no purpose. Headhunting is a solid business, and it's here to stay. Perhaps that's the way to look at it. On a human level, it's hard to swallow anyone's having the right to impede anyone else's right to make a legal living.

## Assessing Potential Staff

Ideally, you will have met and discussed business with everybody who works for you. You can meet casually, assess their suitability, and check their manner.

### A Ready Smile

A propensity for the easy smile is much to be desired. This smile need not reach the eyes, nor must it be a proclamation of eternal devotion. It is merely an easy device, a body-language signal, that conveys a willingness to oblige and please within the context of the moment. Some people wouldn't agree, but smilers are not necessarily losers. In the hospitality industry a winning smile can be an important asset.

Many nations, especially those whose peoples are noted for their dourness and reluctance to smile except when inebriated, are often perplexed by the all-American easy smile, but they perhaps invest it with too much weight and importance. In practical terms it is merely an extension of verbal good manners, which proved very helpful and useful in a nation of immigrants who often found body language easier to interpret than the vocabulary. A mere mechanical baring of the teeth will not suffice, unfortunately, but there is no need to go for the full mother-upon-seeing-her-firstborn effect, either.

The easy frown, or the dead-eyed look that one often, sadly, encounters in the maître d' of a trendy restaurant, renders applicants in the hospitality industry unacceptable, unless they are brilliant chefs who are capable of running large kitchens efficiently but do not come in contact with clients or the public. By convention, and for obvious reasons, such people are allowed to be a little crazy. Many of them extract the last inch of mileage from this indulgence, and the "sacred monster" chef has become one of the more tedious clichés of our times.

## Grooming

You can also discreetly check applicants' grooming. Clean fingernails, shined shoes, and nongreasy hair are the main things to look for. They can smoke their heads off in private as long as they understand that there is absolutely no smoking on the job in this health-conscious age. So strong is the antismoking feeling these days that anyone who simply lights up without first groveling for permission to do so can only be suspected of gross insensitivity. Vigorous gum chewing and failure to remove personal portable stereo headphones or sunglasses are unacceptable as well.

If applicants seem intelligent, confident, and willing, you can take a risk on lack of experience—catering doesn't require rocket scientists. A generally pleasant manner is a major asset, as long as this is not the person's only talent. Once in a while you may have to take a risk, hire a stranger, and just hope the person who shows up is appropriate to your standards and requirements.

## A Smiling Face Is Not Enough

Here is where we have to discuss some bleak realities, though I don't want to preach or discourage. We have discussed the very great importance of smile power. Unfortunately, some people rely on this to the exclusion of all else. They think that as long as they're cute and smile and giggle a lot, they can get away with anything. They rely upon this smile to get them through all obstacles, events, and situations.

Such employees are reminiscent of those brilliant performers in the food industry who, when in doubt as to how to bring their cheap and awful mass-market products to some sort of life, simply add sugar, salt, and monosodium glutemate in mega-dollops.

This curious syndrome affects all classes and age groups. You must beware the cute idiot, and the best way to protect yourself is to interview all potential help and discreetly observe them when they go to work.

Watch out for phonies. In a society where the job is often the holy shrine of existence, most people can manage a smile for the boss, but their manner can

## THE AIRLINE STANDARD OF SERVICE

Flight attendants are among the very best service workers. Some of them occasionally take on a little freelance catering work, but the nature of their job means that they may not always be available. Imagine what they have to do on a full, long-haul flight; yet on most airlines they're ever-obliging and efficient, and at least give the impression of quite enjoying their work—without, one might observe, the added inducement of tips.

The technical side of what flight attendants do is interesting. Airline food has improved greatly on some airlines: its preparation, storage, packaging, and heating by microwave have been brought to a fine art. The best airlines succeed in this area by carefully selecting the things that work best under these cooking restrictions—for instance, fish is out, but cold smoked salmon is doable. The real miracle however, is the quality of service. What do these princesses and princes of the work ethic have that so many don't? In a word—training. Airlines actually take the time and trouble and spend the money to train their staff. Of course, they have to. Caterers and restaurateurs can bluff for many years, and many get away with it for far longer than they deserve, but no airline could function that way. Bad reputations in the travel industry spread quickly.

So fickle are some regular travelers that they'll switch flights, or even airlines, if the one they're booked on is showing a movie they've already seen. At the beginning of the recession one airline chairman nearly had a fit when one of his faceless accountants, spying a bill of $100,000 for cashew nuts served with cocktails in first class, canceled the order. The order was swiftly reinstated. Would a senior executive travelling first class change his airline because he didn't get nuts with his cocktail? Darn right he would. Airlines don't want you to fly with them once. They want you to fly with them every time, just as a caterer should aim to be the one clients call whenever there's entertainment afoot.

Also interesting is the organization of an airline. They are amazingly flexible, even though their service is predicated on the certainty of what a majority of their customers want. They are set up, they are organized. If a passenger has some diet restriction due to health or religion, then—as long as they have some notice—the crew can provide what's required.

Once in a while things will go wrong. Regular fliers are often perplexed by the fact that a flight they take six times a year is, for some reason, chaotic going out yet back to normal high standards coming back. One can only conjecture that some internal, backstage problem has emerged, or that some generally unpopular leader has been on the rampage.

Just occasionally a plane will be short-staffed because managers have combined flights, so there are more passengers aboard than anticipated.

Since such action is often triggered unexpectedly by a mechanical fault in a plane, and since most passengers would rather be on their way than hang about while standby crew are rounded up, the number of cabin crew may be below par.

The scale of airline catering probably represents the biggest business of all in the industry—far bigger than any of the world's major hotels. Here's one of those glib-but-true business success stories.

A certain successful international airline reviewed its expansion and embarked upon an ambitious catering plan to service its burgeoning flights. Once this catering arrangement—premises, staff, supplies—was set up, the managers took another look at the figures and realized, to their horror, that they'd overestimated growth. Though they were expanding, it wasn't as fast as they'd supposed. So they were stuck with more catering capacity than they needed for the time being.

At the same time, a certain less developed country discovered oil and started to boom. Its national airline couldn't cope with the extra catering demand on its flights. The businessman who introduced the airline in need to the one with the ability to provide the service made a fortune. "Have I got a deal for you," indeed.

change dramatically with customers or guests. Some employees have one face for the boss and quite another for their colleagues and, worse, the clients. These Janus worshippers (Janus being the two-faced Roman god after whom the month of January is named) will talk to the boss with smiling sincerity, brows often furrowed with deep and sincere concern, yet ignore their colleagues and go out of their way to insult clients and customers.

This is why you need to learn the art of unobtrusive, discreet observation. No need to breathe down people's necks. Far better to watch from afar while seemingly intent on something else. And don't become paranoid on this issue or imitate some restaurant owners who will often pose as the dishwasher just to get a bird's-eye (or worm's-eye) view of what goes on in the joint. Blessed indeed is the employer who dismisses the dismal old proverb "When the cat's away, the mice will play."

## Looks Aren't Everything

You shouldn't try to impress your clients with the beauty of the staff you employ at the expense of good service. At automobile exhibitions one sometimes wonders what the bikini-clad beauty draped over the hood of the latest model has to do with fuel consumption and horsepower. No doubt Detroit has its reasons. "We don't sell cars—we sell dreams" and all that ancient marketing lore. If, at a mixed gathering, you field gorgeous young servers and bartenders, you risk giving offense to some guests. They may be irritated and made to feel insecure by the sight of their husbands, wives, girlfriends, or boyfriends adopting charming behavior they may not have seen in years.

One caterer discovered what he thought was golden talent when he hired two gorgeous blond sisters, aged around twenty. They were actually good workers and very serious, but their presence at dinner parties for more mature people, sadly, ruined the occasions. The women became huffy as the men went into flirtation mode. Efficient and charming is how your help should be, but not overwhelming in their presence. They shouldn't be the star attraction and dominate the room. If you try to lay on the glamor, you risk shooting yourself in the foot.

## A Possible Scenario

Because of the festive and casual atmosphere of most parties, sometimes the staff lose sight of the need to be efficient in the servicing of the event. Here is a typical recurring nightmare.

A hostess wants to give a cocktail party. She wants to be free to mingle with her guests, so she rings up the local college's employment service and asks them to send a bartender. The party starts at 6:00, she tells them, so perhaps the bartender can arrive at 5:30 to set up a simple bar? The fee will be decided. The magic words "no problem" seal the deal.

On the night of the party, at around 5:45, Steve arrives, with no apology for his tardiness. He is sassy-looking, with a ponytail and a ring through his nose, ear, or eyebrow (sometimes all three), and he has a cute smile and an infectious giggle. An old-fashioned host or hostess might think it a pity he couldn't find time to shave before coming to work, perhaps not being aware of the highly fashionable designer stubble *de rigueur* in some circles. Steve's enormous purple and white sneakers may clash somewhat with his black pants, but at least he got the pants right, and the white shirt, though not ironed, is reasonably clean.

The hostess had better have a corkscrew, because Steve won't have one, his wine experience being restricted to the twist-off cap varieties, and she had better set up the bar herself because he will only have the dimmest idea of what's required. As people arrive, he'll give them the big grin and, if they're lucky, serve them a glass of white wine or a soda. Things slow down painfully when someone requests a complicated drink like a scotch and soda, but after a while the party gets going. Miraculously, everyone has a drink. Dreading being thought heavy and demanding, the hostess may request that Steve clear up empty glasses and perhaps ask guests if he can get them anything.

Not minding in the least that his painstaking repositioning of his pony tail is being interrupted, our hero sallies forth and takes an unconscionable length of time to clear up a little. He then solicits drink orders, one at a time. If, as is not uncommon, the hostess detects nothing amiss, there's no harm done. If, as is sometimes the case, the hostess dares to be displeased; clearly she will look elsewhere for assistance the next time she entertains.

Steve is everywhere. Sometimes he drives a taxi, but forgets the one-way street system and turns a $3 ride into a $5 ride, wasting a precious five minutes. Sometimes he works in a liquor store where, when a customer inquires, "Is this what you'd call a 'dry' wine?" he puts on the big grin and replies "I don't know ma'am. I don't drink."

## The Moral of the Story

The reality is that we live in times when such gross inefficiency is often acceptable. Some blame bosses for not properly supervising and training their assistants. Bosses doubtless reply that they've got quite enough to do already, thank you. But does it really make any sense to go into business with the attitude of seeing just how little you can deliver? You don't want a staff of coldly efficient automatons, but you don't want useless cuties either.

Then again, just in case you thought this was all appearing a bit too simple, on some occasions a host positively requires the catering staff to be the stars of the occasion. However, when we get into this rarified area we are outside the scope of ordinary business and social life and into the somewhat campy and super-sophisticated fleshpots of New York and Los Angeles, not to mention Sodom and Gomorrah.

# Paying—and Getting Paid

At the small scale at which you will probably commence operations, paying the staff is simple. You usually get paid right after the function, and you'll be popular with your help if you can pay them equally promptly.

If a client politely asks you how you'd like to be paid, cash or check, you need feel no embarrassment in asking for cash. Even quite nice people sometimes bounce checks, and usually you simply ring the client who tells you to redeposit it. Sometimes he or she will even apologize for the mishap. The charge for check bouncing is punitive, and the convention is that the bouncer pays you the fee you've incurred. What you're not compensated for is the wasted time and stress involved. (In some countries, including France, bouncing a check will get you banned from having a bank account and possibly a prison sentence, too.) On a larger scale, we get into the area of deposits, bills formally presented, and so on. A big hotel will sometimes demand an advance deposit of $25,000 for a grand function.

Beyond a certain size of operation, if you employ permanent staff, you will have to get organized with insurance, withholding, registering as a business, and complying with any local laws that apply. The details of what you must do vary from state to state, and in any case, unless you have a particular flair for or experience in the area, you'll need the services of an accountant when you expand to this extent. You can still manage things from home, of course.

Also, at this stage you may enter the heavily mined arena of labor relations, whether you like it or not. The accompanying sidebar presents a story, taken from the London *Sunday Telegraph* of October 10, 1995, related simply because it gives an insight into the higher levels of the catering business. It's unlikely that many caterers will ever find themselves involved in such matters. The story is an extreme example of life in the wonderful world of catering.

## WAITRESS "WAS DENIED WORK BY BUTLER CULTURE"

The fashion for British-style "butler culture" in New York high society has prompted a sex discrimination lawsuit from a waitress.

Jessica Weigmann, 31, who is waiting on tables while working as an artist, is suing the society caterers, Glorious Foods, for damages because, she says, she has been denied work in favor of waiters who can better project the image of the traditional butler.

She is being backed by the American Civil Liberties Union and the National Organization of Women.

She decided to sue after being excluded from a lunch for First Lady Hillary Clinton at the Metropolitan Museum of Art in June, where only tall, dark, handsome men were hired to place the haute cuisine before the guests.

"Here's this great women's right advocate and she's being served by all men in discriminatory manner," Miss Weigmann said.

The lawsuit claims that until recently Glorious Foods asked clients to choose between "Women OK?" or "Male Waiters only." The firm, based in Manhattan's Upper East Side, is used by the stars and leading corporate and charity party givers.

The list includes David Rockefeller, the broadcaster Barbara Walters, fashion designers Oscar de la Renta and Valentino, the Metropolitan Museum and the Guggenheim Museum.

The firm turns over about $10 million a year and maintains a roll of about 500 part-time waiters and waitresses, called in when needed for parties or private dinner parties.

The complaint alleges that women were particularly excluded from small functions in private homes, where tipping was best.

"It's absolutely the butler culture. Men are considered more appropriately decorative, and I won't even focus on the racial aspect," said Clark Wolf, a Manhattan restaurant consultant.

Miss Weigmann, who has a degree from Bernard University, says in the suit that two years ago she was dropped "at the last minute" from roster for a party for the designer Valentino and that a colleague later told her that was because "it was an all-male party."

Deborah Ellis, of the National Organization for Women, said the case fitted an historical pattern of discrimination, including the old airlines' rule of hiring only women cabin attendants because they were more soothing. Sean Driscoll, Glorious Foods owner, said the charges were "bull".

# How to Get Business
# and How Much to Charge

C ATERING is a competitive field, but there is always room for newcomers. The reason for this is simply the normal attrition of business. Established caterers expand to a certain size, then rest on their laurels, servicing regular clients and seeking no more. People get tired, and people get lazy. When the founder or driving force dies or retires, often the business disappears, too. Customers sometimes discern a falling off of standards in a caterer's performance, or simply want a change.

Occasionally caterers overreach themselves, take on more than they can handle, and fall flat on their faces. They'll handle a party disastrously—warm drinks, cold food, and precious little of it served on time. If you're loyal to a particular make of car or a certain actor, you'll probably forgive the carmaker if, one frosty morning, the vehicle fails to start, and you won't abandon the actor just because he appears in a movie that fails to please. Most people are much less forgiving in the catering and restaurant area. You'll only get a second chance if the customer realizes that the things that went wrong were beyond your control.

## Occasions That Call for Catering

Company and individual budgets change. Firms that normally throw a summer party and a Christmas party for their staff employees suddenly abandon both. They are not required to offer any explanation for this, but the introduction a few years ago of a legal precedent whereby the server of alcohol can be held liable, for accidents resulting from drunkenness undoubtedly made some companies nervous. Ours is a highly litigious society and, around holiday times, the number of alcohol-related accidents soars. Remember, more than a third of all the alcohol consumed in the United States is drunk in the last three months of the year—the period generally referred to as "the holidays."

However, this is a matter of fashion, and many companies, including some where until recently employees had to request permission to go to the bathroom, are very gung-ho for so-called employee bonding and fall over themselves to entertain workers as well as promote dress-down days when everyone goes to work in casual clothes.

## Catering's Seasonal Nature

At this point one should mention the highly seasonal nature of the catering industry in general. June is usually a busy month, with weddings, openings, and celebrations of all kinds. Through November and December, it is not uncommon for caterers to work for several weeks with no days off, mindful of the business doldrums that will arrive after New Year's Day. At this rate of work it becomes more important than ever to ensure a guaranteed amount of sleep, to maintain a proper diet—and exercise if this is a part of your lifestyle—avoiding like the plague any but the smallest amount of alcohol and reminding oneself of the more restful times to come.

In the long lean periods, the caterer needs to drum up as much business as possible, but it's unlikely that the intensity of the peak periods will ever be achieved. Many other industries share this seasonal factor—notably building and construction, where people will sometimes work seven days straight, week after week, even through the summer, safe in the knowledge that if they want to take a vacation in January, there'll be little reason not to.

## Charity Events

In major cities, a very busy area for caterers is the charity event. These "dos" sometimes come thick and fast, as charities raise money on a regular basis. Some organizations have a big gala and several smaller events—usually cocktail parties but often lunches.

Competition for these contracts can be fierce, especially at the top end of the scale. Imagine a gala evening, perhaps built around a ballet, opera, or theater opening, where a thousand people buy tickets costing perhaps up to a thousand dollars, including drinks and dinner. Clearly the caterer who takes on such a job will find himself and his staff very busy. With experience though, it's amazing how smoothly these things work. The caterer's fees for such events can be considerable, although the charity committee will try to bring in the party for as little as possible in order to maximize profits. However, people who can afford a thousand dollars for a ticket tend to be somewhat choosy, so the committee dare not settle for low-quality food, drink, or service.

**Favoritism and Kickbacks**    There is often much jockeying to obtain these contracts. And yes, the favoritism can be intense. Once again, one can be forgiven for suspecting that, as in so many areas of life, it's not what you know but who you know. Nor should you chide yourself too much for skeptically wondering whether kickbacks occur, because they undoubtedly do. For the blessed innocent, *kickback* is a euphemism for *bribe*. The employed person responsible for buying goods expects a reward for selecting one item over another.

Scarcely any area of the hospitality industry is free from kickbacks. So accepted is the practice that judges have been known to allow it, as a normal part of business. No other industry can expect such indulgence, but the law often takes a realistic view. A problem with the antitrust laws is that they occasionally conflict with reality; all they can do is try to contain outright monopoly and price fixing, though such phenomena occur everywhere.

## Aggressive Promotion

All of this simply underlines the absolute need for the caterer to get out and about, socializing, networking, approaching people with the suggestion that they should hold a function or throw a party, and so on. Many people want to entertain but can't face the preparation and work involved. If you can show them what a piece of cake it can be if they only allow you to make the arrangements, you may well create a regular customer. We are all consumers, and there is a great attraction in set-piece service and instant gratification.

Some individuals have abandoned entertaining in disgust because of the notoriously poor rate of reciprocation of hospitality in these strange times. You don't need to talk to many hosts before you hear grumbling along the lines of "I gave a party for a hundred people—champagne and lavish buffet, with live music. Know how many thank-you calls or letters I received? Three. Know how many return invitations I received from the crowd? One."

Bruised hosts can often be wooed back to the fold, however, by caterers who can offer a good, simple deal. If you can get hold of their guest lists, you may well find that many of the guests would be willing to do more entertaining if only they had a capable and affordable caterer to do their thinking and arranging for them.

Purists might observe that the spirit of *quid pro quo* carries its own doom, but most people who enjoy social life, and especially those who enjoy entertaining in their homes, do hope for some reciprocity, however unworthy that thought may be. Admittedly, in some neighborhoods, towns, and cities, the party circuit becomes boringly predictable to the regular guests—same old faces, the usual suspects. Any caterer, upon being congratulated on the excellence of the functions he's arranged, can be forgiven for flourishing his business card and saying "I'll be happy to do the same for you when you have your next party." In fact, it should be routine.

**Word-of-Mouth**    An enormous amount of catering business is generated by word-of-mouth. Someone wishing to give a party will recall a very pleasant occasion recently enjoyed. He will call up his hosts and ask for the name and telephone number of the caterer, and so the business builds. If you find yourself in the highly desirable position of regularly servicing the same group of people, you can avoid "going stale" by suggesting different items on the buffet or some kind of theme or entertainment. But if people have discovered themselves to be quite comfortable in your hands, they will often want more of same, not exciting changes. It is up to the caterer to assess the requirement. In general, the set-piece party system works best for both caterer and customer. People relax into familiarity, and this creates a comfortable ambiance in which people can get to know each other.

In summary, when you cater any kind of function, always make sure you have a good supply of *business cards* with you, and hand them out generously. These cards should simply give your name, address, and telephone number, and briefly state the available services—e.g. "Full party service—bartenders, waiters, cooks." *Word-of-mouth* is the single most powerful tool, and it's up to you and your satisfied customers to spread the word.

*Advertising*—which need not be expensive—is the next most efficacious method. Company and store—especially liquor store—bulletin boards are suitable targets. You can do some legwork by visiting company offices in person and conveying how pleasant and reliable you are, and by writing to companies to offer them your services.

A *personal letter* will work better than simply sending a printed brochure, and if you can mention a contact within the company who will serve as a reference, so much the better. Especially around Christmas time, some restaurants with space suitable for catering events will hire a temporary salesman to go out and sell the location for parties. There's no reason why you shouldn't do this year-round (this is discussed in Chapter 5).

# What to Charge

Many people embarking upon a catering career are thoroughly confused as to how much they should charge. There's no need to be. Fees and prices vary from region to region and from city to city, but they are usually stable within defined areas. A bond trader, questioned by a curious friend as to what he actually did all day, kept referring to market forces. "What are market forces?" the innocent friend eventually inquired. After some thought and with much furrowing of brow, the trader replied, "Well, market forces are what everybody else is doing."

## Find out the Going Rates

To establish the going rates in your area, simply ring up local caterers and ask them how much they charge to lay on, for example, a cocktail party for 50 with a bartender and maid. Do they provide the liquor? What do they require you, the host, to provide? If your house is well equipped for entertaining, with plenty of kitchen space, refrigeration, and a good supply of food and drink, how much will they charge to simply send an experienced bartender for four hours? And so on.

If you start with the catering company that has the biggest advertisement in the Yellow Pages, you'll probably discover the current top rates. Smaller scale advertisers may charge less. If you call four such companies you'll have an idea of the average current prices.

You'll find that a cheap and cheerful party can be brought in for as little as $15 per head—fruit, cheese, and pâté will be main items, and it's unlikely that people will drink anything heavier than wine or beer. If we're talking sit-down, or station parties, a likely price range will be $40 to $65—which still competes with hotel and restaurant prices. Once we ascend to the heady area of special dishes, pastas, lobsters, and so on, we get into the price range of, say, $60 to $125 per person.

There may be an immediate temptation to undercut the local caterers, but you should approach this idea with great caution. You may simply be foregoing profit unnecessarily. Most people who are affluent enough to spend money in this way are not into penny pinching, though some are, of course.

## The Rubber Chicken Circuit

As you progress to bigger contracts and assignments, however, the picture changes. If the local big charity is planning its annual bash, and one caterer can bring it in for $10,000 while the others are asking $15,000, the committee will obviously be tempted to go for the lower price. We may then risk entering what is rudely known as the rubber chicken circuit, where, in the interests of maximizing cash intake, a charity or political group will lay on a not very pleasing dinner.

Some will say, "So what? Okay, the food and drink weren't that hot, but everybody got together and had a good time anyway, and that's the main thing." True, the purpose of a lunch or dinner is often not a gourmet experience. But many busy sociable people become just a little tired of that basic, cheapest imaginable, lowest common-denominator menu of soup, chicken, ice-cream, and carafes (sparingly distributed) of dubious white wine. However, if a caterer is hired to provide such a dinner, he can only do his best. There is no reason why simple fare cannot be appetizing.

# Acquiring and Paying for Supplies, and Equipment

When you first start out, probably on a small scale, you'll be forced to pay regular retail prices for goods, materials, and equipment hire—if any. Once you achieve a certain size, and if you become a regular customer, things will improve because you'll be able to approach wholesalers. To do this you must inquire about local state laws. In some places you need to acquire a "Sales Tax Deferral," in others a "Seller's Permit." Sometimes the client will provide all the liquor, wine, and food, probably from a source with whom she does regular business. If you, the caterer, are required to lay in supplies, there is nothing to fear—you just have to plan a little, as we shall see. The liquor industry is very supportive in this area, as most stores deliver and allow a sale-or-return deal. Thus, you can take a case of vodka and two cases of white wine to a function, but unopened bottles can be returned and your money refunded. This is handy because you needn't fear running out of liquor or paying for supplies that are unused.

Some supermarkets will even do a similar deal for sodas and beers, though this is not a regular feature of their service. In cases where you are left with unused sodas and beers, you can store them for future use.

If the function is on a small scale, part of your reconnaissance should include the location of the supermarket and liquor store nearest to the party venue. Then, if you foresee running out of some item, you or an assistant can go out and get it. Be careful with this. In the country the nearest store may be twenty minutes away and closed. Even in cities, in the smarter areas, there are often few stores. If you are entertaining on Fifth Avenue in New York, for instance, and you run out of seltzer, you may well be four long blocks from the nearest store. However, local delivery service in such areas tends to be efficient, especially when the deliverer can be reasonably certain of a decent tip.

## Chapter Five

# Locations, Planning, and Staffing

## Locations

Location, for a catered event, isn't quite as crucial as it is for other retail enterprises, but still it looms large. When people call you out of the blue and ask you if you are available to cater a party on such and such a date, you may be inclined to say, after a scrutiny of your calendar, that you are. But the first question you need to ask is "Where is the function to be held?"

Sometimes the proposed venue is so horribly inconvenient that the stress involved in getting to and from it is not worth the candle. If you are intimidated by the prospect of having to trek out to the suburbs or the country and back, then you should say outright that the party is beyond your range. It may well be that your potential client will hasten to reassure you and show how easy it is, offer transportation, or agree to pay to get you and your staff home.

## Transporting Staff and Guests

It is a convention (and in some states, law) that if people work past a certain hour they must be guaranteed safe transport home. This applies particularly to women employees. Of course, many people have their own cars (which you might note on your list of available part-time workers), but if they don't you may have to get them home—possibly at 3 A.M. when public transportation in most places isn't running.

This can be a real problem in the American hospitality industry in general. One restaurant in the Hamptons, the rich Long Island resort area, had to close down because it simply couldn't find affordable labor. Even the local kids weren't available because they were the kind of offspring who receive their first Mercedes as an eighteenth birthday present and complain about the color. So employees had to be transported in from less affluent areas and paid top dollar for their labor. Management was stretched to the limit because no-shows were so frequent, and the suave maître d' often had to abandon his post at the door to bus tables and help in the kitchen.

Clearly there's a chance a caterer may encounter the same problem. Employees may not accept the necessity of traveling long distances because, apart from anything else, they're not getting paid for their time. The fact that millions of Americans travel for as much as four hours a day getting to and from work will not affect their thinking. If a client understands these kinds of difficulties and is prepared to pay the cost of overcoming them, then you simply hire the bus or the taxis and do your thing.

For larger functions, at the top end of the scale, you may be required to bus in some of the guests, too. Luxury buses—with bars and bathrooms—now exist for this purpose. They come into their own for parties held in the distant suburbs of major cities, and the system works generally very well.

Some wary guests reserve the right to leave a party the moment they're bored, and they will resist dependence on buses, which only depart at appointed hours. One can only sympathize—imagine being at a party where the noise is unbearable, there isn't a single person you want to talk to, and the first bus home departs at 1 A.M. Such guests will not usually accept invitations to boat cruises, either, where, once aboard, one is committed to stay until the craft returns to its berth.

## Finding the Right Location

An intriguing service exists in some cities called location referral, that will find you a mansion, a museum, a loft, a ballroom, or terraces, atriums, views, gardens, penthouses, and so on. If such a service exists in your area, it will almost certainly be listed in the Yellow Pages.

**INSTITUTIONS**     Here's an insider tip on locations. In every city or town there are far more available premises where functions can be held than you might suppose. Many institutions have superb locations for parties and will rent them out at extraordinarily friendly prices—provided the event is not for a commercial purpose. The definition of commercial is not terribly rigorous. They might balk at a big corporation wanting to hire them, and, if they agree to cooperate, charge them the same commercial rate a major hotel would charge. However, private individuals, charities, and deserving arts causes are usually acceptable. Such institutions usually don't advertise, preferring to restrict their hirings to a regular circle of clubs, groups, and individuals.

Libraries, and schools are good places to approach. Sometimes the premises do not lend themselves to heavy-duty entertaining—cocktails, beverages, and light refreshments may be the limit. For various reasons, even if heavier entertainment is feasible, the institution may not want it, perhaps because of disruption or potential damage to exhibits and collections. Some art galleries, for instance, invite people to exhibitions on occasion and offer them drinks—but not to be taken into the area where the paintings are hung. It is as well to be particularly circumspect and professional in one's approach to such bodies, because if they get the faintest whiff of irresponsibility they won't let you use their premises.

An advantage of such locations may be that, despite not being terribly central, they are comfortably accessible because they're spared heavy traffic. Also, some dedicated catering locations are just a bit stark, efficiently designed though they may be. You may prefer to adjust to small limitations for the sake of entertaining in a softly and pleasantly furnished room with nonechoing acoustics.

If you're embarking upon a catering career, it will pay you to explore the area for such gems. Then, if you approach individuals or groups with the suggestion that you lay on a party for them, and they demure on the grounds that they have no suitable premises, you can advise them of the possibilities.

**Private Homes**    You may even find individuals who are blessed with excellent accommodation in the form of a large apartment or house, but who are for one reason or another short of cash and so are willing to allow use of their home for an

---

**Some people are really enterprising.**    One caterer recently pulled off a coup in New York that had every restaurateur and caterer in town drooling with envy. He obtained a temporary license and took a short rental on a disused pier that had been a dock for a big ship in the days when the harbor was busier. It was summer, and there was ample parking because there was little residential or commercial property in the area. He laid on utilities, temporary but efficient bathrooms, and enough cooking facilities for a rudimentary menu. He even laid on draft beer—a triumphant step because (you guessed it) the place became an in-place for the ever burgeoning youth market.

**Old hands will smile and nod wisely.**    How do you coax people into granting a short lease on a pier? How do you so swiftly obtain a license to sell alcohol in such a place, bearing in mind all the regulations—fire safety, hygiene, and so on? Clearly through "friends at court." Everybody needs them. Actually, however, the faceless bureaucracies of our city halls are reasonably accommodating when it comes to the granting of occasional licenses for one-time or short-duration events.

evening. Divorced people, for instance, sometimes find themselves in the position of having been awarded a home but are cash poor. Many are very enterprising in the uses to which they put their property—singles club meetings, exhibition parties, and so on.

# PRELIMINARY PLANNING

If you're running a lean-and-mean one person catering business from home, especially in the initial stages many of your assignments will be so small and straightforward that all you need to do is turn up in good time to set up a simple bar and light buffet table without actually inspecting the premises and implementing the grand plan. (The details of how to do this will be explained later.)

You may assume with reasonable safety that, upon arrival, you'll find a decent sized kitchen, a good ice supply, ample garbage disposal facilities, the means of heating hot nibbles, and so on. Your client may cheerfully take on the task of setting up the hors d'oeuvres or canapés, perhaps having done it many times before. Indeed, your main function will be to relieve the host of the necessity of fixing drinks, taking coats, and passing plates so that she can orchestrate, intermingle, and, as the gossip columnists say, work the room. When you escalate to bigger parties, however, it will pay to reconnoiter the location; indeed, it is essential. Certain questions must be answered, and they appear on the accompanying checklist.

It is a good idea to solemnly and formally write down this list and make multiple copies of it. Keep it by the telephone for easy reference, and take it with you when meeting with clients to discuss functions, especially on those Monday mornings when your brain hasn't yet accelerated to its customary sizzling pace.

## CAPACITY AND SEATING

A very important question is "How many people can this room accommodate?" If the function is simply a stand-up cocktail party, then the rule of thumb is simply four people to the square yard. Of course, in making your assessment you'll need to allow for furniture already in place and furniture that may have to be brought in, such as the tables on which you set up your bars or buffets. Often furniture has to be moved out to make room for guests.

A *word of warning*: If furniture has to be brought in, make sure you calculate exactly how many tables and chairs can be accommodated and where they'll be placed. To put it very simply, a room 20 feet by 5 feet will not hold four 5-foot diameter tables, no matter what the mathematics may suggest. The reason is that a 5-foot diameter table is really a 9-foot-diameter table by the time you've allowed a foot (at least) for each guest on a chair and a foot on each side of the table to allow access. This is why skyscraper office moves worked out on a computer occasionally result in chaos. Inexperienced planners sometimes fail to factor in the human space required.

---

## Caterer's Planning Checklist

---

☐ How do my staff and I get to the location? _____
_____

☐ How many guests are expected? _____
_____

☐ What are they to be served? Drinks? Buffet? Dinner? _____
_____

☐ Will guests arrive by their own means, or am I to arrange transport?
_____

☐ Are there stairs? Will this limit the scale of service? _____
_____

☐ Is there an elevator, especially if heavy items such as prepared
foods, ice, and equipment are to be brought in? _____
_____

☐ Is the kitchen adequate to requirements? _____
_____

☐ If not, do I need to bring in other equipment? _____
_____

☐ Is there enough ice on site, or do I need to bring in more? _____
_____
_____

☐ Is there sink space, or are there suitable containers for chilled wine, beer, waters, and sodas? _____

_____

☐ Where are the bathrooms? Are they all in working order? _____

_____

☐ What are the coat/cloakroom requirements? Is it summer or winter?

_____

☐ Are the cloakroom facilities secure? _____

_____

☐ Where are the heating/air-conditioning controls? Do they work?

_____

☐ Do the windows open, and, if so, how? _____

_____

☐ Is there adequate space for all garbage generated? _____

_____

☐ Is there sufficient glassware, china, cutlery, etc? _____

_____

☐ Is clean-up equipment—mops, brushes, pans, and kitchen paper on hand for spills and emergencies? _____

_____

☐ Are there any special factors? Religious considerations? People in wheelchairs or in some other way disabled? _____

_____

_____

**Sit or Stand?**    A decision you or your client must make is "whether people are to sit or stand." At a simple drinks party of short duration, say not more than about two hours, it is often a good idea not to provide more than minimal seating. Of course, you must always have somewhere for the old, the tired, and the suddenly faint to rest, but in general these parties work better if no one sits.

Especially with a youngish crowd, where there's clearly some mixing and matching going on, it's nice if people can move around from group to group easily and without fuss, as opposed to being dragged from the depths of deep armchairs and trundled across the room. Indeed, some experienced hosts dread the sight of people sitting—it means the party has stagnated.

Weddings can involve a lot of standing, often a bit too much for comfort, as delays always seem to occur. It's easy to understand why a bride is always late for the ceremony, but why bridal couples always take so long to get to the reception remains one of life's greater mysteries. Even when the ceremony is in a private home, the proceedings can drag on somewhat, and by the time people sit down to the wedding breakfast they are often ravenous. (Funerals, for some reason, tend to be brisker affairs, and often rather jolly. Perhaps we tend to "whistle in the dark" on these occasions.)

It's important to get seating arrangements right, not only to promote the "theater" of a function but because the consequences of overcrowding can be dire. First of all, if things are too packed, far from thinking "Wow, what a party!" people will look at the jam, their hearts will sink, and they'll merely make an appearance and leave.

If the premises are large enough, a function will sometimes divide naturally into those who want to circulate and those who want to sit. Some hosts are better than others at circulating people and making introductions, but, although an experienced caterer can sometimes give discreet advice in these matters, it's not really his problem.

## Avoid Overcrowding

A common fate often befalls somewhat unimaginative people, or those constrained by circumstance, who decide to return all the hospitality they've received in recent months by giving one big party. If a party is simply too crowded, people lose interest and very little socializing is actually achieved. Such pointless parties are common around Christmas. Some hosts seem to harbor the belief that more is better and that everyone will find something or someone of interest at a large gathering. This is not always true, by any means. One man found himself at a grand reception given by a major bank in a swank hotel. He recognized the beautiful wife of the chairman and naturally paid his compliments and tried to engage her in conversation. To his consternation, she replied to all his remarks in such a low voice that he had to bend down close and ask her to repeat herself. After about the fourth time he couldn't control a brief frown of irritation, which the woman noticed. Beckoning him to come closer, she said, "I'm sorry to talk like this, but I go to two or three of these occasions a week, and I find that if I talk loud enough to compete with everyone else I go home with a sore throat and lose my voice for three days." Such can be the joys of the big party.

As people arrive at a reception or party, or as a restaurant starts to fill, each new arrival has to raise his or her voice a notch in order to compete with those already in place. Many people love this buzz, and for some it's the sure sign of a successful gathering or restaurant. Again, it's each to his own taste, and one must bear in mind that different occasions have different purposes.

When functions are held in hotels, and in private houses or apartments, an incorrect assessment of how many people can be properly accommodated may lead to spillage. Other dwellers in an apartment block may not be amused by seeing the common landings and stairways taken over by their neighbor's guests. They may complain, and someone may have to go around asking people to confine themselves to the designated party premises—which may be very tight indeed.

## The Hazards of Crowding

In the worst cases of party crowd spillover, the police or the local fire department may be called. These bodies have the absolute authority to disperse crowds exceeding the legal posted maximum occupancy if on commercial premises, and may use their discretion to disperse crowds on private premises if they feel that other people are put at risk or have to endure nuisance of any kind.

Many a jolly party has been brought to an abrupt end because of irresponsible overcrowding. You may have noticed lines of people queuing outside bars and clubs, corralled by a rope and controlled by doormen. They are making sure the place doesn't exceed its maximum occupancy. The local police and fire officers tend to note popular places, especially new establishments, which serve only the most rudimentary beverages and are always jam-packed—until that sudden and mysterious day when they are no longer an in-place and become deserted.

FIRE    Stories of fire disasters in which many people died because of excessive crowding are regularly recycled in the press as a salutary warning. Of these, the most notorious is probably the fire at Boston's Coconut Grove, in the 1940s. A recurring factor in such accidents is emergency exits (sometimes fitted with "panic bolts" that enable the door to be opened instantly with one push on a bar), that were firmly locked to prevent entry without paying the entrance fee.

Two major causes of fire are cooking accidents and cigarettes insufficiently extinguished. When people are crowded together, and especially when women are dressed in flowing dresses, the caterer needs to have an eye open for such hazards. Consider the nineteenth-century Wittelsbach princess who fulfilled the mystical prophecy that she and her two sisters would die, one by water, one by steel, and one by fire, by sneaking an illicit cigarette that ignited her lace dress. For this reason the decision to serve dishes flambé—which is actually easy and fun—should be carefully considered and abandoned if the function is likely to be crowded.

## Forestalling Problems

In your discussions with clients, never use the word "problem," unless you're talking yourself out of a party you really don't want to handle. There are no problems to the professional. There are only special factors to be taken into consideration and arrangements to be made.

This is where restaurant experience will be very useful. Running a kitchen for a family of six is one thing. Feeding and watering sixty out of that same kitchen is quite another. For instance, the drips from wine bottles constantly being removed from, and then returned to, an ice bucket can amount to a veritable flood within about 20 minutes if a lot of people arrive at once. For this reason, a modern restaurant kitchen and bar will have a gently sloping floor and a central drainage point for ease of cleaning. Few private homes are built like this. You have to be ready and able to cope.

Brush and pan, mop and bucket must be instantly available to clear up after the unfortunate buffet diner whose plate is suddenly on the floor or whose brimming glass is knocked over. Ideally, reaction is instant, so that hardly anyone notices.

## Serving Food

A very efficient method of serving food to large gatherings is to invite people to sit at their designated tables with their cocktails, having laid out the first (cold) course. Such a course might be smoked salmon, a shrimp cocktail, lobster salad, roll-mop herring, or even just a simple salad. It shouldn't be set out on the tables until the last minute, of course, for food safety and sanitation's sake. When it looks as if most people have finished the first course, the caterer or an assistant can then visit each table in turn to invite those guests to go to the buffet for service of the main course.

At the service point it's a good idea (though not essential), to have a choice of items, to display a menu so that people know what to ask for. Allowing people to remain seated until they're told the main course is being served means that they don't have to wait long in line. The guests have their first course to finish, their bread rolls and butter, and their wine, so, provided the delay isn't too long, there's no reason they should become impatient.

The en-mass lineup for food can have depressing overtones and can be a bit of a bore for the guests if service is slow—as it can be if some guests dither about their choices or stop to chat while serving themselves. A further advantage of the system described above is that it requires fewer waiters on the floor because all they do is clear up and take away—a much quicker procedure than serving individual plates at table.

**Serving Hot Food Far Away from the Kitchen**     Occasionally you may find yourself required to serve hot food to rooms far from the kitchen. The best way to handle this is to use proving ovens—lightweight, cupboard-like cabinets into which you place Sterno lamps (little cans of fuel that burn for some time with an intense blue flame—you see them used in upscale restaurants where food is prepared at tableside).

On this scale, you'll almost certainly employ a chef, and it's up to her to get the timing right. About ten minutes before the meal is to be served, the prepared plates of hot food are taken and placed in the ovens. They will stay hot—very hot—for a long time, but obviously you want to get people seated and served before the food starts to dry out. That is your client's problem, not yours, although you may be required to make the announcement "Dinner is served" at the appointed hour.

# Right-Sizing Your Staff

The key to working out just how many people need to be hired is quite simply "How many guests are there?" The number of workers required is reduced if service can be delivered with super-efficiency, perhaps because the kitchen adjoins the dining room or there's a designated and equipped bar area that is easy to handle. If the function lends itself to tipping, the help will prefer to work with as few people as possible.

The same situation often confronts the restaurateur. Should he put on six waiters, and insure excellent service for his customers, or should he put on only three, thus saving himself a small salary outlay and reducing the number of people sharing the tips, but lowering the standard of service?

## Staff Size and Tipping

A point to remember here is that sometimes (by no means always) the tip level drops significantly with the level of service. Customers and clients who have been able to command barely ten seconds of their waiter or bartender's attention, have established no rapport whatsoever, and have not dared ask any pertinent questions about the menu because this would clearly delay the proceedings, may not tip more than the polite minimum.

One well-trained and efficient worker is worth more than two bumblers who, to everyone's irritation, haven't acquired the knack of just looking at a busy room and instantly seeing what needs to be done, whether it be service, clearing up, or whatever. A caterer's workload can be doubled if he has to constantly instruct his assistants in every detail.

Although one could argue that staff size matters little since the client is simply charged more if more workers are employed, this is not always the case. Sometimes a flat all-inclusive fee will be agreed on, and in this case it's up to the caterer to carve out her own profit. Clearly the smaller the payroll the better, consistent with efficient performance.

## Sealing the Staff to the Event

Accurate estimation of the number of workers required for a function comes with experience. If the function involves a sit-down meal (some call this a station party) with a set menu, one waiter can comfortably handle a dozen guests. If the function is a simple cocktail party with rudimentary food, or a simple buffet, one experienced bartender can handle 40 or even 50 guests. There is always a peak period at a party, but usually the arrival of guests is sufficiently spread out for a caterer to stay on top of demand. But this is bedrock level, and if the service demanded or the complexity of the food escalates beyond this simple level, the caterer may risk chaos without the help of an assistant.

A very common arrangement, and one that works well for cocktail/buffet parties with more than 30 guests, is the butler and maid arrangement. The butler is also the bartender; he greets, takes coats, and serves drinks. The maid prepares the hors d'oeuvres in the kitchen and assists at the buffet.

## Pitching In

There is little room for unionism in catering. The first worker to spy something that needs to be done should take care of it, be it refilling someone's glass, removing a discarded napkin or squashed gherkin from the carpet, or emptying an ashtray. Good workers take everything in stride without having to think about it. They're the kind to treasure—and reward.

## Chapter Six

# Equipment and Entertainment

## Equipment

Oh dear, you may be thinking, proving ovens—where on earth do I get such things? The answer is from exactly the same place you obtain all your special equipment—bigger catering companies. Such companies, often attached to large and successful landmark restaurants, have the space and wherewithal to buy and store their own equipment. You can rent it, usually at very friendly rates.

Mightn't such a company be a bit miffed that you're using their equipment for your own business? The answer is no, they could care less. They'd rather make a few dollars on the hire of the equipment than see it lying idle.

If you become successful and start expanding the scope of your operations, you may eventually buy your own equipment. Storage will then be a problem. You could hire a garage or equivalent somewhere in the suburbs, but then you'd have to retrieve your equipment whenever you need it. This adds one more move to your function plans. It also adds rent and transportation expenses.

### Storage

A golden rule when purchasing equipment is to first ensure that you have somewhere to store it. The vendor may start charging you storage shortly after you buy—this is something you should discuss when agreeing on a price. Here you must take great care. It is unlikely that you will ever endure the following nightmare scenario, which happened to one caterer, but it is a cautionary tale. He found a bargain price job lot of equipment—stove, refrigerator, heavy containers,

43

and so forth—and couldn't resist buying it. Sensibly he first arranged to rent a garage at a cheap rate, simply telling the owner that he'd be storing equipment there. On the appointed day he hired a truck, rounded up some assistance, and loaded up. At the garage, the frowning owner looked over the equipment and promptly refused to take it in, fearing there was going to be cooking on the premises. The caterer was now stuck with the equipment and the truck, so he kept the truck one more day while he feverishly scouted for alternative storage premises. He found it, of course, but at a very unfriendly price—the owner perhaps suspecting dire need. This was very bad luck. "The best laid plans of mice and men *gang aft agley*" and all that. By contrast, a company that rents out equipment will deliver and pick up. One simply has to look at the costs and decide.

## Second-Hand Equipment

The purchasing of secondhand equipment is often an excellent idea. You will occasionally see sales of such equipment, usually from failed restaurants, advertised in the local press. It's very important to keep your ear to the ground if you intend to buy equipment to insure the best choice. The word goes around very quickly, and the moment the padlock goes on the door of a failed restaurant potential buyers will be sniffing around. You can call the local newspaper and ask them if they have any advertisements scheduled for forthcoming editions, or you can ask if certain sections of the newspaper, such as the classifieds, are sold in advance of the issue publishing date. (For instance, as every New Yorker knows, the *New York Times* Sunday real estate section is available by Thursday.) If you are late to the fray you may find that "others" have already bought the best bits, leaving only sad quantities of cutlery and china.

If you are any kind of an engineer, or number one among your acquaintances, you are very well placed to assess the potential of apparently beat-up secondhand equipment. Stories of refrigerators that only needed a good cleaning and half an hour's tinkering to deliver another ten years of service are legion. A prize example is the resuscitation of a discarded espresso machine (a curiously expensive piece of equipment when bought new) that went on to make thousands of cups of coffee and cappuccino before finally expiring.

*Warning*—secondhand equipment is unlikely to be still under warranty. And banks will not usually lend money to purchase it. Sometimes it makes sense for a restaurateur to lease equipment, but few caterers will wish to take on a fixed overhead.

## A Mobile Unit

You may get to the stage where you decide to invest in (either by purchasing new or secondhand, or renting)—a van or truck equipped with cooking equipment from which you serve simple meals such as hamburgers, hot dogs, and beverages. You can then cast about for outdoor occasions that might provide a slot for you— perhaps a sports meeting, a rally, a Highland Gathering, a flea market, or a park concert. An operator's license is usually required, and you have to pay the daily rent for the site. Nevertheless this can be a well-paying business if the weather is good and plenty of people turn up for the event. If it rains, it can be a disaster, but one has to take the rough with the smooth.

Other operators may be well established at regular events, and so you may not be admitted. A certain mild skullduggery often occurs in the area, with the event manager by no means resisting a small reward for his compliance and absolutely insisting on a free hamburger and coffee.

While trying to horn in on regular events, it's a good idea to scout your area for any upcoming events. The sort of people who'll know will be local public relations companies, the tourist office, and City Hall. It won't hurt to establish a rapport with someone in each of these areas—just getting a name and having a friendly chat on the telephone might be enough, but a visit in person may work even better.

## Subcontracting

There may be occasions when you're asked to do a party that takes you out of your depth. This may be exactly what you're hoping for because it is expansion. Don't panic if this happens, because you can always approach a bigger outfit and engage their assistance. Of course you'll be increasing your overhead somewhat, but you can legitimately pass this on and include it in your bill. You'll still get a substantial cut of the proceeds, and you still won't have the overhead of premises, storage, equipment purchase, and all the rest, which the caterer working from home wishes strenuously to avoid. You may think that in such circumstances you're acting as little more than a salesperson for another catering company. But what's wrong with that, as long as you're getting paid? Some of the bigger catering companies employ salespeople whose sole job is to sell the service.

## Equipment for Rent

The accompanying list presents some of the convenient things you can hire (or buy) for catered parties and events. A nice aspect of the huge selection of equipment available is that it expands the variety of themes that parties can have. You can have fancy-dress parties, Wild West parties, Vegas parties, and company picnics. If the guest of honor is from Texas, you can decorate with yellow roses, and so on.

## Hirable Supplies and Services for Catered Events

**Balloons**  Every imaginable shape is ready to be bought, and you can even have special shapes designed if you wish. Of course, if you insist on rivaling Macy's Thanksgiving Day Parade, the manufacturers will need lots of notice. If all you need is Snoopy for the day, Macy's will oblige, but it isn't cheap because such huge balloons require a trained crew to operate them.

**Barbecues**  You can hire various-size equipment if, as would be somewhat unusual, the suburban or country house you are operating in doesn't have one. In town, you might set up a barbecue on a terrace or balcony, but the fume problem can be serious. The police might be called to ask you to put it out, and neighbor relations might be stretched, to say the least.

**Bars**  The range here is from wood and cardboard mockups, which convey the impression of being in a regular commercial bar, to a fully functioning temporary installation with running-water sinks, refrigerators, and so on. Years ago, when Prohibition was recent enough to be a vivid memory, this was considered a naughty, fun item. These days it might fall a bit flat, but it does provide focus and a convenient place from which to dispense drinks.

**Cars**  Most towns have at least one company that can supply cars of various sizes, from regular models (often driven by the owner earning a little spare time cash) to stretch limousines.

**Carousels**  These are mainly for children's parties. Make sure they're properly supervised, and discreetly inquire about insurance.

**Carpets**  All kinds of carpets can be hired, including the long red carpet traditionally used to greet VIPs. At some London stores such a carpet is instantly available in case one of the palaces should call and announce a royal visit. Remember, like parachutes and spinnaker sails, they roll out much faster than they roll up.

**Chafing Dishes**  These come in various shapes and sizes, often with a little platform underneath for a can of Sterno. The purpose of Sterno is to keep food hot, and the cans are decorative enough (usually gold or silvery chrome) to be included on a buffet or dining table. *Important warning*—if you decide your chafing dishes need polishing, make sure they're thoroughly washed in hot soapy water afterwards and rinsed thoroughly. Residual polish will make people very sick, very promptly, even if it is mixed in with hot food. "Hot," in this context, isn't hot enough. Don't leave this precaution to a willing but hapless minion who has never seen a chafing dish in his life, much less a polished one.

**CHINA**  Cups, saucers, and plates of all sizes and types are available. Check on what you'll have to pay for breakage—chances are the answer will be nothing, as catering china, bought in bulk, is inexpensive and vendors allow fair wear and tear. At the top end of society, regular catering china may be inadmissibly coarse and crude, but at this end of the market there'll be plenty of family porcelain to deploy. If the rented china is Okay, just check to see whether it comes in clean or not, and if in doubt, wash it. Never assume anything. If the previous users, or the hirers, simply put a whole load into a dishwashing system, there will be some delinquent items—there always are. The dirty plate, bent fork, or lipstick-encrusted glass will, without exception (such is the power of Murphy's Law), be presented to the guest of honor or, worse, the Client.

**COACHES**  Including horse-drawn carriages. These are fun but expensive, and may throw the timing off, if that's an important factor. They don't work well in inclement weather.

**COAT RACKS**  You may need several. Don't forget the hangers and, for larger functions, the cloakroom tickets and a large packet of pins.

**COFFEE URNS AND HOT WATER (FOR TEA)**  These will usually come in clean, but a quick rinse will do no harm as they may be a bit stale.

**COOKING EQUIPMENT**  Just about anything you can name is available, and it usually works efficiently. You merely need to check its cleanliness.

**CUTLERY AND SILVERWARE**  Though clean, it may be blotched, in which case a quick rinse in hot water and a wipe with a cloth will be needed. One method is for the server, or whoever is setting the table, to have a damp cloth in his hand and simply give everything a wipe as it is laid down. Remember to have a small reserve of cutlery items handy. People drop things, and they should be replaced with clean utensils, not simply retrieved and handed back.

**DANCE FLOORS**  These are surprisingly easy to assemble—simply wooden sections fitted together, usually in a large tent or marquee. Generally speaking, the older they are, the better they are, and it's fun to consider the hundreds of feet that have traversed them.

**FOG MACHINES**  For stage effects, they merely release frozen nitrogen, which turns into harmless fog upon contact with air. They are sometimes fun on the dance floor or around the podium when light-hearted speeches are to be made.

(*continued*)

**Flowers** Need to be arranged well in advance. You can pay the earth for something that only a few may notice, so a careful review is indicated. Some people really like to go to town in this area, and you might arrange a kickback for yourself when you talk to your friendly florist.

**Frozen Cocktail Machines** These can instantly dispense Frozen Margaritas and similar concoctions. Again, a possible amusement for a young crowd.

**Furniture** Chairs, folding chairs, and tables of all types and sizes, including card, kiddie-sized, and banquet. Consider storage, assembly, and lifting as you plan. Try to avoid a hopeless mêlée in which heads, knees, and elbows get cracked on all sides, when, upon breaking down the installation, workers just grab bits and pieces willy-nilly and take them out to the storage area or truck. Get on top of the situation like a drill sergeant. "First we take out the chairs," and so forth.

**Glassware** All shapes and sizes are available. Make sure that your client wants glass and not plastic. Some consideration should be given to the location—glass is not a good idea around a swimming pool, for instance, where people may be wandering around with bare feet either on the festive occasion or at some later time. Glassware is usually expected to be returned clean, which means an extra chore for you or your staff.

**Lecterns** If anyone plans to make a speech, or if there is a slide presentation, you'll almost certainly need one. If it's a big room, you'll also need a microphone, and you should check that it's working well in advance so that you can get it fixed or replaced if it isn't.

**Linen** Tablecloths, cook's aprons, pants, jackets, white hats, dish mops, towels, and napkins are available. This hired-out and constantly recycled laundry takes a beating, and once in a while you'll peel a tablecloth or napkin from a bundle and find it stained or dilapidated. You can hire white waiter's jackets, too.

**Paper Goods** Napkins, party hats, streamers, noisemakers, invitations, place cards, menus, programs, garlands. If you're in the city, printing can often be arranged quickly, but it might take two weeks to produce a menu or invitation cards. Place cards and table plans are usually handwritten because they may not be finalized until the day of the function. You should prepare as much as you can—place cards for people who've definitely accepted the invitation and the table diagram without the names. There will often be last-minute adjustments as people cancel or accept right before the event, and in these circumstances there may not be a typewriter handy. Although the standard of handwriting is not high today, there's usually someone around—as often as not someone who draws or paints—with a fair hand and a proper pen who can take charge of writing menus, place cards, table plans, and so on.

**Party Favors**  These are little presents for the guests, such as small bottles of perfume or cologne, or souvenir badges. At the big charity balls the guests sometimes go home with small suitcases crammed with goodies such as chocolates, champagne, perfume, ties, scarves, liquor, key rings, and pens or pencils.

**Plastic Tableware**  If acceptable, plastic table utensils will save many a move. Nowadays it doesn't have to be airline stark—there are all sorts of designs. There will always be those who swear that a single-malt whisky simply doesn't taste right unless it's drunk from a heavy-cut glass, but they are not a majority.

**Pushcarts**  Hot dog, ice-cream, pretzel, bagel, popcorn, coffee, soup and sandwiches, and so forth. They make for a carnival atmosphere, especially if they're gaily decorated.

**Searchlights**  These can be used for simple decorative purposes, swirling around the sky or pointed straight up, so that the beam can be seen for miles around. This is a trick borrowed from the military, which sometimes uses searchlights to indicate rallying points. It works wonderfully in a suburban area, but in a convention resort area you can see as many as three or four beams shafting heavenwards from various hotels. You think you've arrived at the Mutual Fund Convention dinner and find you're at the Annual Chiropodist's Awards ceremony.

**Sound Equipment**  There are even such things as mobile discos if it's that kind of party.

**Strobes**  These are intensely bright, flickering lights often used in clubs. Outside that area they serve no purpose and can be very irritating to many people.

**Tents**  Above a certain size they are more likely to be called marquees. Make sure the suppliers are prepared to erect and strike them for you; otherwise, you'll flounder as never before. They have it down to a drill and make extraordinarily light work of it.

*(continued)*

**Trays**  The two kinds you'll use most are bar trays for drinks—cork-bottomed so that the glasses don't slip and spillage can be absorbed—and the larger ones on which several plates of food can be placed. There is a certain art in carrying these trays at shoulder level on the flat of the hand, and it isn't entirely ridiculous to practice it. Some restaurateurs simply ask applicants for serving jobs to pick up a tray and walk with it. If they get it right, they get the job.

**Umbrellas**  You may need umbrellas for people to sit under if it's a sunny day. If it's a rainy day, you may need at least a couple of large golf umbrellas for people to shelter under as they step from a car to the safety of canopy or door. In such circumstances, try to make sure people go all the way in promptly so as not to leave following guests in the rain.

**Video Games**  These can be hired, along with slot machines. They may seem an odd accessory for a party function, but the bored young may welcome their presence.

## Car Services: Tipping and Payment

One area you should explore is whether or not the driver will expect a tip. They almost invariably do, but a host may not wish her guests to have to tip the driver of the car that picks them up—in which case she may invite the operator to add a service charge. Few indeed, unfortunately, are the drivers who will refuse an offered tip on the grounds that they'll be getting one from the firm later.

No hard and fast rules have been established in this delicate area. What is the tip requirement of a technician called to repair some equipment who is then driven home? What is the position of a paid guest on a TV show, who is picked up from home or hotel? The simple solution when in doubt is—ask. Of course, if the office says there's no need to tip, the driver may go into one of those dreary, whining monologues about the famous person he once had in the car, rich as Rockefeller (if not Rockefeller himself) who failed to tip. However, consumers have hardened their attitudes in recent years, and most limo companies won't turn a hair if you specify no tipping, no smoking, no radio, no conversation, and air conditioning. They want the business.

Some drivers require payment in cash on the spot. If they are hired at very short notice this is more likely to be the case. An inexorable rule of life is that when you want or need something in a hurry, it's likely to cost you more. Remember, caveat emptor—buyer, beware!

# ENTERTAINMENT

In addition to equipment, you can also hire all sorts of entertainers to make your function more interesting. The accompanying list offers some ideas. None of this information is exactly top secret—it is taken from the Yellow Pages. An in-depth browse through these pages, usually under "Party," "Party Planning Service," or "Party Supplies—Retail and Rental," will reveal the gamut of possibilities.

You or your client must decide whether it's appropriate to bring in entertainment. Some hosts insist that guests must interact and entertain themselves. Also remember that the artists may wish to look at the premises in advance of performance.

---

## People To Hire for Special Events

**Belly Dancers**  A must if you are doing a Middle Eastern theme or have guests from such countries. Other kinds of dancers, from tap to flamenco, are also available.

**Clowns**  They are greatly enjoyed by children and in great demand at certain times of the year, so book early. There are also jugglers and magicians—sometimes all three services are provided by the same person.

**Clairvoyants**  This group includes palm readers and tarot card readers. Their view of the future almost invariably includes liberation of long-frustrated creativity, wealth, and true love. People seem to love it—is not the horoscope page the most popular in the tabloids?

**Disc Jockeys**  Especially for young parties with dancing, they can be a good investment. The music has narrowed to top-forty selections, some of them more than a quarter of a century old ("Dancing in the Street," "Locomotion," etc.), and the DJs know how to get things going. The current fashion for loud music means that you need to consider neighbors and make sure that there is at least one room or area where comparative quiet exists—just in case people want to talk.

**Musicians of All Kinds**  The local music school will probably have a range of student groups who want to make some pocket money. Make sure they play background music, such as lesser known string or piano quartets, not commanding stuff that everyone feels they must listen to. At the same time, music that is too plastic and elevator-style may be equally distracting.

*(continued)*

Soloists such as harpists, guitarists, and pianists, who sometimes also sing, are easy to find. Make sure your musicians understand that they're providing background and that they aren't the focus of the occasion, or they may get a little huffy. It's a party, not a concert.

**PHOTOGRAPHERS**  An excellent addition to a memorable occasion. The host will have other things to do than gather different people to pose, though one group photograph is easy enough to organize. Guests often spend more time worrying about where they've put their $800 camera than actually taking shots. You can have a video done, too.

**POETS**  Will compose odes on designated themes or around personalities. They'll need to know the salient points of a subject's career and personality. Best to stick to sales performance and golf rather than private excesses—unless the host insists. This service can extend to speech writing.

**PORTRAIT PAINTERS**  They bring along an easel, lots of drawing paper, and, usually, crayons. They usually employ the cartoonist's technique of seizing the strongest features of a face and emphasizing them, so that the result is merely a fun caricature rather than a breathtaking likeness.

**PROFESSIONAL PARTY BRIGHTENERS**  These are best hired by recommendation through word of mouth. They are usually attractive and bouncy women who know how to make people interact.

**SKY DIVERS**  They need a fairly spacious drop zone, so this is clearly only for suburban or country parties. The latest parachutes are very steerable, so divers can usually land on target. They're not very expensive. It's up to the local skydiver's club to make the air traffic control arrangements, if required.

**STRIPOGRAMMERS**  Along with kissogrammers and songsters, you must carefully weigh the appropriateness (or otherwise) of such enhancements to your function. There are still a few shockable people left on the planet. It's the client's decision.

# Delivering Maximum Satisfaction

## Client Confidence and Satisfaction

You should regard every client as a potentially permanent fixture of your catering operation, just as the successful restaurateur always regards each customer as a potential regular. Business schools call it developing a good client base. The way you ensure delivery of maximum satisfaction is by concentrating on the matter at hand and exuding professional know-how—not in a fierce or paranoid way but in a way that fills the client with confidence.

### Take the Client's Worries Seriously

You should not be too blithe or dismissive if your client expresses certain doubts, fears, or worries. The professional caterer takes all kinds of functions in stride, but a host at his or her first party is bound to feel somewhat nervous. At weddings, for instance, it's often difficult to say who is the more nervous—the groom or the bride's father.

One senior executive in charge of an event to which even more senior executives had been invited—the very ones who would decide on his promotion—held a final meeting with the staff who were organizing the event. As he ticked off each detail in the arrangements, the person handling it assured him that everything was under control. A pattern of response developed in which every second question seemed to provoke an answer that began with what were meant to be the reassuring words "Don't worry about that . . ." Such was his tension that at a certain point the executive couldn't help snapping "Will you please stop telling me not to worry? I'm very concerned—this is an important occasion and I want it to go well."

If a host becomes querulous, your approach should be twofold. First you should convince her that you do indeed understand the importance of getting this or that special aspect of the function right, making sure that the guests have a whale of a time, or that there's plenty of chilled white wine in reserve. Then you should tell her precisely how you propose to take care of this. "I'll tell Judy—she's my most experienced waitress—to concentrate on that as her sole responsibility. That way there won't be any mistakes." This is where professional *gravitas*, a serious, reassuring straight face and manner—will work for you. But unless you sense that you're working for people who are deeply reassured by *gravitas*, don't wear that face all the time, as it can get a bit gloomy. Some people get through life wearing such a face all the time, but they're not much fun at parties.

## Make Special Arrangements upon Request

It's not uncommon at even quite small functions for one waiter to be told to unobtrusively attend to one person or one small party, to the exclusion of all other duties. When the Queen of England (or even a junior member of the royal family), sallies forth, there is always a lady-in-waiting, or a male equerry, at her elbow in case she needs anything—in addition to the security guards. This yields its funny incidents. It's hard not to smile when some distinguished officer, all sword and medals, is required to hold Her Majesty's pocketbook while she presents a prize and shakes hands, or whatever. Once a young footman, standing at her elbow at the Ascot race meeting, sprang into action when the queen requested some sugar. He returned swiftly with a bowl of loose sugar in a silver bowl on a silver salver. The Queen gave him a withering look. "It's for the horse," she said. "You know, cube sugar."

While caterers in their professional detachment are entitled to derive as much humor from their observations as they wish, the seriousness of the occasion from the client's point of view must be respected. One caterer had the initiative to go out and buy a morning coat (i.e., one with tails), a pair of pepper-and-salt striped pants, and a bumblebee waistcoat. He thus added another string to his bow—that of the perfect English butler, like Hudson in "Upstairs, Downstairs," for those who remember the highly successful TV series. Public relations firms regularly hired him in this sole capacity. Sometimes they'd hold functions in grand hotels and pull him in (at a generous fee) for their business presentations.

The "butler" was not required to serve food or drink, nor was he required to pick up discarded glasses or indeed perform any of the normal duties of the butler or caterer. He was required to perform one function only, and that was to collect a business card from every one of the invited executives sent by the various companies. He was even provided with a silver salver (that's a posh term for a tray upon which originally food was placed for the court food taster, whose job it was to ensure that the king wasn't being poisoned).

Clearly this was not the most onerous of duties. But it ensured that the PR company had the names of scores of executives who were sufficiently interested in their presentation to attend it. It may sound like overkill, but often an invitation sent to one company executive will be passed to another. It's important in business to focus on an individual by name, so our butler's function, though easy as pie, was quite an important one.

# Be As Prepared As Possible

Once again the importance of planning, observation, and anticipation must be stressed. The list of proverbs exhorting this wisdom is endless: "Forewarned is forearmed," "Time spent in reconnaissance is seldom wasted," "A stitch in time saves nine," and so on. There is no other way to combat Murphy's Law, which says that —if something can go wrong, it *will go wrong*. In engineering this bleak rule is anticipated by providing alternatives—no less than three central computers on some planes, dual brake systems on cars, and local generators in hospitals in case the main power supply goes down.

The caterer must play the same game. Every waiter and bartender must be equipped with a corkscrew; there must be more than one supply of napkins; and everyone must know where the cleaning gear is stored, where the telephone is, where the restrooms and cloakrooms are. A true professional in the catering or restaurant industry always has a spare shirt or blouse in her bag, because when accidents happen (such as exploding ketchup bottles) this garment inevitably suffers first and most. If black bow ties are to be worn, then they are best tied, not clipped on, as there is nothing quite so dispiriting as the sight of an accidentally detached bow tie swimming in the soup.

## Have Plenty to Eat and Drink

The sale-or-return service that most liquor stores offer means that there is no need to run out of liquor or wine. With food, if premium items, such as cold duck, smoked chicken, caviar, shrimp, and lobster are offered at a buffet, they will disappear fast. It will probably stretch the party budget to lay on huge amounts of these items (though some hosts will not stint their guests in any fashion), but basics like crusty bread, cheese, and yes, even things that come out of cans, can ensure that no one goes hungry, even if guests don't get the best of what has been on offer.

Think of it as ammunition. This is by no means a perfect analogy because, while running out of ammunition is sometimes unavoidable for a soldier, who cannot always determine the size and scope of an enemy attack, it is totally unnecessary for the caterer and her client, who are not fighting a battle (although it may sometimes feel a bit like that). They are more commonly entertaining a group of friends or, at least, people who share a common interest and general goodwill of one kind or another.

## Open House Events

Woe to the host who simply offers an open house, with no serious idea of how many guests will show up. There is often a dangerous sort of dilution of quality among friends as the acquaintance is extended. You may have known someone for years and trust them implicitly. But if that friend is told he can bring another friend or friends to a function, then the group may casually extend to someone who is not well known and perhaps rather dubious. Open house parties are absolutely hopeless if the host or hosts have any specific purpose in view, such as putting together a sports team or social or business networking. The absence of formal introductions will destroy the value of the gathering.

## Gate-Crashers and Thieves

Gate-crashers can be absolutely harmless. You might get a society gawker who wants a close-up look of some famous person. It has even been known for interlopers of this type to be apprehended by security officers, checked out, and allowed to stay as long as they're correctly dressed and behave themselves.

But there is another kind of gate-crasher—the professional thief. He can be a very smooth operator indeed and look quite smart in a tuxedo, but his target is usually women's purses. The harrowing scenes after a theft often involve inquiries along the lines of "The guy with the mustache . . . who was he anyway?" "Joe's friend." "What friend?" says Joe, "I came alone."

It's a good idea to instruct the catering staff to be on the alert for uninvited guests and ensure their swift expulsion from the proceedings. This is particularly important when events are held in public places. Make no mistake, professional criminals target such functions for easy pickings of handbags and cameras. People are relaxed and concentrating on the event. Alcohol may be flowing, and this always increases the likelihood of mischief.

The professional criminal's most effective weapon is often not a gun but a big friendly smile. He will read the newspapers to review upcoming events. Even a death notice suggests that, at the time of the funeral, a house or houses may be empty for a comfortable length of time, and it is by no means unusual for happy wedding guests and grieving mourners alike to return to find they've been robbed.

There's nothing a professional criminal likes better than a sea of laughing faces and a bunch of people being determinedly informal. On busy Friday and Saturday nights in restaurants, or at busy functions, a cheerful person will often engage the catering manager or maître d' in genial conversation while a partner steals a bag.

# The Usefulness of Formality

Formality may be repulsive to some people, but it has a serious and useful purpose. Far from making people feel ill at ease, it is designed to make them more relaxed by indicating what they should do. Often it falls to the caterer to provide the formality by making announcements such as "Dinner is served," which, if delivered by the embarrassed host, would reduce everyone to giggles. Hosts very often welcome this function, so it should not be ignored.

It really helps if people can be organized. All that is required is that the stages of an event be signposted by announcements. "Please follow me for the video presentation," "The show will be starting in five minutes, so please take your seats," and so on. If formality is abandoned completely, all the ingredients of potential disaster are in place, from stolen purses to a general chaos from which no useful or enjoyable social intercourse can be gained.

Caterers engaged to handle very informal events will do well to approach them with caution; but, having said that, I must add that wherever large numbers of people are gathered, there's money to be made. A swamped bartender may go home exhausted, but he may go home with $500 in tips, which should sweeten his well-earned slumber. Such scenarios are by no means uncommon.

# Common Mistakes That Can Spoil Gatherings

The only suggestion of customer dissatisfaction that a caterer may ever receive is failure to be hired again. One of the things that makes life difficult is the fact that rejection and dissatisfaction often remain unexplained. When someone applies for a job and doesn't get it, it's rare for the true reasons to be divulged. Apart from anything else it's illegal to say certain things—such as "We prefer women" or "You're too old."

It's galling to hear that an ex-client of yours just gave a whopping party—laid on by another caterer—but one shouldn't be driven to the psychiatrist's couch by such events. Sometimes they may be due to reasons entirely beyond your control. A relative or close friend of the client may have gone into the business. Or another caterer may have offered to bring in the party at a much lower fee than you would charge.

This kind of thing is not unusual at charity events, for instance. The committee, understandably, wants to maximize profits There is also the occasional desire for a change. Many caterers find this hard to accept, overlooking the old adage "Variety is the spice of life."

Of course a caterer should try to so engage and impress his customers that they wouldn't dream of hiring anyone else, but you can't win 'em all. There are, however, some obvious pitfalls that caterers should try strenuously to avoid. Occasionally the constraints and demands of the situation or the client will take the initiative out of the caterer's hands, but if correct guidance is accepted, things will go better. Experience shows that functions piloted by an experienced caterer work better than those where there is a lot of interference by the client. As in medicine, detachment helps perspective. Emotional response can lead to faulty decisions.

## Not Giving Value for Money in Refreshments

Although many people will go to a charity affair with a good heart and in a forgiving spirit and shrug off any disappointments, some will be highly critical if they feel they've received poor value for money. For an increasing number of people, the charity circuit is the nearest thing they have to a social life. They go out regularly, looking forward to dressing up, meeting old friends, and perhaps making some new friends, too. If they have a dreary time, they may cross this particular charity off their list.

**Wine and Spirits**   Among the many things people will notice, but probably never mention, is low-quality wine. The policy of events committee members of simply bringing in the cheapest imaginable wine, or in accepting the dubious generosity of a local wine store hoping to unload poor-quality merchandise that isn't selling anyway, is deplorable. Wine drinkers are increasingly demanding of quality, and the available selection is enormous in a highly competitive market.

If hard liquor or spirits—vodka, gin, whiskies, and so on—are to be offered, it's a mistake to bring in cheap, little-known brands. People who drink spirits are often fiercely loyal to their favorites. Now, a catered function is usually not the same thing as a restaurant or commercial bar, and it's unrealistic for a temporary bar to offer six well-known brands of scotch. But you should make sure that the one you offer is a well-known and popular brand, not Old Laird's Special, bottled in New Jersey. Current tastes are such that you are unlikely to have much call for spirits other than vodka, but there are still a few gin, whisky, rum, and brandy drinkers left, so the principle stands. Some people are so brand-conscious and loyal that they bring their own bottle to a party—usually making a joke of it so as not to appear too pompous.

Drinkers are often very health-conscious, contradictory though that may seem, and very anxious to stay with what they regard as clean drinks—the ones least likely to upset them in any way and, specifically, least likely to give them a hangover. Such drinkers will sometimes avoid wine like the plague and stay with vodka. In Chapter 9 we shall examine this aspect of alcohol consumption in more detail.

Nondrinkers or occasional drinkers at a function will hardly notice the tastes or names of liquors or wines—they may dislike alcohol in all its forms, anyway. But those with any kind of palate will undoubtedly notice and feel they've been ripped off. And next time around, maybe they won't buy a ticket to the charity party.

**Food** Skimping on food can cause displeasure—whether people are paying for it or not. A common mistake is to lay on a buffet with one gorgeous centerpiece— a salmon, a duck, a smoked chicken, or whatever—that simply won't allow every guest to have a portion. Those left out will be stuck with the hardboiled eggs and canned ham slices. There's nothing wrong with either of these delicious items— they are common in most people's diet—but it's a bit irritating for someone who relishes small treats and finds there's nothing left by the time he or she gets to the table. This is called the Oliver Twist Syndrome, or OTS for short (Oliver Twist was the Dickensian orphan who dared to hold up his bowl and ask for more food).

One cheerful host used to hold an annual lunch in his pleasant suburban house, which had a nice big garden. Because he'd married late to a younger woman and produced four children, there was inevitably a large age disparity in the family's circle of friends and acquaintances. There were lots of people in their seventies, but many people in their early twenties, and younger. The regular caterer was of the older age group, very experienced and well thought of in the neighborhood. He laid on excellent-quality food and wine, but in despairingly tiny quantities. The older guests, with their smaller appetites, were quite happy with this (though one should never assume that all older people eat less—some are mighty trenchermen), while the youngsters practically starved. The kids found themselves holding out their plates for some delicious roast beef and being given a portion that would hardly satisfy a sparrow.

If there is a polite way of asking not just for more, but for *much* more in these circumstances, it has not yet been devised. Those brave enough to go around a second time at this luncheon received frosty looks, and even smaller helpings. Thus, the first stop for many after this otherwise happy event was the nearest hamburger joint. No wonder some people who've been everywhere and done everything become so jaded that they eat at home before going out to dinner.

The caterer should never take food or wine at face value. There lies the path of disaster. You should taste any wine you're providing and ensure that it's of reasonable quality. As for food, the industry long ago learned the lesson about people first tasting food with the eye, so they've given us huge shiny red apples with the consistency and taste of cotton wool, glowing tomatoes that taste of nothing, and so on. You will soon zero in on the stores that deliver the goods every time at decent prices. A real danger is relying on convenience foods, or on foods—particularly hors d'oeuvres or canapés—that can be bought by the trayfull and merely require a quick nuking in the microwave oven. Though sometimes satisfactory (and rarely better) they are often disastrously awful.

## Overcrowding

One of the most common mistakes that party givers make is to overcrowd the premises. As observed in Chapter 5, some people like to give one enormous party a year—often around Christmastime—and they can be disastrous failures in terms of enjoyment. From the guests' point of view, what is the joy of seeing a familiar face across a room so crowded that you know it will take you ten minutes of thrust, push, and "excuse me" to exchange greetings?

A caterer's advice in such circumstances may be ignored, in which case he can only do his best. At charity functions, again, the desire to accommodate as many paying guests as possible sometimes leads to grotesque overcrowding. On such occasions many people in desperation, buttonhole a server, furtively hand over a $20 bill, and beg "Could you please find us somewhere to sit, a couple of drinks, and a bite to eat?" (Older hands may first state their request, then promise the reward, because often the hapless server can't deliver the goods but will be nevertheless loathe to return the gratuity.)

## No Place for Coats

Cloakroom arrangements, especially in bad weather, can detract from the efficiency and joy of a function. When every single person has a raincoat or overcoat, shawl, umbrella, or hat, and possibly galoshes, a party can become disastrously cloakroom intensive. On one horrific opera night in New York a man waited ten minutes on line at the opera to check his and his wife's coats and a further ten minutes to retrieve them. The cloakroom attendant intoned "Sorry, we don't check rubbers" like a foghorn in November. In London people sometimes book three seats at the theater—one for the coats—but this is rather an expensive cloakroom, especially at the opera, where seats are often $150 or more.

**Handling Coats at Small Home Parties** At a small party in a private apartment, provided the building is safe, there's no reason why you shouldn't simply set up a coat rail outside the front door. Apart from anything else this shows where the party's being held if there are many apartments on the floor. Many people simply designate a bedroom as the cloakroom. Proust—no unpretentious egalitarian he—had a good sniff about this in his novel *Swann's Way*. . . .

> ". . . he had not the actual feeling of being 'at the ball' when he found himself . . . in the bedroom of the lady of the house, while the spectacle of washstands covered over with towels, and of beds converted into cloak-rooms, with a mass of hats and greatcoats sprawling over their counterpanes, gave him the same stifling sensation that, nowadays, people who have been used for half a lifetime to electric lights derive from a smoking lamp or a candle that needs to be snuffed."

**Larger Events** In a house or larger premises, there's usually no problem with space, but if the weather is bad you should employ a cloakroom attendant just to keep things organized. Sometimes an employee can double as waiter and cloakroom attendant, depending on the size of the party and the degree of service required. You'll need lots of hangers and double tickets, which you can buy from any stationers—one goes to the coat owner, the other is pinned to the garment in such a way as not to damage it. Ideally, your cloakroom attendant will have a needle and thread and emergency cleaning materials handy.

**Tipping** Though, in a private house, tipping should not be required from visitors who are not staying over, people are often so in the habit that they'll tip anyway. These tips are usually kept by the attendant. At a bigger, commercial function, however, tips should be turned in to you, the caterer, as they are part of your revenue, and the attendant is paid the regular amount for the shift. Of course, if the clients add a tip to the bill, this should be shared. Remember, in restaurants the cloakroom concession is often bought by outsiders. Sometimes they pay a pretty price for the privilege—and pray hard for bad weather.

## Parking Problems

Parking will not always be the caterer's concern, but even in city centers it *can* be. If the city location lends itself to guests arriving in private cars, but the nearest garage or parking space is some distance away, there may be a need for valets. These are simply drivers who take over a car from its owner, park it somewhere, and bring it back when required. Sometimes, if nearby parking spaces appear while a function is still going on, they'll bring cars back sooner, so the driver is not delayed at all on leaving. These workers are paid a shift minimum and keep their tips—$1 a car is normal, but people in expansive mood will clearly tip more.

You should check the legal standing of this situation. This doesn't mean hiring a $500 an hour lawyer, it merely means asking around. Ask a local hotel or restaurant manager how it works. In some states, such a worker may require a chauffeur's license. In others, as long as the car is properly insured to be driven by somebody other than the owner, then the handing over of a car by its owner to a valet for parking may be seen as a simple verbal agreement between two parties.

In the country, parking arrangements are often appalling. Remember, a country function with 100 guests may well generate more than 50 vehicles. At country weddings, if the venue is near a train station (as it may be in the Northeast but may not be elsewhere) some hosts encourage their guests to arrive by train and provide cars, or even buses, to get the guests to the house. Again, some guests resist this in the interests of independence. They want to safeguard their freedom to leave when they're good and ready, not when the next bus arrives.

If cars are parked at some distance from the house, perhaps on unpaved ground, some people will have to walk a few yards to the house. If it rains or has recently rained, there's a danger of mud, and who wants to walk through mud in their best shoes? A mat should be laid or some other arrangement devised. If it's a high-budget party a temporary duckboard path may be built and also a covered passage. However the easiest compromise is to have guests get out of their cars at the house entrance and have car valets park the cars. You should watch out for wise guys (and gals) in this area, and make sure you hire only people you know and who are accountable; otherwise, a guest's car may find itself on the next freight ship to Hong Kong, especially if it's a Honda, currently the most stolen car in America. Stealing cars to order is a well-established criminal pastime.

## SCAMS

If, as is possible, your catering is limited to cooking things at home and perhaps delivering them, or having them delivered, there's another scam you ought to be aware of. Busy pizza parlors and home caterers often hire people, usually youngsters, in a very casual way—right off the street, as they say, especially on busy weekend nights. Heck, here's this nice young kid with the big grin, not afraid of rolling up his sleeves and doing some work to earn a little pocket money—why wouldn't you hire him? Pity a few more kids around here are not as enterprising.

Pizza is of course a staple food to many, especially those whose concept of Nirvana is a ball game on TV, lots of cold beer in a big bucket of ice, and a few of the neighbors over. When hunger strikes, we may not be talking about slices of pizza, we may be talking about several mega-pizzas. So the order is phoned in to the local pizza parlor, and shortly afterwards the delivery kid sets off bravely into the night, laden with $50 worth of pizza.

The minutes go by. The pizza owner, or home caterer, starts rationalizing the delay—the traffic, the weather, some brief distraction. But after a while he decides to phone the customer just to check that everything arrived Okay. "Why sure," the satisfied customer will say. "Thanks for being so prompt, we'll surely call again. Your delivery boy was so polite—I gave him $5—was that Okay?" Faced with the possibility of making $55 tax-free in one move, more than he could possibly hope to make in a whole long evening of deliveries, the kid has eloped with the total takings.

This is not a descent into tired cynicism or pessimism, nor is it scare mongering. You could live your whole life and never be robbed, never find yourself reaching for a baseball bat to defend yourself against a bunch of 9-year-old children, or see an exposed weapon, etc. But these things happen.

A common variation on this kind of scam is the phony mugging. Some member of the staff goes off to make a deposit at the bank. He or she then hands the money to an accomplice, and musses himself up a bit, and returns to work shaking with shock and crying "I was mugged—it was horrible." Concerned colleagues will be full of concern and sympathy, "Thank goodness it was only the money—at least you weren't hurt." Some cool customers have been known to pull this trick twice. The third time begins to look like carelessness. If someone is going to be handling your hard-earned money, you'd better know enough about them to be sure that the chances of their stealing it are at a minimum.

There is always a risk and references are no protection. Criminals often give each other references, posing as ex-employers. The more worldly-wise you are in general terms, the safer you'll be. The innocent are the most vulnerable.

Unfortunately, the very obvious method of avoiding cash handling by billing the client later is not a realistic one in the world of small business, so it's as well to be on your toes.

# Salvation: The Checklist

The checklist is one of the caterer's most useful tools. Almost everyone uses checklists in some way or another, from the elaborate hour-long run through a pilot has to perform on an aircraft, to the busy shopper with a few items jotted down on the back of an envelope. For many people it is the irritation caused by mounting a shopping expedition and then discovering upon returning home that a major item has been forgotten that first reveals the wisdom of such lists.

Ideally, the caterer will work from a very full list that covers every imaginable factor, but for the smaller gathering obviously a smaller list will suffice. Lists can be lifesavers at busy periods of the year when your head may start to spin. Written information will keep you on course, as you will see from the accompanying example.

This checklist is based on a real-life party given at a house well set up for entertaining and where expense was no object. If the function supervisor were taken ill, a deputy could simply look at it and know exactly what was going on, and there would be no snags. He or she would only need to confirm that everyone knew what their tasks would be. Because a pattern of arrangement already existed, certain matters—flowers, cooking—were not required to be arranged by the caterer. But it won't always be so. Therefore, it's essential to know where to get hold of all equipment and services if you need them. Once again, it's the Yellow Pages to the rescue.

## Party Checklist

| | |
|---|---|
| *Function:* | Carling Vanderfeller's 21st birthday party. |
| *Hosts:* | Mr. & Mrs. Sterling Vanderfeller. |
| *Date:* | September 14, 1999. |
| *Time:* | 8 P.M. |
| *Address:* | The Breakers, North Shore Road, Richville, Long Island |
| *Directions:* | Route 19 to Richville, left at crossroad onto Route 24A. Proceed 2 miles, stop at estate gates and report to security (24 hrs). Signposts in grounds. |
| *Bill To:* | Mr. Sterling Vanderfeller. |
| *Deposit Paid:* | $25,000. |

| | |
|---|---|
| *Total Fee:* | Subject to final review of returns, hours, etc. |
| *Telephone:* | Mr. or Mrs.Vanderfeller. Home: (city) (123) 456-7890); (Richville) (321) 987-6543. Mr. Vanderfeller's office: (765) 987-7654; Secretaries: Sue Riley, Jim Costello. Breakers Housekeeper: (123) 456-7894 (Mrs. O'Riley). Breakers Security: (123) 456-7888. All staff informed. |
| *Guests:* | 400 approx. |
| *Service Bar:* | 3 bars, 2 in house, 1 in marquee. |
| *Disco:* | Host will arrange. |
| *Food:* | 5 food service points in house: pizza and pasta (John Kluger & Margaret); caviar, smoked salmon, oysters, clams (Lyn & Jean) roast beef, vegetables (Steve Smith & Ron); salad (Suzie); Desserts, tea, herbal tea, coffee, decaf (Jose). All food ordered—see separate invoices. Will be delivered to Breakers by Fine Foods Inc. by 4 P.M. Tel: (123) 975-4933, Dorothy or Al. Dorothy or Al, or both, will supervise delivery. |
| *Cooking:* | Client's own staff will do this. Waiters may be asked to help. |
| *Equipment:* | All food preparation equipment, china and cutlery is on premises <u>but</u>: 6 six foot trestle tables ordered from Bingo's will need to be set up <u>by us</u> for food points. Bingo's will provide and set up marquee, dance floor, and all other furniture. Rep is Lorraine Parsons,(765) 465-9826. |
| *Personnel:* | <u>Food service:</u> John Kluger, Margaret, Lyn, Jean, Ron, Steve Smith, Suzie, Jose. <u>Bartenders:</u> Barbara, Nicola, Irene, Steve Hardy, Rodolfo, John Valentino <u>Waiter/busperson:</u> Enrico, Mark, Bill Jones, Polly, Jane, Mercedes. <u>Household staff</u> (Angela and Rinaldo) will assist throughout. Cloakroom: Mike, Val, Sylvie |
| *Linen:* | We will take jackets, aprons, and cloths in van. Mike will coordinate. |
| *Transport:* | Room for 6 in truck. John Valentino, Polly, Nicola, and Ron have cars. Ron will arrange. Regular gas and mileage will be reimbursed. |
| *Report Time:* | 4 P.M. staff meal, final briefing by Alexander. |
| *Parking:* | Client has arranged. Space reserved for our vehicles in forecourt. Attendants informed. |
| *Reception:* | By hosts and guest of honor. Bar number 1 (see plan) will need biggest setup, especially champagne glasses. Ice, iced containers, extra refrigeration in pantry. |
| *Menu:* | See above. |

| | |
|---|---|
| *Wines:* | Dom Perignon '85. Chateau Lafite '87 (red). Bernkasteler Doktor '89 (white). |
| *Spirits:* | Smirnoff vodka, Gordon's gin, Teacher's Scotch, Wild Turkey. |
| *Liqueurs, Etc:* | Grand Marnier, Martell Cognac, Fonseca Port '89. |
| *Beer:* | Grolsch. Fine Foods will deliver to Breakers. |
| *Waters:* | Perrier, Evian. |
| *Sodas:* | Standard setup. |
| *Music:* | Client has arranged. |
| *Flowers:* | Client has arranged. |
| *Fireworks:* | 10 P.M.—client has arranged. |
| *Speeches & Ceremony:* | None. |
| *Dress:* | As for formal function. |
| *Duration:* | All bars and food service, except pizza and number 1 bar can start to dismantle at midnight. Pizza and number 1 bar close at hosts' discretion. Music off at 1:30 A.M. |
| *Pay:* | All personnel guaranteed $100 salary. Any gratuities to be paid on settlement. |

## Other Items for the Checklist

At this point a useful exercise is to imagine other items that might be added to this function checklist. They might include, for instance, cash bar, committee room, decorations, cabaret, cake, toasts, and speeches, a formally drawn table and seating plan, temporary bathrooms, transport, generators, menu cards, place cards, party favors, prize draw or tombola, and so on, to people jumping out of cakes or white doves being released. (Never do butterflies. On one notorious occasion the thousands of pretty butterflies released at a function promptly fried on the lighting. Animals in general, as any old theater trouper will tell you, can be dangerously unreliable. Among the mentionable things they can do, probably the worst is to simply stall refusing to budge, and if it's a camel or an elephant, seamless continuity may be lost.)

Since much of the business a caterer working from home is likely to encounter may be on a much smaller scale—cocktails and buffet for no more than 50 people—clearly the function list will often be much shorter. But while implying no disrespect to the venerable backs of envelopes, it is a good idea to make a formal list to which you refer on every occasion. This will be particularly helpful at busy peak periods. The very least you need to know about a job is where, when, and who's paying the bill.

## The Sad Story of Francois Vatel

Nowhere are the perils of disorganization so starkly illustrated as in the story of a seventeenth century French steward to the Prince of Condé, Francois Vatel. He was employed by the Treasury of France, but high-ranking nobles hired him to put their vast houses in order. He is often referred to as a chef, but his only training was a brief apprenticeship to a pastry cook. At the Prince de Condé's chateau near Chantilly (home of the dessert dish Pear Condé and Chantilly cream), Vatel had his own apartments and servants and was allowed to wear jewels and a sword. The chateau had long been neglected and the job of restoring grounds, chateau, and staff to some kind of order was enormous. Although only in his thirties, he complained that he couldn't sleep and that his head was spinning. Others thought he looked unwell.

In April of 1671 King Louis XIV visited Chantilly with a vast entourage, and Vatel had to take care of accommodation and catering arrangements. On the first evening of the visit, the roast meat ran out and two tables received none. Then the fireworks display was a failure. The next day a small order of fish arrived, and Vatel nearly had a fit when he was told that was all he'd ordered. The thought of another fiasco was intolerable. He went upstairs and stabbed himself to death with his sword. Too late, an assistant arrived to remind him that he had in fact ordered more fish, from another supplier, and that it was on its way.

Poor Vatel, buried in a field unconsecrated for Christian burial because he was a suicide, was clearly an early victim of what's now called "frontline burnout," or simple stress through overwork. But one can't help wondering whether he wasn't carrying too much in his head, when lists were clearly mandated.

# Chapter Eight

# Setting up a Room

## The Room

If you find yourself working for an inexperienced client, you may need to be very firm in your advice. Often clients may not have the faintest idea how to organize functions. They may not understand, for instance, that 20 people simply will not fit into a room which, although 20 feet by 40 feet, also contains several chairs, tables, and sofas. "Oh, they'll all squeeze in somehow . . . " is not a satisfactory approach. That's why at some parties you find people crowding into the kitchen and halls. In England, at country house parties, people sit on the stairs, always a quaint sight and a favorite target for society photographers.

Of course, there is a certain case for closeness fostering the party spirit. Too much space can be alienating for some. Those cartoons in which a man and his wife confront each other frostily from the ends of a long dining table demonstrate an extreme which, though ideal for some, is a bit stark for many. Young lovers may love to listen to each other crunching toast. Those who are not so romantically enmeshed may prefer "more space."

### Storing Furniture

If you plan to remove all or some of the furniture from the function venue, you must first decide where to put it. World War II students (and veterans) may recall the importance of securing landing grounds. It's the same in catering. Nothing should ever be moved until it has a designated place to go to.

Furniture must be stored well out of the way of the arriving guests. Apart from being an impedance to their guests' entrances and exits, with all the threat of medical and insurance problems that implies, the aesthetic appeal of assorted displaced furniture is not great. One should be thinking of evenings at Versailles, not rummage sales. Also, few things are more dispiriting to a guest than when, upon arriving at a party—dressed to kill, programmed to conquer, and with a thousand witticisms at his fingertips—he is asked to help move the furniture.

That priceless Ming vase should be placed somewhere where it cannot possibly be knocked over. Glaring lights should be shaded or removed. Any annoying noise, such as a door that will not gently close but only slam or creak loudly, should be attended to.

Occasionally a caterer will cast a beady eye on a house or apartment and realize that holding a function for the number of people proposed is simply out of the question no matter how much furniture is moved, and another location may have to be found. An alternative is to reduce the number of guests, and many hosts will choose to hold several functions, with different guests, in order to be able to entertain at home.

## Less Is More

At first glance, space in office buildings or hotels that is dedicated to catering for functions, parties, and meetings may seem rather stark, especially if there is no decoration. This shouldn't put you or your client off one bit. On the contrary, you should think positively and be grateful for so much space to play with. You can bring in as much or as little equipment as you wish, but for obvious reasons you should think of minimums.

A small table in each corner with a simple vase of flowers on it is probably as much decor as you'll need, in addition to your bar and buffet table. It's useful if such small tables leave room for the deposit of glasses and even ashtrays just in case someone has the temerity to light up. Even if your host has decided that guests should stand rather than sit, you should at least know where the nearest seating arrangements can be found.

Remember that once two or three are gathered together in animated conversation, the emphasis will be on people, not decor. They become the decor in their party finery, as they interact and provide their own theater.

## Service and Guest Comfort

Milton, the supreme poet of the Puritan ethic, observed:

Imposter, do not charge most innocent Nature,
As if she would her children should be riotous
With her abundance; she, good cateress

Means her provision only to the good
That live according to her sober laws
And holy dictate of spare Temperance.
(*Comus*, 1, 762)

Nevertheless, many people arriving at a party want a drink, and pronto. For a host, it's most important that each arriving guest be greeted and offered something so that even if the conversation is brief, at least their arrival has been acknowledged. When you arrive at a party, especially if you're young and there's no one there you know, it can be heart-sinking if no one says hello. You look around for a moment for the person who invited you, and if they only say hello and fail to connect you to someone, you may be tempted to leave promptly.

Many functions fail completely, to the extent that one wonders why they were ever held, because the guests simply lock solidly into the people they know as soon as they arrive, and little or no social, business, or professional intercourse takes place. Again, it is no part of a caterer's duty to assist the host in this area; indeed, it would be impertinent to try. But you may occasionally find yourself wondering sadly why your client bothered to give a party, as you do your duty and earn an honest fee.

## Places to Park Things

Guests need somewhere to put their plates and glasses when they've finished with them, or wish to exchange business cards, or jot down some information. The caterer needs collection points. Experienced and well-mannered guests at drinks and buffet functions will sometimes show communal spirit and return their glasses to the bar. Failure to provide parking places for glasses and plates is very common at functions in private homes, where the host wishes to impress with a lavish display. The catering staff will find themselves having to look under chairs and behind curtains for party debris. There's also the danger of people treading in, slipping on, or sitting on discarded plates.

Staff should be instructed to automatically gather up used glasses as they go about their tasks. This not only avoids clutter; but if the glasses are real glass and not disposable plastic, they may need to be washed for reuse. Some restaurateurs tell their servers, "Never come back from the floor empty-handed," and this is a good maxim for the caterer, too. If you clean discreetly as you go along, there'll be less work to do when the function is over.

## When to Start Cleaning Up

There is always a point in any function when it starts to wind down, and with experience you'll learn to recognize this. On weekday nights in cities, the moment will be unmistakable, as people who need to rise early the next day depart.

It would be unusual, even in New York, to find many people lingering past 10:00 P.M. On Fridays and Saturdays, however, you may see a very different story, as people linger and often show great reluctance to leave.

When you recognize the beginning of the end of the function, you should start thinking about wrapping up the proceedings, but it's bad form to make your preparations too pointed or obvious. It can be embarrassing to guests, who may be made to feel that they've outstayed their welcome, when the catering staff suddenly go into a flurry of closing down activity. It's a bit like entering a restaurant rather late and having a frowning waiter checking his watch as you sit, or flicking the lights on and off to indicate that closing time is imminent. Almost invariably your client will give you the nod when it's Okay to start clearing up, and only then can you cease to be discreet in your collecting, tidying, assembling, and cleaning.

## Service Positions

Your first general appraisal of the party premises is when you decide where everything must go (See Chapter 10 for the details of setting up a bar, and Chapter 8 for setting up a dining table and a buffet table.) Upon entering a room, most people move to the left, and continue clockwise. Why this is so is uncertain—it may have to do with the fact that the heart is not dead center in the body but slightly to the left. It's why the legionnaires in those old movies who get lost in the desert sandstorm yet stagger blindly on, always return to their starting point, having merely completed a circle. Even when entering guests are required to move to the right to greet the hosts, they will usually revert to their clockwise pattern having said hello and paid their respects.

So, the best place for your bar is often about halfway down the left side of the room. Never put it right inside the door, or you'll risk a jam. Generally speaking, once people have a glass in their hand, they'll move on and greet acquaintances, or introduce themselves—always supposing it isn't one of those tight little parties with everyone grouped in their cliques.

If you have a buffet table, it can be at right angles to the bar, several feet away. It's a good idea to have some separation because at a certain point both bar and buffet may need to take out garbage or replenish supplies, and a traffic jam of heavily laden bartenders and waiters mixing with the guests doesn't make for an elegant gathering.

## Temperature and Ventilation

It's important to consider the ventilation of a room in which many people are due to gather. If it's cool, that's fine; nothing warms a room up faster than bodies. But the problem of maintaining a cool temperature in a crowded banquet room in summer is one that has never been successfully solved. Even cruise ships with their fierce air conditioning systems and available ocean breeze have not been completely successful. What managers usually do is turn the air conditioning on full blast, so that the first guests to arrive may actually be a little chilled. They will not shiver for long as other guests arrive. Then if the air conditioning is left on at full power, the temperature will be at least bearable. Thank goodness most people wear lightweight clothing these days.

If the room is warm even before the guests start to arrive, you might do well to cool things down somewhat. It's not uncommon for people to switch on the air conditioning in the depths of winter if a room is full of people. Sometime before the guests begin to arrive, it's a good idea to open all the windows and let some air blow through the place, especially if there's been some cooking or if the windows have been closed for several days because of the weather. If you or your clients decide to spray with air freshener, this should be done well in advance of the guest's arrival so that the smell is not overpowering, and the brand should be chosen with care. Some products are rather chemical and reminiscent of public lavatories; others are acceptable.

**Overindulging**    An unfortunate feature of the Christmas period is that many people who do not normally drink at all find themselves being plied with liquor, or tempted to imbibe more than they normally would. People in the hospitality industries call them amateurs, and they are a nuisance. What these amateurs sometimes do—after they've taken off their clothes, insulted the boss, and generally expressed their true inner selves—is vomit. With luck they'll get to the restrooms just in time, but you won't always be lucky. That's when you need a really fast cleanup. A bucket of sand is by no means an unreasonable piece of equipment to have on hand at such functions.

One caterer was delighted to be invited to lay on 11 consecutive bar and buffet office parties in the basement of a restaurant over the Christmas period. It was in many ways an ideal location because it was equipped with a full bar, cloakroom, and a dumb waiter for bringing supplies down from the kitchen. Nor was it badly ventilated, given normal occupancy, although the pressure of bodies was huge every night.

After about three days of this festive work season, the caterer found that when she arrived for work, the first thing that assailed her nostrils was a most offensive smell from heavy vomiting in the restrooms. She implored the restaurant management to open all doors and windows in the building. They said they'd attend to it, but did nothing. The restaurant was busy and it was bitterly cold outside. Fair enough—but could the porter perhaps open up and let some air in after everyone had gone home? Well, no one could be found to do this simple procedure. (Only if the owner had shown up at 4:00 A.M. to instruct the porters in what they were to do could anything have happened, and we all know how likely that is.) So the smell got worse as the season wore on. Whether or not anybody ever noticed it will never be known.

If your function is in a room that opens directly onto a terrace or garden, you'll have no problems. Unless it rains, you can in effect expand the premises.

Indeed, some people buy houses and apartments with this facility precisely because of the ease with which they can accommodate numbers of guests.

# Tables, Bars, and Cloakrooms

## The Buffet Table

If the main table belongs to the home or premises and is a fine-looking walnut or chestnut piece, there is no need to cover it with a cloth. If hot dishes are to be put on it, then of course cork mats and coasters must be used to protect its surface. Circular, rectangular, or square will do. However, if you bring in a collapsible, folding table, it will usually have a rough, rudimentary look, and it must be covered—usually with large white linen cloths, which can be rented (as discussed in Chapter 6). Other colors are available, among them lively checks, blue, and nauseating restaurant pink, if you wish to harmonize with the existing decor or a particular theme.

There are such things as disposable paper table cloths. Some restaurants use them, but they are cheap looking, unpleasant to the touch, and make a dreadful noise that sets one's teeth on edge as they're unrolled. However, new products are coming along all the time, and an acceptable disposable table cloth may yet emerge. There are plastic wipe-clean table covers too, but they have an institutional, rather than a party-time, look.

You should personally ensure that a folding table is correctly assembled with all the metal clamps in place. In movies, collapsing buffets are almost as beloved as knocked over fruit stalls and always seem to bring the house down. In real life, it's a different matter. It's fine for banqueting tables to groan under the weight of the lavish fare offered—as long as they stay in one piece.

Sometimes a buffet table can be placed centrally so that people can serve themselves from all sides. If space is limited, it might be against a wall, with perhaps one server attending, although guests will also be invited to serve themselves.

## Setting the Buffet Table

The objects nearest to the guests, on the outside of the table, should be the plates—be they china or cardboard—and cutlery—plastic or real. Piles of napkins, linen or paper, should be alongside. Some high-quality paper napkins have enough weight and absorbency to resemble the real thing. Even so, it's unlikely they'd satisfy the fastidious Humbert Humbert in Vladimir Nabokov's novel *Lolita*, who, given paper napkins by the wife he'd married in order to be nearer her daughter, pined for the "cool, rich linens of the Miramar Hotel" where he'd been brought up as a boy. The truth is, that unless you are in very exalted circles, paper napkins are usually acceptable. If they are not, you may be sure your client will not be slow to say so.

The chairman of a major publishing company, racked with insecurity, used to inspect every aspect of the setup of important meetings and once nearly had a fit when, upon checking the men's room, he discovered that the cleaner, having run out of linen towels, had thoughtfully provided paper ones. Someone was hastily dispatched to buy linen.

Such a host will almost certainly insist on proper glasses too, which means you must ensure a good supply and organize smooth washing and recycling arrangements. The same taboos attach to plastic plates, cutlery, and beverage containers—some people just can't abide them. In the lavatories, even when hot air hand dryers are installed, it's still a good idea to have towels available.

**Observing the Traditions**   If you build an upscale clientele, you need to develop an eye for these snobberies. It's a free country and people are entitled to them. You can score useful points with such clients by making it clear that you understand the subtleties. They'll trust you. Remember, not only do the rich have more money, they entertain more too, which is worth pondering. While on the subject of upscale client preferences, it's a good idea to educate your help in these matters. Some of them may simply not realize that in polite society beer is drunk from a glass and not directly from the bottle.

The simple statement of preference is bewildering to some. They may not grasp the minor but significant importance of guests preferring white wine chilled, hot food piping hot, and fingers kept out of glasses that are about to be filled and served, regarding such preferences a conspiracy to make life more difficult for them. If they wish to sneer at such precious affectation, that is their right as long as they do it in private, and not on your time at your important function. When they're at work, caterers and their staff must observe the traditional rituals and methods.

## Presentation of the Food

Beyond the mechanical means of consumption—the plates and cutlery—comes the food itself. This should be displayed on large plates, as pleasingly as possible. It's nice to have some color—red tomatoes, green peppers, guacamole or avocado dip, a fruit bowl with yellow bananas and red and green apples. Pride of place should go to the large meat and fish platters—the hams, rounds of beef, chickens, ducks, salmon, trout, lobster, and shrimp. Large serving spoons should be provided.

Blank spots on the table can be filled with cheeses and—always a festive look—bunches of green and black grapes. If bread and butter are served, it works a little better if you provide rolls, but if you want to lay on crusty French or Italian loaves, or garlic bread, you merely have to make sure that there's a breadknife handy. After the bread comes out of the oven, it's the work of a moment for you or one of your servers to slice it up into easily detachable portions.

Salt and pepper should be available and, yes, except in super-smart situations, toothpicks. This doesn't mean that you don't have a supply of them discreetly tucked away. Even if the party is given for the famous Four Hundred, there's always somebody in need of a toothpick, just as there'll always be someone with chewing gum to dispose of.

**Carving**  If hosts want to make a thing of actually carving off slices of meat, it's a good idea to have a waiter do it, or even the chef in a jaunty toque blanche (a chef's tall white hat), although this is not essential. Make sure that your designated carver is experienced. It's a simple business, made simpler if you have a really good, sharp knife. Any experienced cook can show you the logical steps, that dispatch the carcass neatly. The carver can also help by serving those items that a guest, encumbered by purse, drink, or whatever, may find hard to handle.

For some reason, many people go to pieces if they're asked to carve. They feel very much "on the spot" especially as many critical eyes are going to be on them. At one time boys stood alongside their fathers at Sunday lunch and learned how to do it, but that was before the fast-food era. Nevertheless, this skill can still be perfected in private, at home. You should try to achieve a degree of expertise where you can carve promptly and before the eyes of an audience, like the server in a serious restaurant who carves to order from the trolley.

The principles of carving birds—chickens, turkeys, ducks—are simple. You need a long strong fork to hold the bird (or joint) down firmly, then you bend the leg outward and downward, cut through the meat, and remove the leg. Do the same for the other leg and the wings. Cut the breast meat in even slices, carving downwards, parallel with the breast bone. The drumsticks and wings can be served whole or sliced.

Taking charge in things like carving is precisely what caterers are for, of course, and the better you are at generating confidence and security in your clients, the more business you'll get. The slight elements of show biz should be acknowledged, not disdained.

It will sometimes happen that you are asked to carve with a blunt knife, and you have left your own favorite carving set at home, not expecting to have to do any carving. When this happens you may have to hack—so it's better if you can do it in the kitchen away from critical eyes, and display the slices on the plates to best advantage. Don't disdain the accompanying sauce, gravy, or vegetables as camouflage for untidy bits if necessary.

**Ease of Eating**  In general, all food, though assembled to look its best, should be easily liftable and eatable, preferably already cut into bite-sized chunks—defined, in company at any rate, as an amount consumed with no more than two chews and one swallow. This can be taken as gospel, since it is taught at West Point when the cadets are being instructed in proper social behavior.

**Tidying Up**  As the function wears on, the buffet table may start looking a little tired or even downright bedraggled. You should tidy as you go, and immediately remove any platters that are obviously finished. Few things in life are sadder look-ing than the picked-clean carcass of a duck, chicken, or salmon—especially if you haven't had any of it.

## Dining Tables

Some hosts like to serve a sit-down meal. This is no big challenge to the experi-enced caterer—in many ways it's easier than the hurly-burly of a buffet. Sometimes you'll find yourself serving to one large table, but often these days a party is broken up into several smaller tables. Because there's a rhythm to table service, you can set up efficiently well in advance. As people finish one course, you simply remove their plates and shortly thereafter replace them with the next course.

Knowing when to clear plates as a course is finished will come with experi-ence. An old-fashioned hostess will push a forkful of food around her plate for ages so as not to embarrass a guest who is eating slowly and holding things up. At the propitious moment she'll discreetly press a button concealed under the table, which will either turn on a warning light in the kitchen or sound a buzzer. This kind of formality is no longer very common, it must be admitted, elegant though it can be.

**SEATING** It's the host's job to make the seating plan, putting people together in whatever he thinks is the happiest juxtaposition. This plan will normally be prominently displayed in the reception or cocktail area of a large function, often on a blackboard on the wall or on an easel. At the tables themselves, place cards should be displayed with the names of guests.

It's part of the caterer's job to show people to their seats so that they don't wander around helplessly. You should take a good look at the seating plan and note where the numbered tables are. In a large room or the banqueting area of a big hotel, these tables will often have numbers prominently displayed on a cen-tral stem. Such equipment can be hired if you want to do it that way.

But in a private home, few tables may be involved and it isn't hard for the catering staff—aided by the hosts—to direct people to their designated places. Beware—at hard-nosed business or professional socialite functions, guests will impolitely play games with the seating plan, arranging to sit next to a target guest rather than accept the place allotted by the host.

Often there will be a spare table set up for last minute arrivals who weren't sure whether they could make the date but were told to come if they could, peo-ple who weren't sure whether their spouses or escorts could make it, and so on. If someone hasn't been placed, they can be accommodated there, and if it isn't the place of their dreams, it isn't the end of the world. At such functions there is often a general mixing of people after the main dish has been served. People disperse, table-hop, and work the room. A guest disappointed not to have been seated next to the star may yet get to touch the hem of his or her garment.

**Mixing**  Sophisticated hosts will tend to mix everyone up, higgledy-piggledy, except where they have some particular ax to grind, in which case the seating may be politically motivated in order to give someone the chance to speak to a specially targeted person or to effect some match-making. Just plain folks will sit families together, husbands and wives together, boyfriend and girlfriend together, and so on, so everything's nice and cozy, and they are spared the often intimidating challenge of having to make conversation with strangers.

By the way, at such gatherings there need be no fear of offending by displaying toothpicks, paper napkins, or even ketchup bottles—as Randolph Hearst used to do at his California castle, much to society's amusement. He excused himself by saying that the sight of ketchup bottles cheered him, as it reminded him of the picnics he'd so enjoyed as a boy.

## Table Settings

Just as some people go to pieces at the prospect of having to carve meat, others dissolve into jelly at the prospect of setting the table. Many a butler, asked by a caterer or potential employer how he will set the table, explains himself only to be turned down because he's got it wrong. Grand restaurants get it wrong. Weighty etiquette tomes get it wrong. The truth of the matter is that there *is* no right or wrong—there is only the house style.

Certain things are taboo at the highest social level—like folding napkins into cute shapes and sticking them in the wine glass. They should be neatly folded flat and set on the place mat where the plate would go, or where the "show plate" (a bit "restauranty" and not often used in a private dining room) will go. Even fish knives are taboo in rarefied circles. At Buckingham Palace—which may be as convenient a reference point as any—fish knives are not set (you use two forks to eat your fish) and the cutlery is laid upside down (i.e., the bowl of the spoon and the prongs of the forks point downward). This may seem eccentric, but it's the traditional house style.

Sometimes at sit-down occasions guests will be perplexed by the absence of butter plates. Many top restaurants simply don't provide them—there's a perfectly clean cloth on the table, why clutter it with unnecessary china? In an upper-class family dining room, there will be neither a butter plate nor a table cloth—you break and butter your bread right on the tabletop.

**Cutlery**  Where does all the cutlery go? Common sense is what you need here. Most place settings should provide a fork, at least for the first course, which is sometimes called "hors d'oeuvre" (that's French for, roughly, "aside from the main course"), "starter," or "appetizer." Often this dish can be eaten easily with one fork. Smoked salmon, the dreaded tasteless gravlax, or a cold smoked trout might require some gentle separation, not amounting to anything as heavy duty as lamb-chop–style sawing—and for these foods a knife is mandatory. Sometimes a deep-bellied soup spoon might occupy this slot, though, except on the rubber chicken circuit, soup is rarely served at dinner. Lord Curzon, Viceroy of India from 1898 to 1905, described as a "very superior person," declared that "no gentleman ate soup at dinner," and who would dare to argue? After all, his Vicereine, Mary Leiter, was an American multimillion-dollar catering heiress.

If the first course is snails or shellfish, then the requisite utensils must be provided—pincers and small forks for snails, small forks (clam forks) for clams, oysters, shrimp cocktails, or lobster salads. In restaurants these special tools are not automatically set on the table because, obviously, not everyone will require them. If such dishes as clams, oysters, shrimp or lobster cocktails, or snails are offered at a private party, it's sometimes simpler, though not mandatory, if they're set on the table in advance.

Working from the outside, the next utensils will be for the fish course, if there is one—a broad-bladed fish knife on the right of the place-setting and a faintly fin-shaped fork on the left (or two such forks, one right, one left, if you're working Buckingham Palace).

Next you have the cutlery for the main course—a plain old knife (right) and fork (left). The knife should have a serrated blade if meat is being served, but a plain blade would be all right for goulash or any meat dish that will not require much cutting to be done.

Finally, there should be a spoon and fork for dessert, if required, often placed left to right at the top of the place setting. Some people include a teaspoon or coffee spoon in this lineup. Others provide spoons along with the coffee, cream, and coffee cups. Often, coffee is served away from the table, back in the drawing room, sitting room, lounge, parlor, or cocktail area—whatever you prefer to call it.

A most useful piece of cutlery that has no official place in formal dining, or even a name, is the small dessert fork with the sharp knife style edge on one side. These utensils come into their own at buffets as a knife and fork in one. The late Kaiser Wilhelm of Germany had a withered left arm due to a birth accident. Whenever he traveled, golden sets of these implements were sent ahead and provided at his table. Thus, his handicap was obscured.

**Glasses**  At the top right corner of the place setting there should be a water-glass and different glasses for the wines to be served. Although there are traditional shapes for every kind of wine, this is often ignored and glasses of the same shape are used for everything. This may seem to be a gratuitous flouting of convention but in fact, the pedigree of the various glass styles is not only not very sound but indeed quite arbitrary. Serving champagne, for instance, in either the traditional glass or the flute sometimes used today doesn't suit the wine. A taller, larger glass, slightly fluted, is ideal, preserving both bubbles and aroma, but most people would rather stick to the prevailing fashion.

Liqueurs, brandy, port, chocolates, petits fours (crystalized fruits and so on), may be served with coffee after the main repast has been consumed. Here, the specified glass tradition is stronger, and small liqueur glasses, small glasses for the port, and snifters for the brandy are used.

The proposed menu determines the table setting at a private function, and not any fuddy-duddy notions of what is "correct." As a simple check on the efficacy of your table setting, just imagine yourself sitting down and consider the courses to be served. Are the requisite utensils in place?

**When to Use What**   From the diner's point of view, the rule for using cutlery is quite simple. You select your irons from the outside and work inward with each succeeding course. The days are long gone (if indeed they ever existed) when people were written off socially by a wrong choice of fork at table. The only exception to this is England, where one of the last remaining possible social gaffes—which may get you written off instantly and, sadly, without a word—is to hold your knife like a pen, instead of with the handle tucked into the palm of your hand. It's rumored that in some circles the letters HKLP (Holds Knife Like Pen) against a job applicant's name are the kiss of death. Clearly one is into an area where there are no dress-down Fridays—almost invariably because, rightly or wrongly, the people running the business insist upon a certain image.

Many Europeans have adopted the American way of eating, in which you do your cutting, lay down your knife, and then transfer the fork to your right hand for transportation to the mouth. This may well be authentic and original manners—one of those delightful bits of Americana that finds echoes in such notions as that Shakespeare works better in American English because it more closely resembles the English of Shakepeare's time.

Should you be lucky enough to be invited to dine at a French aristocrat's chateau, you'll see a small piece of silver at the top right corner of your place setting that looks like a miniature stand of some kind. You rest your knife—your only, all-purpose knife—there between courses. The forks are removed with each course, but the knife stays put—a relic of the medieval style of castle dining where your slice of bread was your plate and knights cut the meat for the ladies. It's called a *porte couteau*—a knife holder.

**Finger Food**   When dishes that must be eaten with the fingers are served—artichokes vinaigrette, for instance, or whitebait (tiny fish deep-fried in batter)—fingerbowls should be provided before the next course. These are little glass dishes containing hot water garnished with flower petals or a slice of lemon. Guests delicately rinse their fingers and dry them on the napkin sitting in their laps (as distinct from stuck in their shirt fronts) or on a special extra napkin that comes, and goes, with the fingerbowl.

People who want to cut a dash or who shrilly insist on demonstrating how unstuffy they are will often drink, or pretend to drink, from the fingerbowl, hoping for and sometimes receiving a laugh. Old hands merely suppress their yawns.

Kind caterers will keep an eye on guests for signs of confusion and embarrassment, especially if young people are present, and discreetly advise if they observe that wide-eyed expression that says, "What do I do with this?"

## Chapter Nine

# Alcoholic Beverages

A BROAD knowledge of alcoholic beverages will be a tremendous advantage, whatever the scope and size of your catering business. You will often be asked for advice on wine, beer, and spirits, and if you're well informed, clients will trust your choices.

Despite the vast number of pages written on the subject throughout the media, and the presence in some cities of a bar on every corner, most people hardly ever drink alcohol except on special occasions and celebrations. People are generally somewhat ignorant of the subject, sometimes dangerously so. More than a third of all alcohol is sold in the last quarter of the year, when Thanksgiving, Christmas, and the New Year are celebrated. Obviously, a large proportion of this is consumed at catered affairs. At smaller functions you can get away with only a cursory knowledge of the subject. So if your ambitions are limited, you need only read the section in this chapter, "What You *Must* Know." However, in business, you can never know too much.

## What to Stock?

A dizzying variety of alcoholic beverages confronts today's party givers. More and more varieties of wines and alcohols are produced every year. In the wine industry, newly producing countries such as Argentina and Zimbabwe throw their hats into the ring. Old producers such as the Republic of Georgia (possibly the oldest wine-producing area), Bulgaria, and others are revived. New vodkas are marketed. Both India and Japan manufacture Scotch whisky.

## Drinkers' Choices

As new players enter the beverage game, the old ones reshape and repackage their products to attract new generations of consumers. Take sherry. The Spaniards twisted and turned to make it more acceptable to American drinkers, to little avail. They sweetened the wine to a grotesque level, which ruined its essential character. Now they've returned most styles to their former authenticity, but some famous brands no longer advertise themselves as "sherry"—which is suspected to have stuffy overtones—but merely as "drinks."

Beverage manufacturers have cleverly grasped that young people today are not nearly as interested in the deep subtle smoky flavors of exotic spirits as in drinks that are sweet and fruity. Thus, Jaegermeister is a hugely successful drink, and new inventions include alcoholic lemonade—a concoction that is drawing heavy fire from people who believe that the young are expressly targeted by this product.

You will not need to carry such items at a catered affair unless they are specifically requested. It's always best to inquire of your client whether there are any special requirements in this area., but nine times out of ten they won't have the faintest idea, so you will do well not to clutter the bar with cases of drinks that almost certainly will not find any takers.

Mercifully, the drinking pattern at a private function is different from that in a commercial bar. People at private parties have different expectations and are denied the anonymity that might encourage them to see just how many Kamikazes they can down in an ordinary bar.

## The Swing Away from Alcohol

Ironically, as the number of alcoholic beverages is increasing, the number of drinkers, especially in Western countries, is steadily decreasing. You will need to be comfortably into your forties to remember the three-martini lunch. And younger people may scarcely believe that there was once a time when hardly anyone wandered around with a huge bottle of water held rather oddly at shoulder level.

Part of the wine and spirits industry's problem is the younger generation. As discerning and heavy drinkers die off, they are not being replaced at the same rate. A recent, very interesting three-part television series devoted to the Scotch whisky industry had other spirit manufacturers ringing their hands with envy, but a whisky executive said, "I could have wept. At a time when we're starting to establish 'Scotch and cola' throughout Europe as the cool, in-drink for the young and trendy, we see three hours of tweedy old retired colonels in misty Scotland sitting by the fireside drinking it—exactly the image we're trying to shed. No blue jeans, no disco music, no bikinis—no nothing."

Counter-intuitive though it may seem, the constant barrage of advertising from the soft drinks industry actually seems to have hurt sales of alcoholic beverages. The vast array of soft drinks available are advertised constantly, and neon signs dominate cityscapes across the United States. Tastes have changed radically in the last decade. These days, any bar or catered function should be sure to lay in a good supply of bottled water and diet cola. Some people drink nothing else, and, because so many profiles of the latest media or software billionaires reveal that their favorite tipple is nonalcoholic it has become a Wall Street fashion. Perhaps, just as overweight people think they've taken a gigantic step on the road to slimness by buying a diet book, ambitious businessmen think they'll get rich by drinking diet cola.

# Alcohol, Health, and Safety

No one should ever drink anything whose origin is in the least bit doubtful. At one extreme, additives such as glycol and methanol are sometimes used by criminal manufacturers of all kinds of alcohol to enhance the apparent quality of low grade liquor and even, as demonstrated in recent European court cases, by old established houses (the companies found guilty of this were heavily fined.). The taste of such concoctions is so repulsive that only the poorer sort of alcoholic is at risk; the point here is that alcohol is a drug and one should stick to reputable sources.

## The French Anomaly

There was great rejoicing when the "French anomaly" was spotlighted a few years ago. The apparent contradiction was this: The French, whose diet traditionally contains a lot of fat, have the lowest incidence of heart disease in the West. The pundits decided that this was due to their high intake of alcohol, citing red wine as the best anti-heart-disease tipple. Oddly, the fact that until recently, 25 percent of hospital beds in the French national health service were occupied by patients suffering from alcohol related diseases got lost in the wash. This, plus the ever increasing accident rate, was the background to French government campaigns to get people to drink more milk and never to drink more than a liter of wine a day. They also provided free roadside coffee stations and expensive roadside courts. The fact that the French are generally an ectomorphic ethnic group (i.e., they tend to be slim, whereas endomorphs tend to go the other way) and that they eat tons of salad lubricated with olive oil, though not ignored, was not given center stage in these explorations.

A quirky fact about France and the French is that they actually drink twice as much beer as wine.

## How Much Is Too Much?

The most generally accepted principle regarding drinking, like diet, is moderation. After the discovery of the French anomaly, a British study actually went so far as to categorically *define* moderation: 21 units of alcohol a week for men, and

14 for women, a unit being one ounce of regular proof spirits or half a pint of regular-strength beer. The difference merely reflects certain differences in the cardiovascular systems of the sexes.

Other doctors then carried out further research. They discovered that people who drank three times more than the moderate drinkers all their lives, died no earlier than teetotalers. At this point, the original team admitted that they had been so constantly pestered to come up with a definition of moderation that they eventually offered one, though the figures they produced were totally arbitrary and baseless. All of this is reminiscent of the [Senator McCarthy-style] character in the movie "The Manchurian Candidate" who, when casting about for the number of card-carrying communists in the United States Senate, glanced at a ketchup bottle label—and settled for the figure 57.

When reviewing drinking habits, it is important to define terms—and also to remember that American spirits are slightly stronger than spirits imported from Europe. The definition of a unit differs from country to country. Puritanical England has the lowest recommended dosage. Its unit is 8 grams of alcohol such as normal-strength whiskey, vodka, rum, gin, or brandy. In France, a unit means 10 grams of spirit, and their recommendations are interesting: a bottle of wine a day for sedentary men, a liter for active men, and half a liter for women in general. In the United States, a unit is 12 grams, and the current recommended limit is two units a day for men and one for women. Clearly one's personal judgment has to be the final guideline in this matter.

## Alcohol's Effects on the Body

All alcoholic beverages, from Armagnac to Zinfandel, contain the same chemical—ethyl alcohol ($C_2H_5O$). This is not to be confused with other kinds of alcohol. Methyl alcohol or wood alcohol, for example, may either kill or blind.

Like any solid or liquid ingested, alcohol is processed by the digestive system and eventually enters the bloodstream via the stomach wall. Alcohol consumed on an empty stomach will pass through that wall faster and thus have a more immediate effect, since it will very shortly reach the brain. In bubbly drinks such as champagne or liquor mixed with soda—gin and tonic, vodka and tonic, scotch and soda, bourbon and soda, and so on—alcohol will also enter the bloodstream quicker.

Alcohol affects the brain as a depressant. The feelings it first depresses are those of loneliness and social inhibition. That's why initial and moderate alcohol intake produces a certain euphoria. Thereafter, it's all downhill, and anyone who's seen a movie or two will be familiar with the scene starring the tearful drunk.

The liver eliminates alcohol at the rate of about one ounce per hour. Thus, in an hour's drinking, if three ounces of alcohol are ingested, it will be a further two hours before the booze is eliminated from the bloodstream by urine, perspiration, and breath.

The presence of alcohol in the system is easily established by analyzing a sample of a drinker's breath—hence the police machine known as a breathalizer. Some countries mandatorily breathalize any driver they stop, and in some places they'll stop anybody, any time. In places such as Gibraltar, the faintest trace of alcohol discovered in a driver can lead to prosecution and loss of license. This is taking the law to the limits because there is a small amount of alcohol naturally present in the blood. In hard-drinking Scandinavian countries, the discovery of alcohol in a driver means loss of license and compulsory attendance at counseling courses for alcoholics (the liquor store owner is also often required by law to record the name and address of all purchasers.).

## Alcohol, Accidents, and Liability

Since so many road, industrial, and domestic accidents and deaths worldwide are alcohol related, one can understand the tight focus on eliminating at least one threat from dangerous modern life.

An important thing for the caterer to understand is that successful prosecutions have been brought against anyone who served the liquor to a person subsequently involved in a fatal automobile accident. The chances of being involved in such horror are small but large enough to be considered. Mercifully, the caterer is unlikely to be pestered by drunks insisting on more drinks, as in a commercial bar. If a stupid host decides that a drunken guest should be given more alcohol, the caterer should disassociate himself from the serving of alcohol immediately.

# Wine

Whether resulting from wine's rumored therapeutic properties or from a generation's preference for a lighter form of alcohol, it is expected that every party bar will offer a good supply of white wine and a slightly smaller supply of red wine. A general familiarity with wines is easy to acquire and will prove very useful to you in advising your clients and finding your way through the confusing array of choices.

How the wine industry, and the alcoholic beverage industry generally, would love to be able to label their wares with the words "Government research has shown that alcohol consumption helps prevent heart disease," instead of killjoy reminders that wine contains sulphites and that drinking alcohol during pregnancy can harm an unborn child. But there is a consumer lobby, staunchly resisted, that would like to see all the ingredients of wine and liquor listed on the label.

In the case of wine, a complete list of ingredients would require a long label indeed, since the average bottle contains more than a thousand ingredients, some of them rather unattractive-sounding chemicals. Most wine is filtered through sulfur to stop it rotting. Red wine is brightened with potassium (thought by some to be the heart-disease preventer). The cheery-sounding chemical potassium ferrocyanide is used as a fining agent, providing a better color.

It is important that wine be correctly stored, ideally in cool, consistent temperatures, and not disturbed too much—hence the notion of the wine cellar, the part of the house that has least human traffic. Bottles of wine should be stored flat so that the cork is in contact with the wine, unless it's going to be used within a week or two.

Once opened, wine should be consumed fairly expeditiously. If a half-consumed bottle is firmly recorked, either with the original cork or one of those gadgets obtainable from most liquor stores, it may last a few days. But wines vary enormously in this respect, and some will deteriorate very quickly.

## A Brief Wine Primer

Wine is the fermented juice of freshly picked grapes, gathered annually, and vintages are referred to by year—a "47 Pommard," and so on. The quality varies from year to year, along with the weather. A long, dry summer is what usually makes for a vintage year because the grapes stay on the vine longer and retain more sugar. They are picked as late as possible, in some cases when they are just beginning to rot. In France this is called "noble rot" (*Pourriture noble*).

If the grapes, and therefore the wine, of a particular harvest are of exceptional quality, a vintage year is officially declared, and the wine often laid down (stored for longer periods) once bottled. Contact with air allowed by the breathing cork is what enables the wine to improve. (How this squares with the recent introduction of plastic corks, invented specifically to offset the ever dwindling quality of natural corks, has not yet been explained by the industry. Do the plastic corks actually breathe? Isn't the whole point of plastic in packaging the fact that it is a perfect seal against all potential contaminants?)

Some wines improve when stored in wooden casks, but not all. It is a matter of experience and the individual style of a particular house or chateau. Wine comes in three colors, red, white, and rosé—nowadays sometimes called "blush." Some wines such as champagne are effervescent, sparkling, or bubbly. This condition in champagne is induced by a secondary fermentation caused by adding sugar to white wine from the designated region, which is the area around Epernay, France. In other sparkling wines the bubbles may be induced by chemicals.

The main ingredients of a bottle of wine are water (85%), alcohol (12%), and sulphites (3%). Small amounts of urethanes (they're carcinogens) are present, as are histamines, which have been targeted by the Australian wine industry as a possible cause of the headaches in some drinkers after a quite small consumption of red wine. The industry is hoping to eliminate them.

How do they produce wine in different colors? Easily—for white wine you remove the grapeskin from the fermenting vat as soon as the process is under way; for blush wines you leave the skins in a while; and for red you leave the skins in throughout the process. The skins form a natural residue eventually, once the liquid has been strained off, and many a tale is told about uses for this by-product, in which the truth about *grappa*, the generic name for Italian common brandy, looms large.

## Wines of the World

Here is a brief rundown of the best known wines of the world.

**French**    There are three broad groups of French wine. They come from the areas known as Burgundy, Bordeaux, and Côte du Rhone. Burgundy is a large region of northern France, with Rheims, Epernay, Beaune, and Beaujolais some of the towns that give their names to famous wines. Bordeaux is both a region and a city. Côte du Rhone means the bank of the River Rhone, which flows into the Mediterranean in a delta northwest of Marseilles and down whose broad valley blows the Mistral, a wind that causes bad weather as far away as the coast of Spain.

Famous red Burgundies, as wines from the region are generically called, include Beaune, Beaujolais, Pommard, and many others. You can't just call any old wine by these names—they are controlled, and the French call these names *appellations controllee*. They must originate from specified areas, although different houses and shippers bottle under different labels.

White burgundies include Chablis and Pouilly-Fuissé. *Chablis* is now used loosely as a generic, nonspecific term for white wine, but strictly speaking only wine from that region should be so called. The best white Burgundies are dry. Poor imitations tend not to be.

Bordeaux reds, often called clarets, include such wines as St. Emilion, Medoc, and so on. These, too, are controlled names. Claret is dominated by famous *chateaux*, or houses, such as Lafite Rothschilde, Chateau Haut Brion, and others. Amusingly, "Haut Brion" is a corruption of the Anglo-Irish name "O'Brien," dating from the days when Bordeaux, like Burgundy, was an English possession by way of royal marriage. Bordeaux wines include Graves, which is dry, and Sauternes, which is sweet. Again, different chateaux create their own vintages within these groups.

Although shapes have changed and become gimmicky in recent years, most Burgundy wines come in bottles with necks longer and narrower than those of Bordeaux bottles. Next time you're browsing in the wine store, you may notice this difference.

**German**    Germany has a huge wine industry, mainly white. It is no secret that, shortly after World War II, the industry decided to concentrate on cheap, mass-consumption wines, but their best offerings are out of this world—like their prices. German wines have two main groups—those from the Rhine Valley, which are called Rhine wines and those from the Moselle Valley, called Moselles. Both come in the traditionally shaped tall and tapered bottle. Nevertheless, they can easily be distinguished because Rhine bottles are brown while Moselle bottles are green. There's no need to be confused—just remember that the word *green* like the word *Moselle* has two *e*'s.

The most famous Rhine wine is the cheap-and-cheerful Liebfraumilch. Another, produced perforce in somewhat lesser quantities, is Schloss Johannisberg—a sublime and expensive wine that falls into the area designated by the German government as Qualitätswein mit pradikat—the highest imaginable quality. The best-known Moselle is Piesporter Goldtropfchen, though the jewel in the crown is the once-tasted-never-forgotten Bernkasteler Doktor.

"Noble rot" (*Edelfaule*) also exists in Germany. The grapes left longest on the vine are called *Trockenbeerenauslese*. If you spy this word on a bottle of German wine, you can prepare your palate for a wonderful experience, and your wallet, or credit card, for a beating.

**Italian**   These vary from the sublime to the ridiculous, but the run-of-the mill varieties are cheap and cheerful enough. Chianti is the best known, usually as a red, and it goes well with most Italian dishes. This isn't a very likely choice for a catered function, but you never know.

Barolo, Gatinara, Bardolino, and Valpolicella are other well-known reds. Popular white wines include Orvieto and Frascati.

Different houses put out wines labeled according to the type of grape used, such as Pino Grigio, Verdicchio, and Pino Bianco. The predominant family of Italian wine is the Frescobaldi clan. They produce gallons of Chianti in thousands of acres of Tuscany, but also the exquisite and rare Montesodi wine, which is only bottled in exceptional years.

**Spanish**   Spain is most famous for its delicious sherries—super-dry (*manzanilla*), dry (*fino*), medium dry and nutty (*amontillado*), and sweet (*oloroso*). But they produce some very acceptable fruity and robust table wines, too, such as Marques de Riscal. In the Iberian Peninsula there is little talk of vintages. The weather is consistent, offering no challenge to vintners. By the same token, the quality of wines is also consistent.

Spain has the distinction of producing the world's strongest wine, in Tarragona, Catalunia. It's red, called Priorato, and made from the *Garnacha* (Grenache) grape, and it achieves an extraordinary strength of 18 percent alcohol by volume. This is not a fortified wine like sherry, Port, Marsala, and Madeira, to which brandy is added. It is probably not possible to make a stronger potion and still legitimately call it wine, for chemical reasons. A lot of Eucharistic wine comes from this region. It's said that Priorato is the Vatican wine of choice, but this hasn't been confirmed.

**Portuguese**   Port, a red, nutty, somewhat sweet fortified wine beloved of the English and Dutch, is this country's best known wine. Some of its vintages are treasured. Fathers in Portugal "lay down pipes" that is, store (casks) of it for their newborn sons.

After Pastis, and cheap wine, Port has the reputation of producing the worst imaginable hangovers. But hangovers are the result of overindulgence, and port, except in France where it is consumed as an aperitif, is usually drunk at the end of a dinner during which other wines may have been drunk, so it is clearly a prime suspect in such matters.

There is also a white Port that commands a small following. Some drink it as an aperitif—the drink before a meal that is supposed to whet the appetite. Others serve it as a dessert wine with water biscuits, cream cheese, and Bar-le-Duc currants. Such a rarified item is an unlikely choice in the world of the caterer, and the information is offered for interest only.

The Portuguese produce some light and fruity white wines called *vinho verde*, literally "green wine." The description alludes to its youth rather than its color.

**AMERICAN**    There can be little doubt that, if they can ever get the price right, American wines will dominate the world market, such is their excellence and variety. California has long produced fine wines, including champagne types. (Some French vintners thought them so good they bought some Californian wineries. Piper Heidseik brought out Piper Sonoma, for instance—a California champagne with a distinct French accent.) The soil along the north shore of New York's Long Island closely resembles that of some areas of Burgundy, and produces some excellent wines that are highly characterful, in the best sense of the term.

**AUSTRALIAN**    White wines such as Lindemann's and reds such as Jacob's Creek are now staple items in the average wine and liquor store. As in America their vintners have the advantage of starting fresh, and they are less concerned with tradition than in establishing what people want from wine and meeting that demand.

# WINE TASTING

While a professional caterer should know the realities behind the world of alcohol, she shouldn't lose sight of the mystique that helps to sell it and is at best harmless and fun as long as one doesn't take it too seriously. Apart from anything else, people often have wine-tasting parties, and if you can demonstrate some flair in the field, this service could become a specialty.

## WHAT CREATES THE CHARACTER AND QUALITY OF WINE?

Three factors determine the character and quality of a wine. The first is the type of grape used—the already mentioned Cabernet Sauvignon, Muscat, Gamay, Grenache or Grenacha, Tempranillo, Montepulciano, Semillon, and so on.

The second factor is the combination of climate and soil. Endless Californian and Spanish sunshine helps to produce wines of consistent quality, but Spain produces no truly great wines and the best of the California vintages come from the northern areas, where the weather becomes a little more challenging.

Most vintners agree that the greater wines have to struggle for existence. The weather in Burgundy, for instance, is often bad, yet this is the area where some of the greatest wines in the world are created. Toward the end of the summer the Burgundy wine producers fly helicopters around, and even fire mortars, to try to dispel rain clouds.

Different grapes fare better in different kinds of weather. The Semillon grape, from which the sweet white Sauterne wine is made in Bordeaux—flourishes in warm, humid weather. The Cabernet Sauvignon, from which many reds are made, doesn't, so that in Bordeaux a vintage year for whites can be a poor year for reds.

Vines planted in clayey soil will yield a flavor quite distinguishable from the flavor of vines grown in gravelly areas such as Bordeaux. Graves is the best known example of this soil's wines.

**The Human Touch**    The third and most mysterious factor is the human touch. Styles and methods vary enormously. Sometimes a winemaker has his eye on the local cuisine. Italian reds, for instance, are intended for tables groaning with herbs, strong cheeses, and plenty of olive oil, so the manufacturer aims for a robust style, rich in tannin, which comes from the grape's skin and gives wine its muscle and stability. One of the factors that makes white wines a little more challenging is that they contain less tannin than reds do because the skins are removed from the fermentation vat early in the process. Sure white wines are thus inherently somewhat less stable, and may travel badly, they are more likely to be laced with various chemicals—an observation that will come as no surprise to anyone who's suffered a white wine hangover after what seemed to be an evening of modest tippling.

Spanish wines such as Rioja tend to be more mellow. Australians find some of the Californian Chardonnays a bit too sweet, while Californians find some of the Australian Cabernet Sauvignons a bit too macho and robust.

Even close neighbors will produce wines of different character. One vintner may leave the wine longer in new oak casks. Another will blend in wine made from another grape, and so on. Many of these variations are closely guarded secrets.

## The Rituals of Wine

Wine lovers have elaborate rituals of tasting. They observe a wine's appearance, color, body, smell, taste, and finish (the aftertaste). At a tasting they'll hold a glass of wine up to the light to assess its color and swirl it around to observe its legs (the extent to which the wine trails stick to the glass). Then they'll stick their noses deep into the glass to get an idea of its nose (or smell). At last, they'll actually taste it—chew it almost—thoughtfully rolling it around the tastebuds. Finally, they'll spit it out into a sawdust-filled bucket, and savor the aftertaste for a moment before making their notes. Then perhaps they'll nibble some cheese or sip some water to cleanse the palate.

It may not sound very attractive, but that's the time-honored routine. What are they looking for and trying to assess?

**LEGS**    The better a wine clings to the glass when you swirl it around, the more full-bodied it is. Good legs, as the streaks of wine are called, imply a full body and robustness. (However, light-bodied wines have a place in the hierarchy too; they are good for casual drinking, and with lighter foods.)

**BOUQUET**    Bouquet, or nose is the next consideration. This is an important ingredient in the pleasureable sensations of all eating and drinking. A chilled white wine (all white wines are served chilled) will have little or no nose until it warms up a bit. Many believe that such wines actually improve as they warm.

Red wines taste better at room temperature and almost all are served like that. Contact with air releases taste, which is why so many people like to open a bottle of red in advance. Exquisite vintage wines should be decanted, as there is often a sediment in older wines that needs to be discarded. Old hands have been known to bring a ho-hum red wine to its peak appeal by pouring it into a shallow dish so that it gets a thorough airing and then putting it back in the bottle or decanter.

However, many Americans are used to drinking red wine chilled and will complain vociferously if it's served warm. Customers are always right in this respect—they can have their roast beef well done, too, if they insist. The French drink Beaujolais chilled. Enterprising bars in the United States offer the New Beaujolais both chilled and at room temperature.

**TASTE**    When it comes to taste, the first consideration is the degree of sweetness. If, during the manufacturing process, most of the sugar from the grapes has been consumed, then the wine will be *dry*—the opposite of sweet. Clearly, sweetness will not be disdained in a dessert wine, like Port, Madeira, or the wildly expensive French Bordeaux white, Chateau Yquem. (Its younger sister, Chateau Y, which comes at a more affordable price, will give you an idea of what the ultimate is like.)

Then there is the aftertaste, or finish—ideally a deeply satisfying one.

**CHARACTER**    Finally, there's the overall character of the wine. Some might find this hard to talk about, but there's no shortage of terms you can use. Wine lovers use such descriptions as fat, thin, fruity, smoky, the right-bankish taste of young Merlot (a variety of grape), lively, spicy, new-turned earth, rotting leaves, good depth, well mannered, good tannin ("to hold it together"), a whiff of coal tar gas, nail varnish, minty, smell of old books, smoky green leaves, cat pee, crushed nettles, and on and on.

While some of this is serious, much of it is simply part of the theater of wine. In stark reality, huge wine tankers trundle through the night all over the world.

Often the wine has no name and little pedigree, but somewhere it will find a home. It will probably be blended and christened with a name far more attractive than that of its source.

You'll often read of wine described as having a "delicious blackberry finish." This is hardly surprising in the case of some ordinary Burgundies (not the famous vintages), since blackberry juice is routinely added to give them more character. Fruit sugar, or sucrose, will almost invariably improve the taste of wine. Many vintners use this, and other additives, as routinely as the food industry uses salt, sugar, and monosodium glutemate. Pesticides and weed killers are also used in the grape growing process.

Some chemicals are used with good reason, however. As many amateur wine makers discover, fermented grape juice is a very delicate liquid. It may simply turn to vinegar if left to its own devices, especially in a warm climate. Sulphur dioxide, for instance, is used as an antiseptic to protect the juice as it turns to wine.

A standing joke in the industry is the regularity with which, at wine tastings—where the wine is not identified until after it's been tasted—cheap, unadvertised, and unknown wines score better than famous, expensive name brands and vintages. However, it is not always like that . . .

At a recent tasting, five champagnes or sparkling wines were offered, four of which were undistinguished and cheap. The tasters were not professionals, just occasional champagne drinkers. While there was much disagreement about the four lesser wines, the tasters were unanimous in choosing the vintage Mumm as clearly superior.

Vintage champagne rarely disappoints, but the same cannot be said for the nonvintage styles of some houses in recent years. A caterer asked to choose an inexpensive champagne or sparkling wine needs to be very careful in his selection.

Television programs featuring wine experts who can identify—and even price—wines tasted at random, reveal uncanny knowledge and consistency of agreement. Cynical reflections, such as those some might entertain in the light of the rigging of old television quiz shows, must remain the private business of the reflector.

## Demystifying Wine

If the world of wine sounds like a minefield, it isn't. It's important to demystify the subject, concentrating on its convivial and gastronomic role rather than nurturing the snooty, upscale aspects that the industry encouraged a century ago. This attitude is summed up in the nineteenth-century cartoon in which a host is serving a guest a glass of wine with the remark "It's just a harmless little domestic burgundy of little or no breeding, but I think you'll be amused by its precocity."

Such a line in a costume drama on public television would no doubt bring the house down—but it isn't the tone of the mass market. The mystique must be diluted if winemakers are to find markets for their immense production.

All the Latin countries have the proverb "A day without wine is like a day without sunshine." Wine quality is instantly apparent with a little experience. The goal and the dream is finding the best quality at the most reasonable price, as in most of the things we buy.

# Which Wine?

It is highly likely that you, as the caterer, will be asked for advice on which wines to serve, and it's by no means uncommon for the choice to be left entirely to you. This is good news because you can not only do a good deal with your friendly liquor supplier but pass on some of the savings to your client. Remember, sometimes your client will be working within a strict budget, perhaps that of a club or company, and the better value in goods and services you can deliver for the money, the more likely you are to be hired again.

The broad choices are between red, white, sparkling (champagne), sweet, and dry. For general-purpose drinking—that is to say, during pre- and postprandial times (i.e., before and after the main meal is served)—you will need above all a good quantity of decent white wine. That is currently the single most likely drink to be requested at a catered function. (In the world at large, of course, beer is the most requested and consumed alcoholic beverage. But except at barbecues, for various reasons beer takes a back seat at most catered occasions. See the section on beer to come.)

Because of its popularity, the market in white wine has become intense, and the quality of some wines offered in restaurants borders on the criminal. Sometimes the wines are so bad, and the customers complain so much, that job lots of dubious concoctions are served only in the form of spritzers—white wine, ice, seltzer, and a squeeze of lemon—to disguise, sometimes successfully, the underlying horror. Wine deeply chilled hardly tastes of anything, but as it warms to room temperature its bliss—or horror—will become apparent.

Part of the problem is that terms like *Chablis* and *Soave Bolla* are generic, and just about any wine can be referred to thus. To get something approaching the real thing you have to request a specific chateau in the case of Chablis, or a specific shipper in the case of Soave Bolla—and the price soars.

So flagrant was the abuse of the popularity of white wine as an aperitif or general tipple, that a small-consumer revolution took place. Through the eighties drinkers started ordering wine by the bottle and closely examining what they got. Better restaurants matched this by offering a selection of white wines—at rather intimidating prices in most cases.

## Ordering Wine by the Grape

It was from this, more or less, that the current habit of referring to wines by the type of grape from which they were made sprang. Where once one talked of a

Burgundy or a Bordeaux (or claret), people now talk of grape varieties. The charming word "varietal," dragged from obscurity, is an adjective meaning "of a certain variety."

The current most popular grape is probably Chardonnay. People will ask for a glass of Chardonnay instead of a glass of white wine. Connoisseurs (and poseurs) will even ask for the Chardonnay of a certain winery or vineyard. Semillon is another grape used predominantly in the making of white wine, in this case sweet white wine, Sauternes, at Bordeaux.

Other grape varietals requested are Cabernet Sauvignon, Pinot Noir (considered by many to be the least conducive to hangovers), Muscat, Merlot, and the uniquely delightful Zinfandel. These are almost invariably red, but there are white and rosé, or blush versions, too.

Almost as many books have been written about wine as have been written about Napoleon. Many newspapers and magazines now have a wine correspondent—most are knowledgeable, and their enjoyment of their work can be quite infectious. Nevertheless, unless you are intrigued by the subject, you should try to keep your mind uncluttered. For working purposes in the catering industry, a sound knowledge of the broad brush strokes is sufficient.

## What You *Must* Know

### Room Temperature or Chilled

White wine, sparkling wines, dry sherries (La Iña, Tio Pepe), and champagne are served chilled. You must be able to chill wine, and keep it chilled, for the duration of the function. Ice supply and the maximum use of refrigerated space are important considerations. Red wine is served at room temperature unless you're featuring chilled Beaujolais Nouveau—the new vintage—which has been built up into a media event in recent years.

### Opening Wine

Your staff should be equipped with corkscrews. The best kind is shaped rather like a jackknife and consists of a small blade, a corkscrew, and a useful lever that, applied against the neck of the bottle once the corkscrew has been inserted, usually allows easy withdrawal. Wine salespersons sometimes hand them out, emblazoned with the name of one of the shippers, or they can be bought quite cheaply.

At a catered affair neither you nor your staff need to go into the theater of wine opening that is required in restaurants—the showing of the label, the examination of the cork (though you should do this automatically even if opening bottles backstage), the tasting of a small amount, the pouring, and all the rest of it. The diners are guests, and it isn't their place to query what's put before them—at least not out loud. However, it's nice if servers know what they're pouring, so that if a guest particularly enjoys a wine and inquires about it for future reference (as drinkers often do—sometimes even requesting a label to take home as a reminder), it's surely nicer and more professional to say, "Chateau de Paris, 1985" than "Gee, I dunno. I'm only a part-timer, and I don't drink."

# Champagne

Champagne has long been the traditional wine of celebration. Sadly, it is an expensive item, some of the more valuable vintages costing $100 or more in the liquor store. Dom Perignon, James Bond's preferred bubbly, is thought to be the oldest. The monk of that name found a wine that had accidentally gone into a secondary fermentation and was bubbling. "I'm drinking stars," he said, or so the story goes.

## Opening the Bottle

The movie and television scenes in which corks pop and the precious liquid is sprayed over the winning team, do a dangerous disservice to the world at large. Champagne requires a firm approach. If a bottle of champagne has been much agitated (i.e., more shaken than is involved by a one-block stroll and removal from refrigerator or container to a table) then, when opened, the cork is likely to be expelled with sufficient force to blind someone if it hits him in the eye (which it does about 400 times a year worldwide—one of those quirky but consistent statistics, along with snake bites and lightning strikes).

It's a good idea to let champagne rest for at least 20 minutes before opening it, in order to minimize the risk of wasting the expensive wine in messy foaming. Before opening a bottle (or Magnum, Jereboam, or Nebuchadnezzar—as the increasingly bigger sizes of bottles of champagne are called), the opener should ensure that he or she has a large glass to hand and—most important—a stout cloth napkin.

Champagne corks are sealed by tinfoil and wire. Before you do anything else when opening champagne, you should gather a napkin around the neck and grip it well to ensure that you won't have to endure the consequences as a cork shoots out. First you untwist the securing wire. Then you gently twist out the cork without agitating the bottle. Strictly speaking, corks should be drawn as silently as possible, since people of refinement consider the popping sound rather coarse and vulgar. However, we live in rather coarse and vulgar times, and many may not disdain the sound of a popping cork but, on the contrary, find it festive and uplifting.

If the champagne gushes, simply pour the foam into a large glass. It will stop gushing almost immediately, and, once it settles down and turns back to liquid, the foam won't be wasted.

## What Goes with Champagne?

It's generally assumed that champagne goes with everything, though many would disagree. It doesn't seem the ideal accompaniment for a hearty beef dish, for instance. A popular custom nowadays is for champagne to be served at the end of a dinner, when toasts are proposed.

At receptions, cocktail parties, and buffets, some hosts like to offer champagne only, or sparkling wines called *Spumante* in Italian and *Sekt* in Germany. This certainly simplifies things and makes for a festive spirit. It's bad news for people who dislike champagne, however, so it's not a bad idea to have a small selection of alternatives, even if only red wine or a still white wine.

It can be irritating for guests who don't like champagne, but politely go along with it, when an old friend of the host arrives and is solemnly served a special scotch on the rocks or a martini, which would have been the guest's drink of choice had he been offered one.

Regular wine drinkers may shudder inwardly if the only drink available is a rather ho-hum nonvintage champagne. This is a notoriously hit-and-miss product these days, to the extent that the Champagne Federation in France has set up a watchdog committee to encourage quality.

# When to Serve Which Wine

The choice of wine, especially at sit-down dining functions, relates directly to the menu. Here is a guide to what wine goes with what food.

| | |
|---|---|
| Appetizers | Champagne, dry white, medium or dry sherry |
| Beef | Hearty red |
| Lamb | Hearty red |
| Veal | Dry or medium white or rosé |
| Chicken | Dry or medium white or rosé |
| Fish, or seafood | Dry or medium white or rosé |
| Dessert | Sweet wine, Port, Madeira |

When you're catering, those guidelines should be adhered to unless the client has some special preference.

Broadly, the rule is simply red wine with red meat and white wine with white meat, fish, or seafood. As far as the individual is concerned, however, these rules are made to be broken. Some veal dishes invite a red wine accompaniment—Osso Bucco, for instance. Many prefer red wine with the more robust fishes such as cod or "scrod" (as it is often called on the East coast, from the days when supplies were not yet threatened and New England fishermen would sell it at a reduced price, calling it "Special catch—Run of the Day").

If Italian or Spanish dishes are to be served, it may be appropriate to serve wines from those countries, since they are, after all, designed around local cuisine. The Greek wine Retsina, for instance, sometimes causes a raised eyebrow because it is somewhat characterful. But when it's served with Greek roast lamb it does seem to find a home. As the apocryphal, affable waiter famously said to the scion of a famous "old money" family at a Waldorf dinner—when complimented on the excellence of the vintage Chateau Lafite—"Cuts the grease, right?"

Eating food and drinking wine are two pastimes that inevitably attract Philistines, at least in the eye of some beholders. Queen Victoria used to spike her claret with Scotch whisky, but clearly there is no reason why she shouldn't have, especially in cold and drafty Victorian buildings. At formal dinners great jugs of Scotch and water, as well as wine, were often passed around the table.

In Spain and France they add water to table wine—not the prime vintages, of course, but the sort of wine the average shopper in these countries buys at the supermarket six bottles at a time.

# Beer

Strangely, the world's most popular alcoholic beverage is neglected, or even disdained, at the majority of catered functions, with the notable exception of barbecues. Perhaps the simple reason for this is that many catered affairs have an upscale aura and beer, delicious though it is, doesn't have quite the festive appeal of wine. Part of the prejudice, if prejudice there be, may be due to the fact that beer is heavy to carry and space consuming (most importantly, refrigerated space).

However, since a number of people will only drink beer, it is often a good idea to have a small quantity available. Guests whose tastes in alcohol are narrow will always be delighted to find they've been catered to. Even so, it's unlikely that you'll ever be required to provide a full selection of beers. Many smart restaurants only offer two—one imported, the other domestic—for their mainly wine-drinking clientele.

If you decide to make available a small amount of beer, your best brand choice is probably Heineken. As well as a popular first choice, it's a common second choice when a requested brand isn't available. (The same goes for Dewars Scotch whisky.) The most important thing about serving beer is that it should be very cold. Often drinkers insist that their beer be so fiercely chilled that the possibility of any taste emerging from it is slight to say the least. But that may be at least part of the rationale, as it is with inferior white wines, whose horrors can be sometimes disguised by chilling it to within an inch of its life.

## Chilling and Serving Beer

If you need to chill beer (or wine) in a hurry, it will be quite cold after ten minutes immersed in ice. Ice used for this purpose shouldn't be used for drinks—that's the law, but people will often request that a bottle be stuck in the ice, and in that case your conscience must be your guide. From the point of view of hygiene, there's no guarantee that the outside of a bottle is sterile; it may have been much-handled or stored somewhere not very clean. Beer glasses must be scrupulously clean and well rinsed, otherwise that ritualistically expected half inch of foam, or head, just won't occur.

**GLASS OR BOTTLE?**    The traditional way of serving beer from a bottle is simply to place the glass on a coaster or "bevnap" (beverage napkin), pour an inch of beer into the glass, and place the bottle on the table. But many people today insist on drinking straight from the bottle, and some younger consumers would wonder what was going on if a waiter went through this ritual. Not long ago drinking anything straight from a bottle was considered the height of bad manners, the province of the humble beeraholic on the street, nuzzling his brown bag and keeping an eye open for the cops. Now it's considered the height of cool in some circles. To old-fashioned eyes there's something a little pathetic in the sight of people dressed to the nines at "smart" parties, guzzling beer from bottles. But the professional caterer needs to keep his or her unfashionable and politically incorrect attitudes clasped to the bosom and never divulged; otherwise, business may suffer.

Caterers must be alert to the fickle finger of fashion, because things change fast, and its victims are alert and enthusiastic. Drinking straight from the bottle, for instance, has almost certainly become acceptable because of the profusion of scenes on TV where it is demonstrated. Possibly because so many actors and writers spend part of their lives in the catering and restaurant industries while awaiting The Call to Fame, many movie and novel scenes are set at catered functions and in restaurants. Serving beer correctly in a movie or TV show would get in the way of the action. It's so much easier to plonk two bottles in front of the embattled protagonists and let them get into their punchy dialogue.

Thinking positive, bottle drinking may save on the dishwashing, and some beer connoisseurs insist that beer actually tastes better and stays cold longer straight from the bottle. A common riposte from bottle drinkers politely offered a glass is "It's already in a glass."

No matter how aristocratic or august the occasion, the old bartender's custom of removing beer bottles as soon as they're emptied should be observed. They make devastating projectiles and, niftily broken as by Burt Lancaster in the movie "From Here To Eternity," handy weapons. Also, removing them is tidier.

# WATERS, SODAS, AND JUICES

The extraordinary demand for bottled waters has been around so long that it may be here to stay. Whatever the case, at any catered event you ought to have some available. Just to make life a little harder, many consumers like their water chilled and won't accept the simple addition of an ice cube or two since the tap water is precisely what they're trying to avoid.

Like everything, bottled waters take up space. You just have to work it out as best you can. Still water seems to have a slight edge on sparkling, so if you lay in a supply of it, you may be able to satisfy those who prefer sparkling water with a glass of the ordinary soda water, or seltzer, as it is also known, which you almost certainly must have as part of your regular bar setup.

Sodas, which are drunk plain and also added to various spirits (which is why they're sometimes called mixers) are an essential item, too. Plain soda is the most important but a diet cola of one kind or another should be available, as this odd product seems to have captured the hearts and minds of half the population of the western world. It is the most requested soft drink in many food service operations. Apart from these two kinds of sodas, you should have at least a token amount of tonic (quinine) water and ginger ale. There are two or three more that you need to stock in a regular commercial bar—lemon-flavored, regular cola, diet ginger ale, and so on—but this is catering, and the parameters are thankfully reduced.

Again, sodas are space eaters, but they don't need to be refrigerated. The large bottles are best. Used at home, unless the family is large, they tend to go flat (yes, even when the cap is screwed back on tight), but in the course of a catered event this won't be a problem.

Juices commonly used in bars, often used for mixing with spirits, are orange, grapefruit, tomato, pineapple, and cranberry. Years ago juices were squeezed at the bar, but that is no longer common. Packaged juices reached an acceptable standard for commercial bar use, though most people would agree that nothing really beats the freshly squeezed variety.

Many juices come in handy cardboard or glass containers usually, and in one-portion containers. Tomato and cranberry juices usually come in large cans, which need to be opened and transferred to smaller bottles that are easier to handle and not quite so starkly functional looking when used in front of guests. Lemon-X—sweetened lemon juice which comes in large cans is now a standard item for the mixing of certain cocktails, such as Whiskey Sours. None of these are standard requirements in the average catering situation, but if you're doing a Sunday brunch, for instance, you might want to offer Bloody Marys and Screwdrivers, the recipes for which are given in Chapter 10.

## Spirits

It is just as well for caterers to be at least acquainted with all the spirits on the market. You will look a bit silly if a client says "I thought we'd serve a liqueur after dinner, Kümmel . . . or maybe a delicious Armagnac, to amuse my new client Monsieur Dupont . . ." or "I thought we'd drink a toast with Metaxa in honor of our Greek friends . . ." and you haven't the faintest idea what they're talking about.

Don't worry—the good news is that although you need a peripheral knowledge of the subject, or at least a point of reference, which this section will provide, in general catering you're unlikely to find yourself dealing with more than four kinds of spirit. This small range is discussed again in Chapter 10.

## The Commercial Bar

Next time you're in a bar, take a look at the array of bottles. Usually the tallest one, shaped rather like the Eiffel Tower, is Galliano, an Italian liqueur concocted from vanilla, anise, and licorice. Often it's the most central bottle of the display, resembling nothing so much as a commander-in chief reviewing a parade of troops. You'll also see half a dozen kinds of Scotch, half a dozen of gin, and half a dozen of vodka. Thereafter, brands will be represented only by single bottles, unless it's one of those big bars with more than one station, each equipped with the full range of spirits.

What on earth are they all for, you may wonder? Good question. Your bartender, if friendly, will reveal that when she does the "breakage" of a morning (i.e., counts the empty bottles in order to compile the liquor list, which she takes to the boss for replacements), the selection of liquors consumed is small. In a moderately busy 50-seater restaurant, with a 12-stool bar a typical breakage list might be: 6 large bottles of white wine (of the "house" variety—the one they use for pouring if no special brand is specified), 6 vodka (house), 1 large red wine, 1 Scotch (house), and 1 gin (house). This would be a typical daily pattern and clearly reflects the general pattern of consumption.

You'll see regular appearances from Stolichnaya vodka, Dewars Scotch, and the other half dozen well-advertised brands, but all other brands would require replacing only occasionally. You're looking at a shelf full of Cinderellas. There is also draft beer and beer by the bottle to remember. The draft kegs are in the cellar, and the empty beer bottles are disposed of separately.

There are many exceptions to this pattern—one bar in South Carolina famously gets through 300 cases of Jaegermeister a month—but the message is simple. Drinking tastes have narrowed drastically in the last two decades. Wine and water have boomed, while spirits and cocktails have slumped.

## What You Should Know

The only justification for the presence of so many bottles in a bar is that there are always a few who remain loyal to a now obscure brand, and you never know when you're going to be flooded with a young crowd demanding outlandish cocktails. The industry jumps through hoops to unload some of its less popular products, and one of its time-honored ways is to invent a new cocktail of which the core ingredient is some obscure liqueur. In fact, the taste of the core component is completely obscured by the time the other five or six "essential ingredients," plus sweetened lemon juice and maybe some cream, have been added. You will hardly ever be required to produce such exotica in the ordinary run of catering, and although one must consider the worst-case scenario of a host who insists upon having a Piña Colada party, there's no need to hold one's breath while awaiting the call.

The following long list of well-known liquors and liqueurs is offered for interest and reference only. It does not represent an essential body of knowledge, but "should know" or maybe even "could know" information.

**Vodka**   This is the most popular spirit in the United States. It is simply grain spirit, though some vodkas are distilled from potatoes. Because it contains so few ingredients—water, alcohol, glycerol, and trace elements of carbohydrate and protein—it is generally regarded as the "cleanest" drink, that is, the one least likely to produce a hangover. This purity is achieved by filtering the spirit through charcoal, often several times. An early advertising slogan in vodka's march to the top was "It leaves you breathless." While it's true that vodka isn't very noticeable at the superficial level of mouth contact, lunchtime imbibers who have to go back to an office often take no chances and have a good gargle with mouthwash before returning. Also, alcohol is partly excreted through the breath, and if enough is consumed, especially on an empty stomach, hydrochloric acid is produced and this causes halitosis.

Vodka features in several cocktails still regularly requested—Screwdrivers, Vodka Martinis, and Bloody Marys—simple cocktails that are discussed later. There were 4,000 brand-name vodkas at one time, some so crude they had to be flavored with fruit or sprinkled with pepper to be palatable. Absolut introduced lemon- and blackcurrant-flavored vodkas called Citron and Kurant. Other prominent brands are Gordon's, Stolichnaya, Tanqueray, and Smirnoff.

**Rye, and American, Whiskey**   Rye whiskey was originally made from fermented mashed rye grain. As other grains became available, they were used too, and now rye, blended, and American whiskey mean more or less the same thing. Different companies use different blends to produce their own distinctive style. They mix various grain spirits and add flavors such as juices from prunes and other fruits. These whiskeys are usually drunk on the rocks, or with mixers such as ginger ale, 7-Up, or soda, and they feature in certain cocktails, of which the only one still regularly requested is the Whiskey Sour. Prominent brands are Seagrams 7, Four Roses, Schenleys, and the Canadian whisky, Canadian Club.

**Bourbon Whiskey**   This is sweeter and darker than Rye, distilled from a 51-percent corn mash and aged two to six years in charred oak barrels. In the same family but slightly different are Tennessee whiskeys like George Dickel and Jack Daniels, which, before aging are filtered through maple charcoal. All Bourbons, such as Maker's Mark, and Wild Turkey, seem to command fierce "brand loyalty" from their consumers. They are often drunk on the rocks or with soda, and feature in cocktails such as Bourbon Manhattans and Sours.

**Scotch Whiskey**   This is a blend of malt and grain whiskey, characterized by a smoky peat flavor. "Malt" means from barley, and it is the drying of the sprouted barley over smoky peat fires that creates this flavor before the distillation process is begun. Different distilleries use different, secret blends to create their own style. Basic regular Scotch doesn't display its age, which might be as little as two years. There are eight-year-olds, such as Moncreiffe, and twelve-year-olds such as Chivas Regal. Although the older whiskeys are inevitably more expensive, many prefer the younger style, and again there is fierce brand loyalty.

Many Americans prefer "light Scotches" such as Cutty Sark or J&B. "Light" in this context refers to the color, which varies according to the amount of caramel added to all scotches and has nothing to do with their strength, which is almost always around 86 proof—like most spirits.

**Single-Malt Scotch Whiskey**   These are the ultimate Scotch whiskies, consisting of one pure liquor, as distinct from blended. They come from the dozens of small distilleries all over Scotland, many of which welcome visitors. The local water, peat, and subtle variations in preparation methods and ingredients produce a wide variety of distinctive tastes and aromas.

Although the popularity of these expensive whiskeys is increasing, they are rather wasted on nonconnoisseurs, like many vintage wines and some other spirits. They are drunk neat, sometimes with plain ice, or water. In a seriously Scottish household or club, where the carpets, furniture, and, not uncommonly, the very walls are covered in tartan, whiskey is served neat, or plain, in a short glass accompanied by a glass of water. Bells is the current best seller in Scotland, though Famous Grouse is not far behind. Worldwide, Dewars and Johnny Walker Red and Black are well-known. Whisky is now made in both Japan and India, with the jury still out on their authenticity of taste.

**Irish Whiskey**   Jamesons claims to be the oldest whiskey on the planet, and the Irish version is quite distinct, being distilled three times instead of two, as is the case with Scotch, and not flavored by smoking peat. Thus, it's very smooth and many drink it for its own sake. However, most Irish whiskey finds itself tipped into coffee and topped with whipped cream to create Irish coffee. There is an Irish single-malt whiskey, recently launched, called "The Tyrconnell" after a racehorse that won the 1867 Queen Victoria Plate, the Irish classic race at that time, though it had been rated a 100-to-1 outsider.

If you're catering to Irish clients or celebrating something with an Irish theme, you might be requested to serve Irish whiskey, but it isn't a standard item in the catering field.

**Rum**   White rum, such as Bacardi, is the best known in the United States, most commonly served with cola and a squeezed wedge of lime. It also features in certain cocktails, notably the Daiquiri, still a regular request in commercial bars. Most white rum comes from Puerto Rico.

There's also amber-colored and dark rum, such as Myers, which comes from Jamaica, and Goslings, which comes from Bermuda. These are mixed with colas or orange juice. Goslings mixed with ginger ale is called a "Dark and Stormy" in Bermuda, another of whose contributions to world cuisine is the custom of serving sherry bitters with soup.

All rum is distilled from the fermented debris of crushed sugar cane or molasses and must be aged a year. Dark rum is made dark by adding caramel and is usually the standard 86 proof. By tradition, however, most extra-strong rums are very black.

**Gin**  This was once among the most popular spirits, mainly because it was so cheap. In London, in Victorian times, there was an advertisement for gin, "Drunk for a penny. Dead drunk for tuppence" with sometimes the further offer of "free straw." No wonder it's nicknamed "Mother's Ruin." A "gin mill" is of course somewhat pejorative slang for a bar.

Gin is simply grain spirit, like vodka, flavored with juniper berries and various dried fruits and herbs (quaintly called "botanicals") such as coriander, licorice, orange and lemon peel, almonds, angelica root, orris root, and cassia bark. Different brands use different, secret mixes.

Beefeater, Gordons, and Tanqueray are the best-known imported London gins, but there are various domestic products, too. Since the most common way for the spirit to be drunk is with sweet and bubbly tonic water, sometimes called quinine water, with a squeezed wedge of lime or lemon, any old gin will do for most people. Martini drinkers are likely to notice if they're given something other than their requested regular tipple, but caterers won't find themselves serving this cocktail often.

**Sherry**  This fortified wine from Spain is served as an aperitif in its dry and medium forms in small traditionally shaped glasses, called *copitas*, and as a dessert wine in its sweeter forms. "Fortified" means that brandy has been added to it. This was done originally to stabilize the wine for transportation, but it became its accepted style long after such problems had been ironed out.

**Port**  This is a sweet fortified wine from Portugal, usually drunk after dinner. Some of it is vintage, for example, an '89 Cockburn (pronounced *coe*-burn).

**Madeira, Muscat, and Marsala**  These are also well-known fortified dessert wines, often used in cooking, e.g., Chicken Marsala.

**Tequila**  This spirit comes from the Mexican town of that name and is made from the blue agave plant, a member of the amaryllis family that is often incorrectly referred to as a cactus. It is used in cocktails such as Margaritas and Tequila Sunrises, and sometimes consumed in an elaborate ceremony in which salt is spread on the inner thumb and licked, then the liquor is drunk, and finally a wedge of lime or lemon is chewed. It's not a caterer's standard item, you'll be relieved to learn.

**Brandy and Cognac**    Brandy is the generic name for the distilled spirit that comes from grapes. It's manufactured worldwide, including in the United States. Spirits such as Cognac, Salignac, and Armagnac must be certified as coming from those areas. A Cognac is a brandy, but a brandy isn't necessarily a Cognac.

In the same family, but very different, are such drinks as Kirsch, or Kirschwasser, a German brandy made from black cherries—a favorite over fruit salads. Slivovitz is a plum brandy. Marc is a French brandy, aged and very strong, made from the husks and mush that remains of the grapes after the winemaking process has been completed. It's a cousin of Italian Grappa, made the same way. Metaxa is Greek brandy, and Calvados is apple brandy, made commercially and in legal private stills in the Normandy region of France.

**Vermouth and Wine Cocktails**    Vermouth comes in two versions, sweet red and dry white. It's simply wine flavored with wormwood and is used in various now somewhat obscure cocktails. The dry sort, of course, is used in minute quantities to make dry martinis. No one has ever been heard to request a Sweet Martini, but the red version does find a home in Manhattans from time to time.

Dubonnet, a red wine mixture, is served as a chilled aperitif and is used in a Dubonnet Cocktail. The white version is seldom seen in the United States. Lillet is another kind of aperitif, usually served with a slice of orange. Suze, though well known in France, is a rare bird indeed in America.

**Bitters**    Campari is the best known in this genre, an Italian concoction of roots, herbs, fruits, and artificial flavoring. It finds a home in several cocktails. Angosturas is more concentrated and is described on the label as a stomachic. Indeed, it is a good tummy settler, sometimes drunk with soda water, and is used in a couple of cocktails. Others are the Italian Fernet Branca, the French Amer Picon, and the German Underberg and St. Vitus.

The herbs and fruits added to wine to make these drinks are, of course, top secret.

# Liqueurs

There is an outside chance, especially if you're catering a dinner, that you may be required to serve liqueurs. Also called "cordials," these are intensely flavored and characterful spirits, served in tiny glasses often alongside after-dinner coffee and not infrequently tipped therein. They are almost invariably intensely sweet, and some irreverently believe that their only true role in the gourmet pantheon is as flavorings for vanilla ice cream.

Liqueur ingredients are shrouded in secrecy, and, so their labels would sometimes have you believe, passed on by the abbot to his successor, with his last breath.

## LIQUEURS TO KNOW

Here's a brief roundup of some of the most famous liqueurs.

BENEDICTINE    A dark golden liqueur with a unique taste.

BENEDICTINE AND BRANDY (B&B)    It's exactly what it says. Some prefer this as being less sweet than pure Benedictine.

CHAMBORD    This raspberry liqueur comes in a collector's-item orb-shaped bottle, and a dash added to champagne makes a Kir Royale.

CHARTREUSE    This comes in two versions, green and yellow, and has an intriguing flavor.

COINTREAU    This is one of three orange liqueurs, the others being Grand Marnier and Triple Sec.

CREME DE CACAO    Cheerfully pronounced "cream o' cocoa," this comes in two versions, dark and white chocolate. The dark kind finds a home in the creamy cocktail Brandy Alexander and the white in a Grasshopper. These are highly unlikely requests, except in a restaurant on Mother's Day, along with Bailey's Irish Cream, a waistline-challenging mixture of Irish whiskey and cream.

CREME DE CASSIS    A blackberry liqueur added to white wine to sweeten it up in a cocktail called a Kir.

CREME DE MENTHE    This is a generic name for mint liqueur, which comes in two styles, white and green. The green version is used in a cocktail called a Grasshopper, the white in a Stinger.

CREME DE NOYEAU    An almond liqueur which enjoyed a brief flight as the central ingredient of a cocktail called a Pink Squirrel, now a dim memory for most people.

DRAMBUIE    A sweet liqueur based on Scotch whiskey. When added to ordinary Scotch it makes a cocktail called a Rusty Nail.

FRAMBOISE    A dark raspberry liqueur.

**Frangelica**   A liqueur based on hazelnuts, sometimes mixed with coffee and occasionally topped with whipped cream.

**Fruit Brandies**   These are available generically in the following flavors: blackberry, apricot, peach, banana, pineapple, plum, cherry, apple, strawberry, and pear.

**Pear Brandy**   The most famous brand is called Poire William, and there's a pear in the bottle. How does it get there? The bottle is placed over the pear, when it's still tiny on the tree, and tied to the tree branch. The trees look like something devised by Dali.

**Galliano**   This Italian yellow vanilla–anise–licorice liqueur is hard to miss in its tall triangular bottle, but it's unlikely to darken a caterer's doorstep.

**Grand Marnier**   The most authentic and expensive of the orange-flavored liqueurs.

**Jagermeister**   This amber, sweet German liqueur is nostalgically reminiscent of a European concoction known as "Gripe Water," given to babies to stop their crying until it was discovered that it contained alcohol and was promptly banned. It still exists in the wild islands of the Caribbean, where mothers desirous of a night's rest use it with gratitude. Jagermeister is a big item with the youth market, often drunk in neat shots and chased by beer. A caterer will usually incur no disapprobation if, upon request, he regretfully admits that none is available. (Unless the client has stipulated "This is a Jagermeister party, of course . . .")

**Kahlua**   This is a coffee liqueur that, although originally perceived as a cheeky rival for Tia Maria, has achieved a life of its own by asserting its presence in Black (and White) Russians. Helpfully, the recipes for these concoctions are printed on the back label, but a caterer's bar need not carry this item unless specially requested.

**Kummel**   The generic name for a liqueur flavored with caraway seeds. There are several brands.

**Midori**   A Japanese melon-based green liqueur. Its tall bottle rivals that of Galliano on a commercial bar shelf, and it is used to make a cocktail called a Melon Ball. As with most liqueurs that have carved out a niche in a specially invented cocktail, the recipe is on the back label. Unless a caterer is servicing a post-concert reception for the famous, eponymous young fiddler, it's not an essential item.

**Pernod and Ricard**   Green-yellow in appearance, these French brand-name liqueurs are almost invariably drunk with ice and water. When mixed this way, they turn bright yellow. Called "Pastis," the cocktail commands a following in France and among francophile Americans. The flavor, of anise and licorice, is based on a diluted version of absinthe, the wormwood-distilled highly potent liquor that was the nineteenth-century alcoholic demon of France and an inspiration of poets such as Verlaine and Baudelaire. Both Pernod and Ricard are owned by the same company.

**Ouzo**  This is a Greek version of the pastis described above. It turns white-milky-cloudy when water is added.

**Sambuca**  This generic Italian licorice-flavored liqueur is usually drunk in a "snifter." By tradition, three coffee beans, representing the Holy Trinity, are floated on top. They are for decoration, not consumption.

**Sloe Gin**  This dark plum-flavored neutral-spirit liqueur is featured mainly in a cocktail known as a Sloe Gin Fizz, still occasionally requested at Golden Anniversary celebrations, and the like. A sloe is a small fruit from the plum family, more like a damson, with a deep intriguing taste.

**Southern Comfort**  Usually drunk straight or on the rocks, this is a brand-name gold-colored Bourbon with a mild peach flavor. Not everyone would agree that it qualifies as a liqueur, but it has its faithful followers.

**Tia Maria**  This is a brand-name coffee liqueur, rarely drunk straight but occasionally employed in now obscure cocktails. Like other liqueurs it can be poured over vanilla ice cream with great effect, and for the truly wicked a teaspoonful or more on top of chocolate mousse imparts extra flavor.

# Chapter Ten

# Setting up a Bar

I F the event you're catering is small—say not more than 40 guests—in a house or apartment, you may simply set up your bar in the kitchen and operate from there. That's where the sinks and running water are, and that's where you'll find the refrigerator, usually. You may find yourself playing the part of butler, greeting the guests as they arrive, asking them what they'd like to drink, retiring to the kitchen to prepare the beverages, and bringing out the drinks on a tray.

With a little practice you'll be able to take the orders from as many as six people with no effort at all, and clearly it's much more efficient to serve as many people at once as you can. Indeed, serving people one at a time is the sure sign of the amateur or, certainly, the inexperienced.

Restaurant bar experience will prove invaluable in this area, as in all others. The essential factors in the efficient running of a bar of any kind are to be well set up and know what you're doing.

## Prompt Service

Speed is of the essence at a catered party, just as it is at a restaurant, if for a slightly different reason. When people are paying for their drinks the sooner they get what they ordered the sooner they'll be ready to order the next. Don't forget that one of the reasons for the frenetic loud music played in some restaurants is to make people eat and drink faster—it's called "turnover."

At a private function, there is no "turnover factor." The need for prompt service is more the need to attend to people and make them feel welcome so that they can relax into the spirit of the proceedings. Also, the sooner you take care of one task, the sooner you can attend to the next. If your bar is in the kitchen and you're also preparing appetizers or light refreshments there, you'll need to move seamlessly from one task to the next.

Of course, you may occasionally find yourself operating a cash bar. At galas, for instance, it's not unusual for a cash bar to be available even though cocktails and wines have been offered before and during dinner. If there's dancing, people may want to have more drinks than are basically provided for the ticket price, and it's not reasonable—especially if the event is a fundraiser—to lay on an unlimited supply of free alcohol.

But even in these circumstances it wouldn't be appropriate for a caterer to approach customers with empty glasses in the spirit of "Ready for another round here, folks?"—unless your client has given orders for you to sell as many drinks as you possibly can, which would be unusual to say the least.

**Head Counting**    If your client requests a head count, that is, if she wants to know how many people showed up, there's a device called a "clicker," which looks a bit like a stopwatch. Every time you press the little knob, the read-out increases. You can get it at a store specializing in hospitality merchandise, and it may enjoy a grander nomenclature than plain old "clicker," but they'll know what you mean. Make sure you don't double- (or quadruple-) count those people who bob in and out of the proceedings for one reason or another.

# Setup

If you're well set up and organized, it doesn't really matter how busy you are, all will be well. Being "well set up" means knowing where everything is and having all your supplies to hand and arranged in order of requirement. The bottle of white wine—usually the single most requested drink these days—should be at your pouring elbow, but the more obscure drinks, if any, can be safely placed further away since you won't be reaching for them very often.

## Access to Space and Supplies

The first thing to consider is access. Working out of a house or apartment kitchen can be somewhat constraining. There isn't much space to work in, and there's usually only one exit and entrance. Refrigerated space will soon be full. Dirty glasses will accumulate, and so will garbage.

First, you need to "clear the decks" by removing anything that is not required and likely to be in the way. Create as many working surfaces as you possibly can so that you have somewhere to put things.

You need to ensure that all the plumbing is operational—hot and cold water flowing and sinks not blocked. You need a supply of garbage bags, and you need to know exactly where they can be placed, or hidden, once they're full or so heavy that it becomes dangerous to put anything else in them.

You need a mop, bucket, brush, and pan handy for the instant cleanup of things dropped and broken. Apart from anything else, we all know that if we remember our umbrellas, it's much less likely to rain.

## Making Space for Work and Supplies

If, as is not uncommon, the house or apartment has a dedicated bar, or one of those kitchens with a hatch, or a bar-style counter, then things are much easier. It's important to maintain a distinction, in all forms of catering, between guest areas and functional service areas. Ideally the twain will never meet; everyone has a much better time if these boundaries are respected. A well-meaning but bumbling impatient guest straying into your space intent on self-service can slow you right down sometimes.

That's what a *bar* is all about. In law also, the word *bar* originally referred precisely to that necessary physical separation between judiciary, plaintiffs, accused, and witnesses.

If you're lucky enough to be catering in a well-appointed house with a dedicated bar, there'll be plenty of space, and the placement of your bottles and equipment will be logically indicated. Instead of wondering where the heck am I going to squeeze in a big ice bucket, you'll pour the ice right into the appropriate sink. Your reserve supply of ice, by the way, can find a happy home in the bath or shower, preferably with the curtains drawn if guests are using the bathroom. You can also empty ice into the bath and put white wine in it. Ideally white wine and beer are placed in ice at least twenty minutes before serving, and half an hour at the very least if they are being chilled in a refrigerator.

Try not to turn the house into what looks like an emergency relief post. A room with nice pictures and windows should be dominated by them and not, for instance, a pair of huge black plastic buckets. Remember, a New York hostess once used to have a maid stationed outside the bathroom ready to enter as soon as a guest left to sprinkle rose petals in the toilet. Naturally one wonders how she coped with a customer in a hurry who couldn't wait for this ceremony to be completed.

A *word of warning:* if you have a large amount of wine on hand that you've brought in from the liquor store or wine merchant on a sale or return basis, remember that labels on bottles placed in ice will come off after a while. The liquor store can't be expected to take these back. So, if your reserve wine has been brought in the spirit of "just in case" and there's a good chance it won't be used, try and chill it in a refrigerator so that the labels remain intact.

## The Makeshift Bar

A common situation you'll encounter, however, if you have to set up a bar is that you'll be working off a folding table that you've supplied, or sometimes a large dining or library table, covered with a cloth both to protect it and to disguise its stark functional appearance. It's best to set it against a wall, with enough space left between table and wall for you to comfortably move and bring in and take out supplies and garbage. At a busy event, don't forget that there'll be an accumulation of empty bottles of one kind or another, too.

You need an ice bucket close to hand, so that you can put ice into drinks as you serve them when required. This could be a large three-foot plastic bucket on the floor with a bag of ice placed in it or, more elegantly, a big silver punch bowl full of ice on the table. Such a bowl will require refilling from time to time, but it's the work of a moment.

Space permitting, it's not a bad idea to have a smaller ice source somewhere at the guest side of the table. There's always someone who needs more ice, and if they see a source, they won't bother you.

Ice    If you're setting up tables, chances are the ice will have to be brought in by supplier. Ice companies are used to emergency calls, usually from restaurants whose refrigeration has broken down, and they will usually react promptly. However, it's best to order ahead of time, especially if there's a heat wave coming in. Many supermarkets sell big bags of ice and some deliver.

But definitions of "delivery" can be quite quirky. Some people only mean curb-side delivery—getting the sofa to your top floor is your problem. Sometimes, if ice is delivered before the catering staff are on premises it may just be dumped, and not in a particularly convenient place, so the caterers have to hump it.

This can be a heavy job—don't leave it to little Suzie, put big Steve in charge. It's usually the heaviest job to be done, closely followed by bringing in liquor, beer, and soda supplies. Apart from anything else, the heavy ice bags are often strongly stapled, making opening them not the ideal task for a female server or bartender who manicured her nails for the occasion. It's normal for any heavy work to be done by the male members of a catering crew. Have no fear, there's plenty of work to keep the females busy—setting tables, cutting fruit, and so on.

Lifting and Carrying Loads    If you find yourself working with a regular crew, you might give them a two minute seminar on lifting—it's valuable knowledge. When lifting something heavy you should approach it squarely, bend the knees before you lift, and lift with your legs, not your back. Defensive lifting can save a lot of pain and wasted days in bed. Remember, too, that back incidents are often the result of repetitive bad habits, so the threat builds with each successive straining lift.

Another prevalent bad habit in catering is for people to carry enormous loads in order to save a journey. Wise old hands would rather travel twice than lift too much. Again, your initial reconaissance should include the location of elevators, and if there are none, you should allow time and energy for bringing in any heavy supplies or equipment.

Try to avoid having to set up in too much of a hurry; otherwise, everyone gets sweated up. And try to get any heavy work out of the way first. You can be discreetly arranging bottles or cutting lemons as the first guests start to arrive, but you shouldn't be humping furniture, ice, or cartons of food and drink. There's something unattractive about overworked, harried staff—the juxtaposition of those who are at work and those who are relaxing is uncomfortably reminiscent of Roman senators being serviced by their slaves. As far as possible, staff should be relaxed and smiling at all times. It looks more professional. Putting on their white jackets (if appropriate) and bow ties should be the last thing a crew does, five minutes before the most eager first guest would dare to arrive.

**Glasses, Bottles, and Condiments**   Having prepared the table and the ice supply, the next step is to set out your glasses, real glasses of various shapes or plastic and disposable. Plastic glasses, by the way, no longer have to be airline stark. Some very festive-looking ones are so attractive that (say it in a whisper) their proud owners will wash them and use them again instead of throwing them away after one use.

Then you set out your bottles, putting the most frequently used closest to hand and none, if possible, more than a gentle stretch away. You should also be aware of where you've put the backups, or replacements.

If you're going to be serving simple cocktails such as Martinis and Gin and Tonics, you'll need small containers of olives, lemon and lime wedges, and lemon peels handy. This is not a restaurant bar, so you can skip the onions, the orange slices, and the cherries unless you have been specifically requested to provide them.

# The Well-Stocked Bar—Commercial and Catered

For contrast, reference, and an overall view of the bar operation, we present two lists. The first is a comprehensive inventory of the spirits, wines, beers, sodas, equipment, and miscellaneous items a commercial bar must carry. It's worth a quick scan whenever you are catering a function because requirements sometimes vary. Occasionally you may just have a hunch, even though your client has not mentioned it, of some slightly unusual requirement—and you'll always score "bonus points" (which help bring in repeat business) by meeting strange requests readily and with a smile.

The second list contains items required by a caterer for a party given in a private home for 30–40 people. Only drinks and appetizers, or "nibbles," are to be served, and, although some of the guests may linger, the majority should leave by 8:30 P.M. This is a very typical operation for someone who's catering from home—indeed, often your bread and butter.

The inventory and equipment listed will suit your needs.

## COMMERCIAL BAR INVENTORY AND EQUIPMENT

- RYE or AMERICAN WHISKEY—several brands such as Seagrams 7, VO, Crown Royal, Canadian Club.
- BOURBON WHISKEY—several brands; Tennessee whiskey.
- SCOTCH WHISKEY—Dewars, J&B, Cutty Sark, Johnny Walker (Red and Black) Chivas Regal; Teachers, Ballantines, Black and White, Famous Grouse, Bells.
- SINGLE-MALT WHISKEY—Glennfiddich, Glenlivet.
- IRISH WHISKY—Bushmills, Black Bush, Jameson's, Canadian whiskey.
- RUM—Bacardi (light and dark, Black, Gold) Myers, Mount Gay, Captain Morgan's Spiced, Goslings, etc.
- GIN—Beefeater, Gordon's, House of Lords, Tanqueray, Boodles.
- VODKA—Smirnoff, Gordon's, Tanqueray, Stolichnaya, Wyborowa, Finlandia, Absolut, Icy.
- SHERRY—dry, sweet, Manzanilla, Amontillado, Tio Pepe, La Iña, Harvey's Bristol Cream.
- PORT—Cockburn, Taylor Fladgate, Sandeman's.
- TEQUILA—Cuervo, Cuervo Gold.
- COGNAC and BRANDY—Remy Martin, Courvoisier, Cordon Bleu, XO, apricot, blackberry, cherry, Armagnac, plum, Marc, Metaxa, various Spanish brandies.
- BITTERS—Campari, Angosturas.
- VERMOUTH and WINE COCKTAILS—Lillet, Suze, Dubonnet, Cinzano, Noilly Prat. Stock, sweet and dry.
- CORDIALS, LIQUEURS, and MISCELLANEOUS—Bailey's Irish Cream, Chartreuse, (green and yellow) Chambord, Cointreau, Creme de Cacao, (cocoa, dark and white) Creme de Cassis, Creme de Menthe (white, green), Creme de Noyau, Curaçao, Drambuie, Frangelica, fruit brandies, Galliano, Grand Marnier, Khalua, Kummel, Midori (melon), peppermint, Tia Maria, Jaegermeister; Pernod, Ricard.
- CALIFORNIA WHITE WINE—Chardonnay, Puligny Montrachet.
- CALIFORNIA RED WINE—Cabernet Sauvignon, Zinfandel, Merlot, etc.
- GERMAN WHITE WINE—Moselle, Reisling.
- FRENCH RED WINE—Beaujolais, Pommard (from Burgundy) Margaux, Mouton Cadet (Bordeaux red wine, or claret), Côte du Rhone.

(*continued*)

- FRENCH WHITE WINES—Chablis, Pouilly Fume, Pouilly-Fuissé, etc.
- ITALIAN RED—Valpolicella, Chianti, etc.
- ITALIAN WHITE—Soave Bolla, Pino Grigio, etc.
- ROSE—Tavel, Anjou, (unless it's the house practice to put a splash of red wine into a glass of white wine . . .).
- HOUSE WINES and SPIRITS—cheap versions of brand-name beverages, which are served when no brand name is specified.
- BEER—bottled, draft, and nonalcoholic (Buckler, Caliber).
- CHAMPAGNE—(domestic) Korbel, Piper Sonoma; (Imported) Moet, Mumm, Krug, Dom Perignon, Piper Heidseik Ruinart.
- SODA—colas, diet colas, lemon, ginger, tonic, seltzer, etc.
- JUICES and BOTTLED WATERS—orange, grapefruit, tomato, cranberry, lemon (Lemon-X) pineapple, lime juice (Roses), Evian, Perrier, Saratoga, etc.
- PERISHABLE SUPPLIES—milk, heavy cream, Worcestershire sauce, Tabasco, salt, pepper, cherries, olives, onions, lemons, limes, oranges, cream, coconut cream, nutmeg, sugar, castor sugar, horseradish, coffee beans, bouillon.
- MISCELLANEOUS—Glasses, mixing equipment, blender, corkscrews, bottle openers, sharp knife and cutting board for fruit, straws, beverage napkins, coasters or both, stirrers, straws, large dinner napkins, matches, bar mops, towels, toothpicks, pens, paper, ashtrays, cigarettes, business cards, mop, broom, dust pan, reference book with cocktail recipes, telephone directories, dictionaries, atlas, Guiness Book of Records, TV guide, local entertainment guide, daily paper, town map, first aid kit, local health and hygiene notices, muddler (a six inch pestle, looking like a miniature baseball bat, for crushing fruit in an Old Fashioned)—a spoon will do), watch or clock, calendar, crazy glue, feather duster, ice buckets, stands, tongs, electric brushes, gloves, standpipes, licenses displayed, pourers, stoppers for opened champagne, wine glasses, menus, cutlery, ice scoops.

## Caterer's Bar Inventory and Equipment

- WHITE WINE—Large bottles are best, 6 will probably be enough; if you bring 12 you needn't fear running out.
- RED WINE—2 large bottles should be plenty.

- VODKA—3 liter bottles should be enough. You can buy large jugs of most spirits now, which are more economical in price but they're a little ungainly and heavy for pouring before guests.
- SCOTCH—2 liter bottles will suffice.
- DRY VERMOUTH—This enables you to provide what is probably the simplest cocktail on the planet and also the one most talked about— the Dry Martini—a drop of vermouth, two ounces of gin or vodka, ice, and an olive or lemon peel is the on-the-rocks recipe. Guests who want it "straight up", i.e., chilled but without ice, can be accommodated with a little manual dexterity as you pour from one glass to another. You don't need to bring a mixing glass, shaker, bar spoon, or strainer.
- DIET COLA, SELTZER—3 large bottles of each.
- GINGER ALE—1 large bottle.
- BOTTLED WATER—6 still, 6 fizzy, or all 12 fizzy.
- ORANGE JUICE—a quart carton.
- BEER—as requested.

This small list will make available the following popular drinks:

White wine

White wine spritzer

Red wine

Vodka on the rocks

Vodka and soda (Vodka Ricky)

Vodka and ginger ale (Moscow Mule)

Vodka and orange juice (Screwdriver)

Vermouth on the rocks

Scotch on the rocks

Scotch and water or soda

Beer

Soda, water

This is a better than adequate selection of drinks for a private party, and guests whose personal tipple isn't included can surely find an acceptable compromise in it. Remember, the caterer's role is somewhat different from that of the restaurateur. The guests are simply not in a position to say, "What do you mean you don't have any Old Atlanta Bourbon? What kind of a joint is this?"

**Punch**   The caterer's simple setup can be augmented by a fruit punch in a big glass (or silver) bowl, for which you need a big ladle. There are a thousand recipes—fruit punch, rum punch, wine punch. You can make it up as you go. A basic recipe might be:

> 1 bottle white wine
>
> 1 fifth vodka (or rum)
>
> 2 pints orange juice
>
> Apples, oranges, melon, mint, etc.—various fruits cut up
>
> Ice (not too much or the mix will soon become watery)

Some hosts will have their own favorite recipe. Don't let mischievous people "spike it" with more hard alcohol, which will go undetected because of the general fruity sweetness of the mix, also found in so many of those dangerous sweet cocktails so beloved by the younger, inexperienced drinker.

# Special Requirements

Sometimes there'll be a special requirement. As mentioned, some clients will insist on serving champagne only. If this is the case, be prepared to do some mopping—some spillage is inevitable if you get busy.

If it's a young crowd, you'd better lay in some beer—one kind only will do. Put it in big plastic containers with ice, or fill the refrigerator, or both.

## Bloody Marys

For a weekend brunch or barbecue, the client may suggest that guests be offered a Bloody Mary. The recipe for this simple cocktail is:

> 1 ounce vodka
>
> 1 teaspoon lemon juice
>
> salt
>
> pepper
>
> Worcestershire sauce
>
> Tabasco
>
> Tomato juice

Mix all ingredients. Shake the mixture and serve with ice in a tall glass, with a squeezed wedge of lime or lemon. You may add horseradish sauce, a stick of celery, or celery salt. Sometimes people request Danish Aquavit—a kind of schnapps—gin, or even rum in the drink.

In some commercial bars, a huge fetish is made of this cocktail by making each one individually. It's a boring aspect of the Sunday brunch shift. Why some owners insist on custom-built drinks is one of the industry's greater mysteries, because a busy bartender may get careless and sloppy if he's turning out a large number of Bloody Marys. Plaintive cries of "Did you put any vodka in this?" and "Too much Tabasco" are common.

However, there is a mix available. It comes in big cans, the same size as plain tomato juice, and is of excellent quality. Tastings show again and again that drinkers prefer the cocktail prepared with the ready-made mix to the individually prepared version. The reason for this is obvious. The prepared mix is made at leisure, to correct proportions, and is tasted by a panel who decide whether it's okay or not. Consistency of quality is established. In any case, if a drinker wants a touch more Tabasco, or whatever, it's easily fixed.

If you haven't managed to get hold of any of this mix, you can make up your own ahead of time, give it a good shake and a stir, and put it in a big bottle with a lid (fruit juice bottles are ideal for the purpose) so that you can give it an extra shake when you serve it. You pour a shot of vodka and some ice in a glass, add the mix, and *voila*, another satisfied guest.

## Requests

It's very common nowadays for party hosts to offer nothing more than sodas, wine, and beer. There'll usually be a few guests who really prefer a vodka or a scotch, and since they're so easy to accommodate, it seems a shame to disappoint them. A possible reaction to this is "So why not also lay in bourbon, rum, brandy, and everything else? Where do you draw the line?"

The answer is at vodka and scotch. People who are fixated on some other liquor long ago learned that it sometimes isn't available, and if it's so important to them they may carry a hip flask. If a guest's tastes are known to the host, of course, they'll usually be accommodated. It can sometimes cause a frown or two when a guest at a "wine only" party, who's dying for a scotch, suddenly sees the host breaking out the scotch for that Very Special Person.

The only other supplies you need to check for at a caterer's bar are wedges of lemon and lime, lemon peels, and possibly olives; napkins, corkscrews, ice supply, and glasses. This is assuming that the appetizer or buffet side of the party has been taken care of in the kitchen or at a separate table.

# Operation

If you or your assistant bartender have worked in a commercial bar, then working a catered function will be a piece of cake. If you haven't got this experience, it's still easy enough once you're organized. This is a sort of instant crash course in bartending.

When you're working at a bar set up on a table, you have everything that a restaurant bar has except running water and sinks. Therefore, you must ensure access for taking out accumulated dirty glasses, garbage, and empty bottles.

If it's a bigger function and you have a crew of several assistants, you should instruct one, or all, to check the bar regularly to see if the bartender (who at some stages will be quite busy) needs anything. More chilled white wine or beer? A full garbage bag to be removed? More ice required? And so on.

## Doing What Needs to Be Done—Everybody's Responsibility

Trained and experienced personnel know perfectly well that they need to help each other out, to fill in while one person goes backstage for a cup of coffee or to the bathroom, or even—heaven forfend—for a smoke. They do things automatically and easily. But you may be working with rookies, and if so you must imbue them with the need to keep a general eye on the proceedings as well as attend to their own allotted tasks.

As a caterer, you simply cannot afford to allow the attitude of "It's not my job," which is the curse of the restaurant, hotel, and many other industries. If anyone sees something that needs to be done—be it a table strewn with dirty glasses and dishes that needs to be cleaned up, a crumpled napkin, a full ashtray, a guest with a problem, or a floundering bartender—they must learn to leap to action stations.

## Self-Service

The principle of self-service is firmly established in American life and indeed helps to make entertaining simple. Many a host will ceremoniously pour a guest a first drink and then say "Please help yourself." This frees the host from watching all his guests' glasses and plates to assess their current requirements. It also frees the guest from the sometimes unwelcome encouragement to drink more than he or she wants. These days "one for the road" is the drink to avoid.

Because guests are not usually shy about helping themselves, you can, with your client's approval, set up self-service subsidiary bars at points around the room. These bars need only consist of an opened bottle of white wine in an ice bucket, a few glasses, and some paper napkins or bevnaps. Some hosts will extend this to a bottle of vodka, some lemon peels, and a bottle or two of soda. Even parties small in the number of guests can become quite crowded in an apartment, and a source of refreshment at the far end of the room will save some guests the trouble of having to struggle through the crowd to get to the bar. This is entirely an option—some hosts will resist it for fear that it will discourage people from circulating, rather in the way some hosts remove all the chairs so that guests won't be tempted to sit down and stagnate. If all of this smacks more of "stage management" than catering—so be it. It's the reality.

**Opening Wine Bottles**    You need to acquire the ability to open wine bottles quickly, and it doesn't take long. Watch an expert in a restaurant and you'll see how it's done. The main thing is to approach the task with total confidence and make sure the blade of the corkscrew goes in deep enough to get a good grip on the cork. Sometimes corks simply jam or break. No need to panic. Extract the corkscrew, and take another bottle. Later when you get a breather, go back to the problem bottle and see if you can extract the cork cleanly. If you can't, push the cork into the bottle. This will introduce little bits of cork into the wine. Taste the wine, and be prepared to spit it out if its spoiled as a result of faulty corking. If the wine tastes okay, but can't be served directly because of the bits of cork floating in it, filter it into another jug or any kind of container—coffee filters are ideal—and then you can use it. If you're too fastidious to drink it, it may still find a home in the cooking of Boeuf Bourgignon, or Coq au Vin.

## Organization

Knowing where everything is will really help you save time and work more efficiently. A professional bartender, entering a new bar, will put his hand on every single bottle there is so that he builds an instant memory. How often one rents a car and speeds away, only to find oneself, a few hours later, wondering how to make the headlights dim—or even come on at all.

The caterer's inventory of equipment is so small it really isn't a problem. But especially as you expand you must get into the habit of formally briefing your crew, and one of the things they need to know is where everything is, from the ice and wine back-ups to the bathrooms.

A golden rule for the bartender is to return everything to its proper place, like an airplane mechanic or a doctor. After a while you can almost reach for things without looking, but you should always look, anyway.

**Keeping Things Moving**    Unlike a commercial bar, the caterer's bar doesn't have any "show-stoppers" that can bring operations to a crawl. No orders for "Three Pina Coladas, Two Margaritas, one up, one down, no salt on the down, and Two Sex-on-the-Beach, easy on the Peach . . ." This is the sort of order that sounds throughout many a bar at about ten past five on a Friday night.

However, several guests may arrive together, and at functions such as weddings, for example, it may literally be a case of "the bus stops," as fifty hungry and thirsty guests debouch into the area. That's when you smile (as opposed to gritting your teeth) and just do it.

# Keeping Guest and Client Happy

Again, one of the factors that make a caterer's life so pleasant is that a majority of guests are in a benign, indulgent, and uncritical mood, surrounded by friends, family, or colleagues, and most unlikely to rock the boat in any way at all. Part of the reason for this attitude may be that, whatever the goods and services they are delivered, they usually won't be getting a bill for it—a thought that may inspire the spirit of tolerance and forgiveness in the meanest breast.

But when it's a charity do, a fundraiser, or some function for which the guests have actually paid, this buffer is not so protective. People may not voice their instant complaints, but they may *think* "The tickets were $100 each . . . I mean, I believe in the Society but . . . standing on line for flabby white wine, that awful fried chicken . . ." Some clients, especially commercial ones, may impose a budget so miserably tight that a caterer is hard put to deliver a good-quality function. The caterer can bring some pressure to bear, but only so much. If for instance, a client proposes a sit-down dinner on a meager budget, you might talk her into a simple buffet and bar arrangement.

Ideally a caterer will pretend that every one of the guests is actually a customer and thus deserving of the best. Remember also, when you cater a function you should approach it with a view to repeat business. Every guest at a function is a potential client. If you're a harassed club secretary or PR executive, or a climbing socialite or busy executive, imagine the bliss of being able to ring someone up and say "Tuesday the fourteenth—about fifty people for drinks and nibbles at my premises—can you handle it?" and simply tick off a problem on your crowded agenda. Caterers who deliver the goods make a good living, and some make fortunes.

## What the Server Can and Cannot Handle

A word to those who may not have had time or opportunity to acquire restaurant experience. It's perfectly okay to handle ice. Yes, you should have an ice scoop, because that's the quickest and neatest way of getting a few ice cubes into a glass, but don't be afraid to handle it if necessary. The one thing you should never do (but it's commonly done) is to put a glass into a pile of ice cubes and scoop them up. With tedious regularity, a glass will break and all the ice will have to be thrown out in order to make sure that the guests aren't chomping on broken glass—a lawyer's dream.

Another thing to be avoided at all costs is putting fingers inside glasses, no matter how clean your hands or how urgent the order. It just isn't done. Nor, ideally, will you put your fingers in glasses that have been used and that you are merely clearing away. It looks sloppy and unprofessional.

Of course, the bartender's hands are supposed to be scrupulously clean, and indeed they usually are. They're very much on show, plopping olives, squeezing limes and lemons, and so on. Some professionals make an absolute fetish of their hands—French cuffs, dazzling cufflinks, and professionally manicured nails.

## Chapter Eleven

# Kinds of Parties

## Barbecues

Because barbecues are almost always determinedly informal affairs where leather shoes and shirts with long sleeves—no matter how far rolled up—may be considered the height of pretension, caterers don't get much of a look-in. The ritual is now so deeply a part of American social and business entertaining that it has a sort of life of its own. The supermarket shelves are awash with barbecue-dedicated products. Each family seems to have its own views on the subject and favorite recipes, too. Besides, what on earth will people talk about if they can't fuss about the state of the charcoal, the way to get best results, or the imminent arrival of the spareribs?

But many an upwardly mobile, crafty social climber will have sniffed out the fact that a demonstration of unpretentiousness (apparently there really is such a word) may win hearts and minds more easily and efficiently than all the black tie dinners in the world. Some business moguls these days, when "nerd power" (at least in the computer business) has reached its apotheosis, may feel that they're risking their "I'm just a regular guy" image by attending such a function.

So the barbecue in all its potential delight—and disaster—is here to stay. Bleak overtones of campfires and opening up the West shouldn't be exaggerated. Many barbecue guests approach the function with some insecurity of spirit, wondering whether perhaps they may be so ill-fed that they will have to visit a restaurant on the way home or, worse, cook for themselves when they return.

## The up and down Side of Barbecues

A perfect barbecue might be one at which people are not only entertained, introduced to fascinating new people, and reassured as to their unpretentiousness, but also satisfactorily "fed and watered." It's easily achieved.

The potential delight can be found when the weather is perfect (though there should always be a sudden bad weather backup plan to move indoors), the food is zestily cooked with hearty overtones of charcoal flavors, and is served promptly in a way that enables the guests to actually relax and enjoy it. There should always be enough tables or other surfaces to enable guests to put things down, even if they don't actually sit down, so that they're not totally preoccupied with juggling cardboard plates, drinks, napkins, cigarettes, and business cards.

The horrors and pitfalls are well enough known. Many of us have attended disastrous barbecues where we froze, and barely got fed at all. Such food as is served on these occasions is often dangerously undercooked and frankly revolting (See Chapter 15.) Sometimes unlucky guests can't wait to get home for a bite to eat and a drink. We are reminded of that old dirge "If only the chicken had been as warm as the wine, and the wine as cold as the chicken . . ."

The barbecue's attractions are total informality of dress and manner, food that has an aura of all-American authenticity, and, above all, that wonderful word again, "unpretentiousness." The barbecue host isn't strutting his stuff. He isn't required to prove anything. He isn't baring his soul or showing the world what he can do. He's even allowed to get things a little bit wrong. The barbecue is one of the few remaining areas in life where gentle amusement can be derived from failure. His guests share with him the element of fate and chance—at least as regards the weather—and are warmly (one hopes) and spiritually (perhaps) unified in the grand endeavor.

It's totally possible that there are at least a few people on the planet whose hearts warm more to the prospect of a special occasion such as a formal black-tie dinner, provoking an effort to look their best and carrying with it the intimation that something special in the way of food and wine may be on offer. However, this is an entirely personal matter.

## The Caterer's Job

If a caterer is hired to handle a barbecue he can be sure there's more to the scene than meets the eye. The client clearly wants to be free of the necessity of discussing the exact nature of the fuel employed or the recipe of the marinade for the various meats.

**Safety**   The first and major concern of the caterer at a barbecue is the danger of naked flame. Often this is the client's concern, too. He wants someone to be stone cold sober and *in charge*, so that the possibility of someone being burned is entirely removed from his responsibility. This way he can relax and schmooze, network, and socialize to his heart's content.

Burns are a major hazard at barbecues. Oven gloves are a godsend in preventing minor accidents. Remember, when in doubt assume that anything you're about to handle (except perhaps wine bottles and paper plates) is very hot. And keep the mass of guests well away from the fire. Total physical separation is the best way. Ideally, the food should go from the fire to a table, beyond which the guests wait, sitting or standing, and are served. Just in case, you'd do well to know beforehand how to handle minor burns.

**Good Food**    The second concern of the barbecue caterer is to produce reasonably edible food for the guests. No chicken wings blackened on the outside but salmonella-red on the inside, or any other of that dangerous amateur nonsense.

Say it in a whisper . . . some hostesses are so concerned that the food may prove inadequate that they covertly cook items in the kitchen and bring it out for a little ritualistic baptism by charcoal fire, in order to convey barbecue authenticity. Given the chemical ingredients of the average bottled barbecue sauce this is a bit rich, but these are the realities.

**Equipment**    A barbecue client will almost always have the necessary equipment installed in the yard, or on the terrace if we're talking city penthouse apartment. But if this equipment is not in place (for instance, if you're running a barbecue in a designated public park area), it can be hired.

Hired barbecues are usually about 3 feet long by 2 feet deep, so you may need more than one. The charcoal needs to be lit well in advance of the time you want to serve the food. Methylated spirits is the approved fuel because it's the safest and imparts no trace of taste or smell. It's all right to poke, rake, and apply a little bellows power to the charcoal, but not when cooking is in progress.

Camp stoves and lamps can also be hired.

**Service**    There's no need to panic about super efficiency of food service. A byproduct of the informality of these occasions is the goodwill and patience of the guests. But one shouldn't assume this—it is a cushion for absorbing small hitches in the service.

Many restaurants lean heavily on the goodwill and pleasant disposition of their customers. One can seethe inwardly after some atrocious display of bad service or bad manners, and one's irritation is compounded by the fact that good manners, and reluctance to inflict unpleasant confrontational scenes on one's guests, prevent one from making thoroughly justified complaints.

Caterers simply won't get away with this kind of thing, because what they do is on a more personal level and reflects directly on the client who, though presumably tolerant of human frailty, will on the whole prefer things to go with a pleasant swing.

**The Neighbors**   An experienced caterer will always consider his client's neighbors—just in case his client doesn't. Angry reaction from smoked out or disturbed neighbors can put a cloud on an otherwise successful party.

The single best course is to invite the neighbors to any kind of social function that is likely to generate fumes or noise, but clearly this won't always be a solution. The vicissitudes of real estate and the juxtaposition of people are not always happy arrangements.

In most cities, noise is supposed to stop by 11:00 P.M., and any offensive generation of smoke or fumes can invite instant intervention by police or fire department. So it's always as well to have an eye to the neighbors.

## Suitable Barbecue Foods

Suitable foods for barbecues include chops, steaks, sausages, and burgers. Fish steaks, or even whole fish, work very well if they're wrapped in tin-foil (with a little oil added) and placed right in the smouldering embers. Most barbecue hosts will find this a bit too much of a production, but if there aren't many guests and its Friday—it's a possibility.

Lamb works very well, as long as someone is appointed to baste and turn it—perhaps dipping sprigs of rosemary in the oil and painting it onto the meat. Kebabs can be prepared in advance and marinated if desired. Don't pour that marinade away—use it to make gravy or barbecue sauce. Baked potatoes can be cooked in advance and stored in a box. Salad, the ever-popular and satisfying coleslaw, bread rolls, cheese, and fruit are further options.

Other possibilities are sweet potatoes, corn on the cob, and mushrooms. Fruit will do fine for dessert.

Remember, you can get away with quite a minimalist menu at barbecues. Better, surely, to offer a limited choice of items, all of which are nicely cooked, than a selection that will keep the staff so busy that there is dilution in quality. Why invent work?

**Drinks**   It's a mistake to serve one's best wines at barbecues, just as it is when serving curry or chili. So robust and piquant are the flavors of barbecue foods that the subtlety of your best Pommard might be wasted. Better to stick with beer, robust red wine, and cider.

Coffee and tea may be served, though often they're not. Soup in mugs is a further possibility, especially if there's a nip in the air. Fun-but-fussy items might be a wine fruit cup, punch, or even hot spiced ale.

Here's a sample menu from a very successful barbecue.

Barbecued lamb and mushroom kebabs (you could add onion chunks)
Barbecued chicken legs

Corn on the cob

Coleslaw

Baked potatoes

Barbecue sauce

Candied baked (barbecued) apples

Cider, beer, Chianti (red and white)

The barbecue ambiance doesn't really suggest anything more adventurous than the tried and true. Better a successful humble hamburger than an unfamiliar dish that doesn't quite hit the spot with fresh-air–sharpened appetites anyway.

You'll need plenty of paper napkins, and the paper plates should be of good, robust quality. The cooks will need heavy-duty aprons, heat-proof oven gloves, just in case, and a selection of long-handled slicers and forks.

## Beast Roasts

If your catering ambitions border on the heroic, you might consider making the spit-roasting of whole beasts a specialty; but be warned this is a major production. Of course, after you've done it a couple of dozen times, it may seem a breeze.

The critical area is the construction of the grill. The fire box must be off the floor to allow for an ash pit. So that the heat is reflected forward onto the item being cooked, there must be a wall at the back of the fire. Since this operation will be taking place in the open air, the current wind direction should be borne in mind during setup and assembly. Wind directions, remember, can change at very short notice, especially at ground level.

Despite the spectacular nature of this kind of cooking, the culinary results are often very disappointing. Venison, for instance, when served to people who haven't had it before, often produces a number of dubious frowns and wrinkled noses. Once less than hot, the meat tends to be a bit greasy, and no matter how cooked, its consistency against the teeth somehow doesn't feel right. "Al dente" (i.e. slightly resistant to the teeth) string beans is one thing, but it doesn't work for meat. Suckling pig, often done on a small spit over a regular barbecue fire, is a rather mouth-watering prospect that often disappoints. There's lots of fat but not so much succulent meat. No doubt in former times this prospect was pleasing—some primitive, and not so primitive, people ate and drank solid animal fat because it helped keep out the cold. But few of us have that kind of taste or appetite these days.

The carcass—be it heifer, horse, camel, ox, pig, deer, lamb, or boar—is impaled on an iron pipe and wired so that it doesn't slither about. A wheel is fixed to the end of the pipe so that the carcass can be turned in the flames. The meat must be basted, and long-handled ladles should be provided.

You'll need a well-aged carcass that isn't too big. About half the gross weight of it will be lost in the cooking as water and fat are dispersed. Since a 200-pound ox takes more than 12 hours to cook, we are clearly into a highly specialized area of catering that requires very careful consideration.

Charities like to do this sort of thing sometimes, and such a monumental service will yield an excellent fee. If you see an event like this advertised, it might be interesting to attend it and talk to the professional roaster in charge. There's no reason why you shouldn't include his talents in your list of available services.

# Wine Tastings

Wine merchants are the most likely people to host such events, and the guests are likely to be potential customers or sometimes even wine students—ordinary people who'd like to know about wine. Occasionally you may find an amateur wine lover holding such an event for friends.

These affairs are often held in wine cellars or stores, but other venues might be selected, and you might be asked to provide one.

## Supplies and Equipment

Often a lecture is given, so there'll be a need for chairs set out in theater or classroom fashion, as well as a lectern or the traditional green-baized table, with a glass and a carafe of water (often a popular brand-name bottled water these days). There may also be a requirement for visual aid equipment or display boards, or a blackboard and easel.

If wines are to be tasted while the lecturer is talking, then tables will be required for glasses, notes, and literature. Although tasters are clearly responsible for their own pens and paper, it won't be a bad idea to have some in reserve.

When there is no formal lecture, or if the actual tasting takes place afterwards, the room must be set up under rather unusually strict conditions. There must be "No Smoking" signs displayed, and there should be ashtrays at the entrance to the room so that in the (nowadays unlikely) event of someone arriving with a lighted cigarette they can dispose of it instantly. Tobacco smoke distorts the delicate tasting process.

Ideally, there will be a separate table for each wine tasted. Sometimes this might be as many as a dozen, but that is about the absolute maximum for most tasters to consider, as the senses are soon exhausted and differentiation becomes impossible. A plain white cloth should cover the table.

Daylight or ordinary white light bulbs are fine; candlelight isn't very practical. Contrary to popular supposition, most tasters are more likely to hold a wine up to a piece of white paper to determine its color than to a candle flame. Office type pale blue fluorescent lighting isn't acceptable as it distorts the color of the reds.

Yes, spittoons are required. This is improvised easily enough by filling a box or a bucket about three quarters full of sawdust. Tasters will swirl wine around the glass—an ordinary five ounce wine glass with a stem is fine—then swirl it around in their mouths, make disgusting glug-glug and gargling noises, hold the wine to the light or a piece of paper, and spit it out. They then make their notes. Squeamish would-be caterers may well prefer to pass on the wine-tasting front.

Sometimes tasters will stick to the same glass, but often they'll require a fresh one, so a decent reserve should be established.

## Food and Staff

The only food you need to supply is cubes of cheddar cheese and plain biscuits, but sometimes a host will want a bigger selection of cheeses (though none should be strong).

Remember, the white wines need to be chilled and the reds must be at room temperature. For this reason, the wine should be delivered well ahead of time. Red wine coming off a truck in the middle of January may be chilled, while white wine arriving in July may be unacceptably warm.

So limited are the requirements for a wine tasting that one caterer can handle the whole thing without assistance. Even a more elaborate event would rarely require more than two; however, the decision of how many staff to assign is entirely subjective and can only be decided when the client has stated his requirements.

Wine tastings are easy to lay on and interesting to a caterer who wants to learn about wine. A frequent source of amusement is the "blind tasting" where people are asked to taste and grade wines whose labels are hidden by a napkin tied around the bottle.

Remember, anyone attending a wine tasting is likely to be the kind of gregarious person who, from time to time, will wish to entertain. There's no reason why you shouldn't be his or her caterer on those occasions, so it's important to have your business cards ready to hand out.

# Dinner Dances

A certain formality attends these functions, which are often annual celebrations by clubs or companies, but this doesn't create any extra difficulties. On the contrary, formality makes things much more simple. In these "anything goes" times, some people are intimidated by the faintest level of formality, to the extent of becoming tight-lipped, (or getting a fit of the giggles) if anyone even extends a hand to shake. If you get a chance to attend, or even observe, a formal dinner at a major hotel or club, you should do so.

Service officers reunion dinners are an interesting subspecies of these events. The guests are so well trained in the routine that everything goes like clockwork, and the staff find them very easy to work.

At a huge dinner held in a Hilton Hotel, one budding caterer checking out the form was amazed to see how relaxed the staff were. Seeing that he'd cleared his plate, one of the waiters even asked him politely if he'd like a second helping. Contrast this with the cold-eyed, unsmiling, sweating staff of the average in-restaurant on a busy Saturday night.

At a dinner dance the band will usually play light music during the meal. If this is the case, the caterer should arrange with the client when the musician and other staff should eat—this could be during speeches, cabaret, or interval.

The simplest arrangement is usually to allow the band (and the rest of your staff) the same dinner as the guests, usually before the guests arrive. It is hardly morale boosting for employees at a function to have to settle for chicken wings and rice when the guests are having smoked salmon and filet mignon. (In many so-called upscale restaurants the waiters and staff never taste anything on the menu, though they're still supposed to be able to inform the customers as to what the various dishes consist of. One magazine used to run a weekly feature in which they printed the menu served to the staff at famous restaurants—hamburgers, hamburgers, and hamburgers was roughly the story (and none too fresh at that).

This general rule may have to be changed at a really big do, with perhaps several bands playing all night. The host/client may object to so many sampling his best Beluga caviar, lobster, and champagne. In this case a separate, but decent, meal should be provided, and a source of coffee and refreshment laid on.

## Setting up for Dancing and Handling Intervals

Sometimes it will be necessary to politely ask the guests to leave the dining room while it is quickly revamped for dancing. Often, the very guests who were most reluctant to take their seats at the beginning of dinner will be the very ones loathe to leave them at the end, but that's human nature. A firm but tactful toastmaster will usually get them moving cheerfully.

At a club event with a cash bar, stages and intervals may deliberately be built into the proceedings in order to provide propitious moments and opportunities for buying drinks. This is no problem as long as you're well set up.

Next time you're at the theater or a concert in the city, notice how well (usually) the bartenders cope with the instant crush that occurs during the main interval. The secret is to be well set up, to supply only a modest range of the most popular beverages, and to just dive in. You go from customer to customer at a steady pace. Rude though it would be in ordinary company, there is sometimes even a case for designating the next customer by pointing at him, like the President at a press conference.

The precise arrangement of the room for dancing should be planned in advance, and the moving staff briefed. This is particularly important when there's a wish to keep certain parties together, and where you're displaying numbers to differentiate the tables. Once the dancing gets going, people usually start mingling, table-hopping, and going to the bar, so there's rarely a problem in this area despite the tenacious definition of territory insisted upon by some at the beginning of the proceedings—sometimes, in certain circles, marked by chairs ungraciously tipped up against the table.

Many people nowadays, conscious of the dangers of drinking and driving, like to offer tea, coffee, or even soup in the later stages of a dance. At parties in France the host will often, at a certain point, politely ask her guests if they would like a drink or a liqueur and, having served these drinks, remove all alcohol from the scene, replacing it with delicious fizzy fruit drinks and coffee. This serves also as a polite intimation that the party's over.

# Wine and Cheese Parties

These events are becoming more and more popular (some jaded types think a bit too popular, perhaps) and for very good reasons. They are festive and an excellent informal way of entertaining a relatively large number of people inexpensively. From the caterer's point of view, it's an easy solo operation, depending on the number of guests envisaged, of course. Even if the number of guests is large, only a small staff will be needed. Once the party is set up, it only needs a supervisory eye on the proceedings. It's more or less self-service all around, except that things need to be tidied, bread cut, dirty plates whisked away, and wine bottles opened.

## Food

A good selection of cheeses is essential. Everyone loves cheese—it has a Mr. Clean image in the dietary one: protein, calcium, and all that good stuff. It's also "sticks to your ribs" fare and complements the tastes of various wines admirably.

There is much visual appeal in cheese, and it's best if the cheeses displayed are left whole as opposed to being completely cut into wedges. One wedge can be cut and laid on top of the 9- or 10-pound round, so that people will get the message that it's available for consumption, not merely for decoration. Some of us are reluctant to, as it were, deflower food that is so plainly and immaculately *intacta*.

At the end of most of these parties, a lot of cheese is left over. The bigger the remaining portions, the better their use for leftovers. Half a Brie can go into the refrigerator and be used up as and when required. It might also be taken home by favored guests, of course.

The variety of cheese offered can include hard, soft, mild, strong, cream, blue, and smoked. One shouldn't go to the extremes of cheesemanship by offering port-soaked rotting Stilton or expensive items such as *crottin de chavignol*—a French goat cheese that is the most expensive in the world and yet so esoteric in its appeal that not everyone likes it. In general, exquisite foods should only be offered where they're likely to find an appreciative audience. Don't waste money.

**Accompaniments and Utensils**    Excellent accompaniments to cheese are tomatoes, radishes, celery, spring onions, thinly sliced onion rings, and fresh fruit. These items should be set out separately, not mixed in a salad.

A good selection of bread and biscuits should be offered. We are now into the world of water biscuits, cream crackers, and digestive biscuits. Crisp-breads, black bread, pumpernickel, and wholemeal bread are also appropriate.

The correct cutting instruments—bread and cheese knives—should be available, as well as small plates and napkins.

The initial setup should look attractive and appetizing. After a while it will look a little dilapidated or at least frayed at the edges. As the party progresses, the caterer should tidy up discreetly.

Remember to allow surfaces here and there for setting down plates and glasses as guests cut pieces of cheese or replenish their glasses. There is sometimes a tendency to overcrowd tables and rooms so that people are trapped with both hands occupied and no place to put anything.

## Wines

Super-expensive vintage wines will be wasted on these occasions, though, if the client insists, the caterer will naturally have to go along with the required standards. The average consumption rate is one 5-ounce glass of wine every fifteen minutes, up to a maximum (an absolute maximum) of six glasses per person. A bottle of wine once opened is committed to eternity, but unopened bottles, provided they haven't been soaked and lost their labels, may be eligible for return to the wine merchant.

Fruit juices and nonalcoholic thirst quenching drinks should be readily available, and although overindulgence is rare at these innocent affairs, coffee should be made available toward the end of the event.

# A Few Ideas for Theme Parties

## Burns Night

Sixty million Americans and Canadians are of Scottish or Irish (or Scots-Irish) ancestry. They are generally found at the more affluent end of society and tend to be gregarious, enjoying a drink and a party. Three clan chiefs are Americans, and they naturally relish the role. Many American Campbells are on the clan computer and receive regular greetings from their clan chief, the Duke of Argyll.

Why not approach potential clients and suggest a Burns Night party? It isn't a solemn concept. On the contrary, it's just an excuse for a gettogether with a few traditional overtones. People usually get dressed up for it as part of the fun.

Robert Burns, Scotland's most famous poet, was born on the 25th of January 1759, and this anniversary is much celebrated in Scotland. The story is that he needed to raise nine guineas to buy a ticket to Jamaica to get away from personal problems, and so he printed a book of his poems called "Poems, Chiefly in the Scottish Dialect," which he intended to sell to friends. The book was so successful that he decided to stay in Scotland and earn his living as a poet.

**Food and Drink**   The sit-down dinner must include a course consisting of haggis with mashed turnips or swedes and potatoes, served with a tot of whiskey. Haggis is liver and onions cooked in a sheep's stomach: Sounds disgusting, tastes delicious. Other Scottish foods can be served, too, and the haggis course doesn't necessarily have to be the main one. You could do roast beef or grouse—a bird sometimes available in America that can usually be provided if sufficient notice is given to an upscale butcher or gourmet store. Remember, if you say a dish is Scottish, then it's Scottish. Scotch whiskey and wine are the normal drinks served.

Although it's customary to write the menu in Scots dialect, not every Scots-American will be amused by "whigmaleeries" for "petits fours" or "an' a plither o' ither odds and ends" for "garnished," so don't be too strident in the Scottishness.

**The Rituals**   The Selkirk Grace (some call it the Kircudbright Grace) written by Burns is recited by the Chairman of the dinner:

> "Some hae meat and canna eat, and some would eat that want it, but we ha' meat and we can eat, sae may the Lord be thankit."

A little ceremony attaches to the serving of the haggis, main course or not. It is carried in accompanied by a piper in full Highland dress, if available, playing some traditional tune such as "Scotland the Brave." The chairman who is usually the host or a specially honored guest, then toasts the chef and piper, and all three drink.

In Scotland, the Loyal Toast would then be drunk to the Queen, but this is clearly inappropriate in the United States. Some have been known to toast the German Duke, who would be the King of Scotland had the Stuart dynasty not come to such an untimely end. Others make the gesture of passing their hands over a glass of water, meaning "Here's a toast to the king over the water—Bonnie Prince Charlie." Then a toast is drunk to "The Immortal Memory"—of Robbie Burns, of course.

The local Caledonian Society may well have someone who can do the Scottish dialect (Edinburgh version) and can invariably be prevailed upon to read some poetry such as the one dedicated "To a Louse":

> O wad some Power the giftie gie us
> To see oursels as others see us!
> It would frae monie a blunder free us
> An' foolish notion:
> What airs in dress an'gait wad lea'e us
> An' ev'n devotion!

Such performances are usually done in impeccable dialect and with great relish, to the immense enjoyment of everyone who loves language. However, some younger people may not enjoy this kind of thing and will develop set, grim faces, which mask a brain seething with the fear that they may have forgotten to set the VCR for their favorite show. Nevertheless, these dinners are almost invariably different and fun.

## Other Ideas

The scope for theme events is limitless. You can do fancy dress parties, Halloween parties, Texas parties, Wild West parties, and so on. Almost every country has some kind of a national day that offers an excuse for celebration, from Bastille Day (July 14, France) to St. Patrick's Day.

Many potential clients who would not otherwise give parties can be persuaded to do so if an amusing theme is provided for them. An amazing number of people are just too shy to entertain, and having a theme offers a focus for conversation, a commodity in desperately short supply these days.

# Chapter Twelve

# Weddings

C URRENT morals have somewhat diluted the drama of the wedding day. Many priests actually recommend that young couples who come to them to discuss marriage should live together for a while before tying the knot. The wedding night of lubricious folklore may well be a thing of the past in a society where it's not unusual for a couples' children to accompany them on the honeymoon. Sadly, it's not unusual to hear executives bragging about how briefly their wedding ceremony interrupted the business day.

Nonetheless, so important is this category of function that it deserves a chapter to itself. Despite the divorce rate, the formal wedding ceremony followed by a reception where food and drink are served is alive and well. The number of people who will marry at least once in their lives remains at around 90 percent, although current trends suggest that this figure will reduce somewhat over time. Even so, although the number of single people who will never marry is increasing, and many "marriages" are sacrosanct only in common law, the multiple marriage syndrome ensures that there will always be a steady demand for the ritual and its attendant celebrations.

Some may envy the caterer who took care of the festivities at each of a client's five weddings—one proudly advertised as having eleven children (by the spouses from their sundry unions) in attendance. It is no part of a caterer's duty to comment on such things. Her job is simply to make sure everyone at a gathering gets fed, watered, generally looked after, and sent home with the warm feeling of having had a good time.

# The Secrets of Successful Wedding Catering

The secrets of success in catering weddings are organization and practice. Once you establish the routine of a set-piece function, you can repeat it effortlessly again and again. Watch the professionals, such as the banqueting staffs at the major hotels, whenever you get the opportunity to do so. You'll notice that they don't sweat and that their stress level is clearly minimal.

Notice the procedures on a good airline. Everything's rehearsed, everything's been done before. There's nothing you could do to surprise them. Even if you go berserk, the flight attendants have drills for that and available handcuffs. If you do anything as old hat as having a heart attack or giving birth, don't be offended if they have to stifle their yawns while efficiently going about their duties. This is the kind of preparedness that makes for a successful wedding. The caterer must keep his or her head while those all around them are losing theirs.

## Wedding Settings

The law in the United States, and in many other countries (but by no means all) allows the marriage service itself to be conducted just about anywhere. Thus, one sees people marrying underwater, in trees, at home, on golf courses, on the beach, on boats, in church, registry offices, and even—or does exuberant imagination delude?—skydiving through the air. Captains of ships, and possibly of aircraft (though this has not yet been tested in law) have the authority to conduct weddings.

This freedom of venue has led to catering establishments that specialize in marriages to the exclusion of all other functions. Some are very elaborate. The room is set up like academy awards night, the bride enters, is spotlighted so that guests may admire her dress and general attributes, and walks down a red-carpeted catwalk to the ceremonial venue, which may or may not be an altar. In the wings, the manager anxiously consults his watch and prays the happy couple will not fluff their lines, like the hapless Princess Diana who (memorably, for all who watched her wedding to the Prince of Wales on television) couldn't quite remember all her groom's given names), or that the preacher will not go on too long, since the next couple and their guests are already in the waiting room awaiting their turn. Some might think it reminiscent of a busy day at the funeral home but it is equally, one might argue, a part of life.

## Wedding Styles

Unlike other catering situations, the wedding is not one where you can talk to the host and simply inquire "Do you want the same thing as last year?" Although Orson Welles telegrammed to his ex-wife, the actress Rita Hayworth, in response to her invitation to a subsequent marriage—"Sorry, can't make this wedding. Will try to attend the next."

The wedding in question was that of Hayworth to the international playboy and heir to the title of Head of the Ismaili Muslims, Aly Khan. There is of course much competition to be "The Mother of all Weddings" but this occasion could certainly be a contender (see sidebar).

---

## THE WEDDING OF RITA HAYWORTH AND THE ALY KHAN

The wedding took place at the town hall in Le Cannet, near Cannes, on the French Riviera. Under French law all marriages must take place in public at the town hall, if not held in church. A church wedding was out of the question at that time because both parties were divorced and Aly was a Muslim. Permission to hold the ceremony at the Aga Khan's chateau was not granted, such is the rigor of French bureaucracy (as an example, the "prefet" may refuse the use of names at baptism considered unsuitable).

Because the groom was awaiting confirmation of his divorce, no date could be set, and so the invitations were printed without a date, which was filled in later by hand. With guests coming in from as far away as Hollywood and Brazil, in the fifties, long before the Boeing 747, the scope for chaos was enormous. The groom took a personal interest in the luncheon arrangements at the chateau after the ceremony, enlisting the services of senior executives from the Cannes Casino.

Aly personally checked the shopping list: 40 lobsters, 110 pounds of cold meats, 10 pounds of caviar, 25 pounds of salad, 1,500 cookies, 40 pounds of petits fours, and a 120-pound wedding cake. He reminded the chef not to serve that normally standard item, ham, because of the religious rules of many of the guests.

One might notice the simplicity of the menu. Above all, everything was cold—totally suitable for an open-air lunch on a sunny Riviera day. One would guess that it was prepared off-premises, probably at a local hotel, and brought to the chateau in refrigerated vans. However, for such a big do, it's possible that they brought in extra refrigeration and stored food there. Since very few of the senior participants on this famous occasion survive, it would be hard to get the whole picture. But so far as the catering arrangements were concerned, there was nothing unusual about this wedding. It was a top-of-the-line, no-expense-spared function.

*(continued)*

The bar manager from the local Carlton Hotel was in charge of wines and cocktails. (The muslim sect to which Aly belonged, the Ismaelis, allows alcohol consumption, though they are not very enthusiastic consumers). He invented a new cocktail for the occasion called the "Ritaly": two-thirds Canadian Club, one-third Italian sweet vermouth, two drops of angosturas bitters, and a cherry. If you can find a bartender who knows how to make an Old-fashioned, you will get something that will taste more or less like a Ritaly. There's no reason why you shouldn't do the same for your clients, where appropriate.

Because of the huge crowds of spectators and journalists who turned out on the beautifully sunny wedding day, the police were on duty. The local mayor had declared a public holiday. Aly arrived at the town hall in a gray Alfa Romeo, driven by his brother. Aly was wearing a black morning coat with grey striped trousers. The groom's father, the Aga Khan, arrived in a green Rolls Royce, wearing a cream-colored suit and a red rose and his wife, the Begum, wore a pale blue sari. Rita Hayworth arrived in a white Cadillac convertible, in a blue dress and hat. The ceremony took eight minutes. Eyebrows were raised when the groom kissed his bride on the mouth—this was not then the custom in France and was considered wildly American.

Back at the chateau, thousand of flowers had been set out all over the garden. Two hundred gallons of eau de cologne had been poured into the swimming pool, in which two giant floral wreaths floated. One was in the shape of an A for Aly, the other an R for Rita.

## Another Kind of Wedding

In extreme contrast with an international marriage of Hollywood to royalty, the kind of wedding you are more likely to cater is typified by a recent one involving a middle-class couple who'd lived together for a year or two and decided to tie the knot. They borrowed a friend's large apartment for the occasion. The groom wore a blazer, and the bride a wedding dress especially chosen because it could be readily made over into something that could be worn on other occasions. A character in Oliver Goldsmith's "The Vicar of Wakefield" says "I chose my wife , as she did her wedding gown, not for a fine glossy surface, but such qualities as would wear well." All wedding clothes can now be rented, of course, including wedding dresses.

The couple were of different faiths, so were married by a licensed preacher of the Unitarian faith. After the brief ceremony, there was a simple buffet dinner in the apartment—Southern fried chicken, lots of salad, fruit and cake, and red and white wine. People dropped in after work, several still in working clothes and some in T-shirts.

# The Caterer's Responsibility to Clients

Although, as a hundred movies testify, there can be a funny side to these functions, the caterer should above all remember that a wedding is a major occasion in a client's life and one that may be fraught with doubt, fear, and insecurity. The received wisdom seems to be that when it comes to a wedding, the major sufferer is the father of the bride—a sentiment to which a million television sit-coms will attest. Nevertheless, there's also evidence that many brides' fathers very much enjoy the organization of their daughters' weddings, reluctant though they may be to admit it.

A wedding caterer may find himself in complete charge of the function. It will sometimes be a first time for the major participants—bride, bridegroom, and parents of both. With luck, parents may have enjoyed their own weddings, but they may not have much experience supervising the weddings of their offspring.

As always in catering matters, it is important to write down a plan. This should include minute detail and be reviewed from time to time. The more you plan, the less likely anything is to go wrong.

# The Caterer's Wedding Timeline

## Well in Advance

Two months before, decide the date and the venue of both the service and the reception (they may be different). Book the premises, if necessary. Remember, almost everyone wants to get married in June. Even a private home may have other claimants if it's a big family or some other event is being celebrated. Of course, some flexibility is possible at this stage if the church or reception venue is not available on the date you prefer. There's still room to maneuver, look around, and find another place.

Only when the dates are fixed can the bride's parents, or sponsors, make up the guest list and send out the invitations. They should keep a record of the replies. This is your guide to the numbers involved so that you can have ball-park figures for making other arrangements such as transport, food, drink, and perhaps accommodation.

In these strange informal times it isn't a bad idea to include with the invitation the request for a reply by a certain date "so that catering arrangements can be made." If you don't know the number of guests expected, chaos can result. Of course, there's always some flexibility. Up to six unexpected guests can usually be accommodated at most weddings, but more will impose stress and strain. You should try and book staff or assistance at this stage and also order any equipment you may need to hire, and the wedding cake, if required.

The wedding guest list isn't the caterer's responsibility, but it's highly likely that clients may require general advice. After all, a caterer may have the experience of a thousand weddings while his client has none but her own.

Clients may require help and guidance in many areas, and if the caterer can provide this, it won't do the business any harm. Catering can be an intensely personal business. That is precisely what makes it so much more fun, in terms of engagement and human interest, than many other businesses.

## One Month Before

Start shopping, order flowers, and check on ice supply. Plan transport arrangements, and remember to have a fallback plan in case something goes wrong such as a driver being unavailable, vehicles breaking down, or the limousine company suddenly disappearing. For some reason this is a flaky industry, and you will do well to establish good standing with a reliable local car firm, preferably one that's been in business for some time and has a good reputation.

## One Week Before

You should have a fairly tight idea of the number of people who plan to attend the wedding by now, always presuming people have politely replied to their invitations. Sadly, it may be necessary to call or write people reminding them of the invitation and asking them for a reply. This process sometimes reveals the death or disappearance of distant friends or relatives. Remember, at larger functions you'll be wise to set up a table without place cards, for "waifs and strays", or undecided guests who simply won't know until the last minute whether they can make it or not, or whose spouses have walked out on them, or who've suffered some accident. (This is often the most fun table of the function, but that's another matter . . .)

At this stage you should review the whole sequence of events and timings, and make your final shopping list.

## The Day Before

Finish off the shopping, particularly of highly perishable goods and foods such as caviar and fish. Check all arrangements from ice to flowers to transport, and tick them off on your checklist (the one from Chapter 7). Don't leave any blanks. If you get sick and somebody else has to take over, it's no use to them if they pick up your clipboard and see no entry whatsoever. Opposite TRANSPORT it should say "Joe's Limo Service, 6 cars ordered and confirmed, to be available throughout.

Telephone (999) 676-4567, Pete Shapiro or Suzie Wong." If you don't need a toastmaster, then opposite TOASTMASTER it should say "NOT REQUIRED." Remember, as Samuel Goldwyn almost said, a blank checklist isn't worth the paper it's written on.

If the reception and/or service is to take place at home, arrange the furniture and remove breakable ornaments.

## On the Day

Complete the final decorations, chill the wine, check everything one last time.

# The Various Duties of a Wedding Caterer

If the father of the bride was in the army for three minutes, or has ever been in charge of anything, you may find in him a staunch ally who'll actually enjoy attending to the details and minutiae of the wedding arrangements—wet weather alternative plans and all. It's perfectly all right to assume that the wedding day will be one of perfect June sunshine as long as you have alternative plans in case it pours relentlessly and is bitterly cold. Some parents treat a wedding as a creative event, which isn't unreasonable since it often is. They actually enjoy the whole production, demanding of time and thought though it often can be. But you may equally well have to nurse a whole nervous family through the proceedings.

However, the joy of catering is the successful completion of a function to everyone's satisfaction. You have the psychologically beneficial feeling of having done a proper day's work for a well-merited reward—a sensation denied to many. Flexibility and advance planning are your main strengths and defenses, and every wedding plan will be a bit different. However, the basic requirement will always be the efficient gathering together, entertaining, and dispersal of a body of people, so that in this respect most weddings are the same.

## The Ceremony

The actual religious, or spiritual, ceremonial part of a wedding is not usually the caterer's responsiblity. The caterer is mainly responsible for the reception. However, where the ceremony is to take place in a private home, as is by no means uncommon, obviously the caterer will need to keep an eye on the general arrangements since the spiritual (the service) will lead seamlessly (one hopes) to the temporal (the wining and dining) within the same walls. These two aspects of the occasion need to be separated. For instance, the room in which the ceremony takes place shouldn't be set up for the meal, though once the formalities have been completed, there's no reason why tables shouldn't swiftly be brought in and set up. Usually a wedding ceremony won't be held in a private home unless it's reasonably spacious. It works better if the dining and reception areas can be set up completely and separately from the ceremony, in rooms that allow efficient service and access to the kitchen.

## Transportation to the Reception

In a majority of cases, guests proceed from the wedding ceremony to the reception—sometimes in the next room, sometimes at a house some distance from a church or office. Remember, if the reception is held at a distant location, every single person at the ceremony will need transportation. If you hire one more car than you strictly need, it will be no bad thing. It can be a lonely feeling for dear old Aunt Mabel, who's flown all the way from Idaho, if nobody seems to want to get her to the reception.

## The Reception

Remember, existing space is often temporarily expandable by use of tents or marquees, and canopies. If an apartment has a terrace, a canopy can be put up so that, even if it rains, the space is still available. The obvious thing to do is to install it and review the weather at the time of the wedding. Then you either roll it back or leave it in place. Make sure someone in your crew, or a member of the party, knows exactly how to do this quickly and expeditiously, if the vendor's crew won't be handling this. A marquee is an excellent space extender, especially if placed on a lawn near large bay windows. Once it's erected you have protection if it rains, and you can set up a bar or buffet there if you wish.

Marquees vary in size, and some are most elaborately decorated. If the weather remains fair then you'll want to roll up the sides, and it's important to check that this can be done with your marquee. Whether or not you install a temporary wooden floor depends on the state of the lawn. Remember that if the proceedings go on after nightfall, as is likely, you'll need to provide electric lighting.

You should book this equipment well in advance, especially if the wedding is taking place between May and July, which is the high season for weddings. This is not an inexpensive exercise, but weddings are the sort of functions where the hosts—usually the bride's parents, but not always—have to grit their teeth and dig deep into their pockets, praying that it will only be a once-in-lifetime affair. It's probably the labor charges incurred by having to employ a crew to erect the marquee that bumps up the price. You must establish the proposed route from kitchen to marquee well in advance if you decide to serve food therein.

Make sure the marquee is well aired before the guests arrive. They can sometimes be a bit damp and musty smelling, which can take the edge off the scent of flowers, perfumes, and colognes that are often part of the memory of a day which, for many, is the happiest day of their lives.

## THE RECEIVING LINE

At the reception, guests are customarily greeted by the bridal party, who form a receiving line, usually in the following order:

The bride's mother
The bride's father
The bridegroom's mother
The bridegroom's father
The bride
and (last but not least)
The groom

A gap of ten feet is usual between the bridegroom's father and the bridal couple. The best man, bridesmaids, and ushers usually hover in the vicinity with the one special duty of maintaining the flow of guests through the receiving line, some guests, notoriously, being more talkative than others.

None of these arrangements are written in tablets of stone, but they will serve as useful guidelines. Remember, the best man—if he's conscientious—should be aware of what's going on generally, and the ushers are at his beck and call for the carrying out of any small errands. They are actually working, not relaxing. Their reward is the opportunity to meet the bridesmaids and other interesting people.

## KEEPING THE GUESTS HAPPY

At a discreet distance from the receiving line, liquid refreshment, often including champagne, is usually offered. The discreet distance helps to ease congestion—every occasion needs space and pace. Naturally, particularly at a home wedding, such refreshment may well have already been liberally available, so it should not be assumed that receiving line escapists are necessarily dying of thirst or hunger. Nevertheless, fresh offerings—either of food, drink, speech, or entertainment—are the natural punctuation of formal affairs.

A basic discipline of all catering is constant monitoring with regard to the possibility that guests may be thirsty, hungry, cold, hot, or just plain *bored*. In general terms it's a matter of keep 'em moving and keep 'em occupied and everyone will be happy. Functions can grind to a dismal halt when guests are nursing their third, in many cases, unwanted cocktail while awaiting the signal to sit, eat, listen, applaud, or leave.

# The Wedding Meal

The formal sit-down lunch or dinner is sometimes called the "wedding breakfast." The best man or toastmaster—which might be you, the caterer—will announce that luncheon is served, and when people have found their places he (or she) might (only rarely these days) invite people to stand to receive the "bride, bridegroom, and retinue."

Seating is often *ad hoc* and informal (without regard to Montagues and Capulets, the names of the respective bride and bridegroom's families in Shakespeare's play *Romeo and Juliet*) though it's normal to have place cards with the guests' names inscribed. It must be conceded however that, in a majority of cases weddings will tend to divide into two groups: the bride's family and friends and those of the groom. In church, too, it's still common for the groom's family to sit on the left of the aisle and the bride's on the right.

Quite often the caterer will merely be asked to lay on a buffet, of varying degrees of elaborateness, so that people can circulate freely. This makes sense, for instance, if there isn't to be a dance.

As for the menu, for the average wedding you'll usually have to work within a budget, but once you get your eye on costs this isn't a problem. It shouldn't be because it's part of the job. With practice you'll be able to envisage a suitable menu, bearing in mind seasonal factors and price changes throughout the year. A hotel will often offer a printed menu showing what they could lay on for say $30 or $50 a head. Above this figure it's probable that expense is no object and you can even start considering luxury foods such as lobster and caviar.

## The Head Table

If the reception includes a sit-down dinner or luncheon (as distinct from a buffet, which is okay for a second or third marriage, usually there's a top table where the leading participants of the wedding and members of both families sit in traditional order:

Preacher or whoever conducts the ceremony
Bridesmaid
Bridegroom's father
Bride's mother
Bridegroom
Bride

Bride's father

Bridegroom's mother

Best man

Chief bridesmaid, or maid or matron of honor

Any variation on this is permissible. Not all couples have both, or either of, their parents still alive, for instance, and they may want more people at the head table. There needs only be a focus on the head table, where the bridal party will sit. Apart from anything else, this is where the speeches will be made, so it needs to be visible and audible to the guests.

Broadly, the choice is between many separate tables each seating up to a dozen people, or an n-shaped arrangement, with the guests sitting alongside each other on the vertical legs and the horizontal bar as head table. If there are several tables, it may mean that some guests will have their backs to the bridal party's table from which speeches may be made. But since speeches aren't usually made until the last course has been served, people can swivel their chairs around.

## The Toasts

At the end of the meal there are usually three toasts and three speeches. The first is the toast to the bride and bridegroom, usually proposed by the bride's father or an old friend of the bride's family. With luck this will be short and sweet. The bridegroom then responds to this toast. In his speech, which traditionally includes or even begins with the words "My wife and I," he thanks the guests for their presents and the hosts (usually, but not always, his just acquired in-laws) for the reception. Finally he proposes a toast to the bridesmaids.

In the old days, when women didn't usually make speeches at weddings, it was up to the best man to respond on their behalf. Nowadays, the bridesmaids are likely to speak for themselves, leaving the best man to do the same. His speech is traditionally lighthearted. He may read some of the letters or telegrams of congratulation, where these still apply, and should end by thanking the bride's parents, or whoever are the hosts, for their hospitality and proposing a toast to them.

## Cutting the Cake

Either before the toasts or at the end of the meal, as a signal that the bridal couple are about to leave the table to change into their going-away clothes, the wedding cake is cut. The bride, assisted by the groom, cuts the first slice from the bottom tier, often to the accompaniment of flashing cameras. If this first slice has already been cut by the caterer and disguised by a thin layer of icing, this little ceremony will go quite smoothly. The cake is then taken away to be cut up and distributed to the guests. Traditionally, the top tier of the cake is saved for the baptism of the couple's first child. Some slices may also be sent by mail to absent friends and relatives. A standard portion is $1\frac{1}{2}$ to 2 ounces, so that for 100 guests a 100 pound cake is needed.

## Tossing the Bride's Bouquet

Upon leaving to change, the bride can throw her bouquet to the guests—the tradition being that the person who catches it will be the next to marry. They should then depart on their honeymoon by tradition, but increasingly bridal couples don't want to miss the fun of their reception and stay on—especially if there's a dance—and take off the following day.

# Services Provided by the Caterer

Working from home you can probably handle a small home wedding reception of not much more than forty guests by yourself. If you expand to bigger operations, you may well find yourself being asked to provide more than food and drinks—the full package.

At weddings, the caterer can provide a comprehensive service that will be useful in getting more business. Ideally, he can arrange the dinner, the dance, the wedding cake, the transport, and the accommodation for out-of-town visitors.

## Photography

Another area in which the caterer can take a hand is the pictures, by providing photographers, a video crew or both. It's best to have professionals on the case, despite the fact that many guests will be taking their own pictures. Sound recordings of the reception can be made easily enough these days with the camcorder. If you want a record of the service, of course, you need the permission of whoever is officiating.

## Parking

Parking may or may not be the caterer's responsiblity. If it is, she must have wet weather plans, including, most importantly, a door man with a large umbrella, as well as a canopy because the guests will be wearing their finery, and their shoes are unlikely to be L.L. Bean country gear.

## Flowers

Flowers may be chosen to harmonize with the bride and bridesmaid's dresses, and unless the caterer has this specialist knowledge, the job is best left to the experienced florist, who will take it in stride. Other decorative possibilities include good-quality paper napkins imprinted with the names of the bride and groom or specially printed bookmatches. In Europe, each guest is often given a white net bag of sugared almonds, tied with a white ribbon.

## WINE

Occasionally, a client with a big wine cellar, or friends in the business, will insist upon providing his own wine. This obviously eliminates the caterer's markup and profit.

It is customary in such cases for the caterer to charge "corkage" on the wine—that is, to levy a small charge per bottle to make up the profit she would otherwise forego. If you take your own wine to a restaurant that has its own liquor license and wine list, the same system applies (though not to an unlicensed establishment where you bring your own). Of course, a caterer may feel diffident about demanding such a charge, as do many restaurateurs, and prefer to waive it. It's up to the individual to decide.

On one famous occasion, a family agreed to pay corkage on each bottle of their own wine. The family then turned up with magnums of red wine and a single "Salmanazar"—equivalent to 12 bottles of champagne. The caterer billed them at the rate of the equivalent number of regularly sized bottles. The family objected, proposing to pay only one corkage fee—even for the Salmanazar. At the time of writing, the case had not been resolved.

## THROWING RICE

Rice and confetti have a bad image these days, mainly because they are such a pain to clean up. Some churches actually forbid them, so be sure to check. Outdoors, rose petals and bird seed are better ideas.

## SECURITY

Someone must be put in charge of the receipt and security of presents that guests will bring along. Usually a table is designated for that purpose. In a private home there may not be a security problem, but with the unavoidable comings and goings of staff, drivers, and guests, there's always a chance for a wise guy to sneak in. At a hotel or any place where the public may have access, some kind of security watch is mandatory.

A special caution applies to weddings that have met with fierce opposition from certain parties, often on religious grounds, or where potential inheritors feel challenged. Shakespeare's *Romeo and Juliet* tells it like it can be. Where such opposition exists there's always a slight chance of disruption of the ceremony. Fights and worse are not uncommon at weddings.

## Stag Night

If you are hired to lay on a stag dinner for a bridegroom and his male relatives and friends, then the best thing you can do is reconcile yourself to a rather childish and not infrequently bawdy evening. Young women have been known to jump out of cakes not always correctly attired.

The single best advice you can give to your clients, if requested to provide this service, is that it should take place not on the eve of the wedding, but on the day before. Many weddings are shadowed by the fact that some of the male guests, and not infrequently the groom himself, are not in the very best of shape because of overindulgence and a lack of sleep.

It will be no bad thing if you establish a somewhat serious presence, as things can get out of hand. If drinking bouts are the order of the day, don't be too shy to impart the wisdom that a fifth of liquor such as whiskey or vodka is a comfortable lethal dose for even a healthy young man, if drunk in one go. The fact that in late stages of alcoholism people can do two bottles a day and appear sober is irrelevant in this context. Hearty food will go down best at this kind of function—not quiche and salad.

## Summary

Even when cocktail parties, dinners, reunions, and dances have long disappeared from the social scene, there will always be weddings, and it's important to put on a good show in order to get repeat business as a result of word-of-mouth recommendation. Most weddings go off reasonably smoothly and happily. A major setback can be a change in the weather, which is why, even when a wedding is planned for June, wet weather plans are absolutely essential. Murphy's Law being what it is, one might say that the more meticulous the wet weather plans, the less likely it is to rain. Always take the most cautious route. If, as an experienced caterer, you are querulously asked for general advice on arrangements tell your clients, for example, that guests should arrive in town the day before the event if they wish to be sure of attending. Twenty-four hour delays on flights are not uncommon. Traffic accidents and quite trivial events can cause crippling delays.

## If You Run Out of Real Weddings . . .

So appealing is a wedding, and so strongly are people drawn to attend one, that there even exists an international company offering interactive weddings which are really a sort of theatrical charade. Nobody actually gets married—they just pretend. They work like this: A room is converted into a chapel with stained-glass windows, altar, and pews. Guests pay about $50 a head to sit through a wedding ceremony performed by actors, complete with organ music, sermon, vows, and confetti, and then move to a reception. The men dress in tuxedos and the women have elaborate hairdos. Presents (including Cadillacs, they say, but perhaps a grain of salt wouldn't be inappropriate) are lavished on the happily "married" couple. Thirty-five other actors are also present to make conversation with the guests. The impresarios, or perpetrators, say that everyone loves a wedding because it's such a "great opportunity to observe people." Would this idea work in your town? Think about it.

# Chapter Thirteen

# Food

A LL caterers need a good general knowledge of food, its preparation, and serving. If a client says "We have some French guests—wouldn't it be fun to serve escargots?" and the caterer doesn't know what that this is French for edible snails, he's in trouble. But this general knowledge, coupled with a precise knowledge of a small repertoire of dishes will provide ample expertise that can be widely exploited.

## The Menu

If you only intend to sell yourself as a cook who goes into private homes to prepare dinners and lunches for small numbers of people, it really doesn't matter if you only have one menu in your head. Your special soup, rack of lamb, or roast duck, followed by a dessert of Greek yogurt with walnuts and a drizzle of honey, and finished by a savory of miniature toasted bacon, cheese, and tomato sandwich, may become the talk of the town.

If you restrict yourself to a small repertoire of dishes, you'll soon get to the stage where you can cook for large groups with hardly any stress or strain. Practice makes perfect. Also, a consistently high quality of cooking is more easily maintained with a small menu. The truth of this is evident in any restaurant that features a large menu. Inevitably, there will be some hit and miss, with some dishes far outshining others. By contrast, restaurants that offer one dish only, be it fish and chips, steak, French fries and salad, or duck, often achieve high quality.

Contrary to the impression that one might gain from the ever burgeoning media coverage of food, the simple truth is that most people are somewhat unadventurous in food matters. Army caterers jump through hoops to get their men to eat a "balanced diet," but the salad and the oily fish are all too frequently disdained, no matter how attractively presented. Burgers, fried eggs, French fries, and pizza remain firm favorites. What does General Schulzenower have for lunch? A diet cola and a slice of pizza. What does Private Doe have for lunch? A diet cola and a slice of pizza. One police force recently reported that the single most popular drink in its huge cafeteria was diet cola. Enormous amounts were consumed—much more even than coffee.

## Following Trends

Of course, there is now an element of fashion in food, as in so many other consumer items. Where are the spinach salads, sprinkled with chopped bacon, of yesteryear, and where the smoked chicken, the kiwi fruit, and the grilled goat cheese? Mashed potatoes are currently big, simply called "mash" on many menus, by some spontaneous international agreement. But long after fashionable dishes have been forgotten, the old favorites will still be popular. We have not seen the last of baked potatoes or broccoli.

However, these realities should not lull the caterer into ignoring new trends and not regularly reviewing dishes and menus. Remember, you can experiment on family and friends, or yourself, but don't serve chocolate coated grasshoppers to your client's guests unless requested.

The constant media exhortations to try something *new* and *different* would fill pages. There is not much merit in their advice so far as the caterer is concerned. People have been cooking food to a high level for about 400 years now, and there is nothing new under the sun, though the constant trickle of once complicated and time-consuming foods that can now be prepared simply is very helpful—frozen pastry being one excellent example.

Not until your client sighs and says, "Let's do something different," should you go into full creative mode. And even then you should keep your feet firmly on the ground. Twelve people to dinner for a menu of caviar and lobster mousse with oysters, roast goose, Caesar Salad, a multi-layer gateau, and individual cheese souffles sounds wonderful, and might well be. But you'll need to be well paid for taking on such a demanding menu, especially when something much more mundane might go down just as well. Smoked salmon, beef ragout with rice, peach Melba, and a nice brie, for example, will be far easier and less expensive to do. The caution notwithstanding it must again be observed that if you can bring the production of an interesting, elaborate menu to the point where it's actually easy for you to prepare, then why not flaunt it? It's all a question of balance.

**Novelty**    In addition to the generally prosaic tastes of most people, which comfortably reduce the challenge to the cook and caterer, there's another helpful factor—novelty. Every cook just naturally has a certain touch and brings a certain style to dishes, even those classic dishes for which, theoretically, only one universal standard should apply. Novelty alone will help to give food a certain zing. Of course, there is a quixotic contradiction here, since home cooking is partly loved because of its dependable sameness. George Bernard Shaw observed that "There is no love sincerer than the love of food". Perhaps, where natural appetites are concerned, occasional excursions strengthen loyalties, as in other areas of life

An important thing for caterers to remember is that they are not required to paint the ceiling of the Sistine Chapel when they produce a dinner. Ordinary satisfaction is what's required, not revelation or culinary breakthrough. There is no reason to put your professional life on the line by attempting to provide something new and different every time you sally forth in business. More of the same— provided it's of good quality, is more likely to be the requirement.

Even if you corner a small portion of the market by cooking for intimate, upscale dinner parties, roast goose and chocolate mousse should represent the outer limits of your repertoire. The challenge is not to reinvent the wheel but to provide general satisfaction. The more elaborate the menu becomes, the greater the scope for things to go wrong. This is one of the reasons that chefs in "fancy" restaurants are so notoriously temperamental.

## A Few Suggestions

This is not a cookbook, but a few suggestions will help the caterer to explore ideas and possibilities. There are also some general observations that even the best cookbooks often fail to mention.

### Use the Best Ingredients

A truth not fundamentally recognized by many is that few prepared dishes can exceed the quality of their basic ingredients. Of course, a lot of cooking has this precise objective—the wonderful things you can do with chicken gizzards, lamb hearts, and so on. The original idea of sauces was to disguise the inferior quality of the basic foods, especially the meat and fish. It is said, though no pundit has yet pronounced on the burning issue, that the rationale of Indian curry was originally simply to disguise appalling meat.

**Using Available Ingredients**   The French definition of a good cook is one who makes the absolute best of available ingredients. Napoleon's chef, after the battle of Marengo, only had a chicken, three crayfish, and a small selection of vegetables to work with. He produced Chicken Marengo, which the emperor greatly enjoyed. (On battle days, in total contravention of modern dietary advice, he didn't eat at all until after the slaughter had been accomplished).

Later, back at Les Tuileries in Paris, the emperor requested the same dish. The chef, sensibly realizing that the conjunction of crayfish and chicken was absurd, omitted the fish and augmented the vegetables. Napoleon complained bitterly, protesting that interference with the original recipe would bring him bad luck.

**Improvising**   Paul Bocuse, the French chef who wore kitchen whites and a *toque blanche* when he was invested by the President of France with the Legion d'Honneur, said on one occasion, "Like a painting in a gold frame, an omelet should be gilded and varnished." Considered by some to be the greatest chef in the world, he once found his omelets sticking to the pan. He was out of practice, he complained—an interesting observation. But, at the propitious moment of serving, he took a linen towel and shaped each omelet to perfection.

## Poached Salmon

Poached Salmon is a festive and professional-looking dish that will provide an excellent centerpiece to a buffet table. The tired proverbs such as "Please the eye and you delight the palate" are true—and, in general, food should always look good. Few sights are more appetizing than a whole fish on a plate.

Inevitably there are contradictions here. Many a restaurant kitchen crew dines happily on tasty food that just isn't pretty enough to be sent out to the customer's tables. Quite how you make a winkle or a steamer visually appealing is something of a challenge, but the intense taste of these fruits of the sea is unforgettable. Food lovers can have no trouble relating to the character in a popular novel who, dining in a trendy New York restaurant, looked at the plate set before him and couldn't decide whether to eat it or frame it.

Wild salmon is widely available in the summer months. Farmed salmon is available year-round. If you intend to serve a classic Poached Salmon, you should check with your local fish supplier well in advance to ensure its availability. When you collect the fish it should be resilient and firm to the touch—sparkling skin, pink gills, and full, bright eyes. Salmon meat is rich, and a 3-ounce portion per person is plenty. A 7-pound salmon will serve as many as 15 people.

**How to Do It**   Poaching is considered by many the absolute best way to serve salmon. Place the fish in a large, deep pan, sometimes called a "fish kettle" and cover it with water. Add a sliced onion, a sliced carrot, 2 tablespoons each of cooking oil and white wine (or lemon juice). Also add a bayleaf, a sprig of parsley, and a dozen black peppercorns. Cover the kettle with a lid and bring it gently to the boil over medium heat. When the liquid starts to boil, time one minute—no more—then turn off the heat. If you intend to serve it hot, it will need a few minutes to cool before serving. If you intend to serve it cold, leave it somewhat longer. This method works with any size of fish.

**Presentation**   Lift the fish out of the liquid and place it on a serving dish. Ease the skin off one side, using two fish sheers, and flip it over. Then remove the skin on the other side. Use kitchen paper to mop up. You can leave the head and tail in place or remove them, as you prefer. If you leave the head on, make sure you cover the now rather unappetizing looking eye with garnish. Overlapping slices of cucumber are a popular decoration, as are piped rosettes of mayonnaise.

**Storage**   The fish should be stored in the refrigerator and covered with a muslin cloth if there is much delay between preparation and serving—cucumber tends to dry quickly. You can brush the whole fish with oil or even cover it with a thin layer of aspic (easily prepared from gelatin powder) if you wish. Finally, you can add a few sprigs of parsley, watercress, or tomato slices to complete a delicious and festive-looking dish. Flavored butter (when served hot), mayonnaise, chopped dill, parsley, and tarragon are suitable condiments.

**Microwaving**   Yes, there is a microwave option here, for smaller fish. But you'll need to experiment to get it right, such is the variation in times and results. Some believe that the microwave does wonders with fish. Others are not so sure, and a few rightwingers believe that the microwave has no more important function than a warming device. Whatever your true opinion, you'll find the microwave a blessing as it can very quickly heat up preprepared dishes.

If, as happens in even the best regulated families, the fish breaks up in preparation, the garnishes can be used to disguise its reshaping. There is an apocryphal story about the society hostess whose butler accidentally dropped the huge salmon he was about to serve at dinner. "Really Hudson, don't make such a fuss," the imperturbable hostess said. "Just clean it up and bring in the other one."

## Beef Stew

Beef Stew is an immensely versatile standard that can easily be prepared and stored, or even frozen, without damaging the flavor. Add sour cream and you can call it Boeuf Stroganoff. Add paprika, a tiny amount of caraway seeds, a pinch of marjoram, and a clove or two of garlic, and you can call it Goulash. Add secret ingredients and call it anything you like, such as "Ragout a la Suzie." Lace it with red wine and include onions, and call it Boeuf Bourgignon. We're talking about a satisfying, hearty dish that almost everyone will enjoy or at least find acceptable. Purists may raise their eyebrows and think, "Hey, you're cutting a few corners here . . ." It may be true but it doesn't matter. Few diners' eating experiences are ruined by the absence or addition of some minor ingredient. If the general effect is appetizing, they won't even notice. Authenticity isn't the crux of the matter. It depends on whether their mission is to eat or to criticize.

The crucial factor in Beef Stew, as in so many other dishes, is the basic quality of the meat. Some butchers and supermarkets offer stewing steak that proves to be inedible. Heaven knows which part of the animal it comes from. None of the traditional cooks' methods of turning sows' ears into silk purses, or the inedible into the edible, seems to work. You can marinate it in a herb and wine mix, beat it with a tenderizing hammer, cook it slowly with tender loving care, and the result is still appalling—the meat tastes stale, and even if vaguely chewable, resists the teeth in an unpleasant, plastic, greasy way. So risky is the red meat area that many beef lovers will solemnly buy the very best filet mignon steak and cut it into bite-size portions or even grind it for hamburgers in order to be sure of acceptable results.

Assume nothing about meat. You can buy a steak with optimum color, well marbled, and all the rest of it, and still find yourself saddled with tough meat. Your best chance of a tender result with beef is to make stew, and the more slowly it's cooked, the better.

If you find a butcher whose stewing beef is acceptable, then stay with him. You need to discover and cultivate a reliable supplier. The underground whisper that the best cuts of meat go to restaurants and hotels is true. They are a wholesale butcher's prize customers because they buy such huge quantities, and thus command the best, whereas the individual consumer is somewhat disdained.

**How to Do It**    The method of preparing any of the variations on Beef Stew is the same. The quantities given here are to feed four people. To feed more, simply multiply accordingly. You'll need:

1 beef stock cube

1 pound stewing beef

1 pound assorted vegetables (carrots, mushrooms, etc.)

1 large onion

Pepper mill, Worcestershire sauce, Accent, etc.

Potatoes, rice, salad on the side

First, dissolve a beef stock cube, or cubes, depending on the number of people you need to feed, in half a pint of boiling, or at least very hot, water. More people means more cubes and more water. Even the fast-melting cubes seem to take ages to liquify. Of course, there's a liquid version available, but most cooks seem to prefer the cubes—a basic essential for many dishes.

Allow about 4 ounces of meat per person, not less. Big, young football players will eat a bit more, petite, elderly ladies somewhat less—usually. One pound of beef will feed four persons. Remember, there'll be accompanying juice and vegetables, and some will eat more or less than others. Ask the butcher to chop the beef into bite-size chunks, if he doesn't do this automatically, as is usually the case.

You can marinate the meat in red wine, chopped garlic, and onion overnight, if you wish, but experience suggests that the improvement afforded by this process is much exaggerated in some cookbooks. How many cooks do you know in real life who rave about marinade?

Brown the meat by frying it slowly with a little oil, or butter, with some chopped onion, to a level that, if you were grilling a steak, would be deemed "medium," that is, a certain redness apparent but not *saignant*, rare, or bleeding. At this point, drain off all the fatty liquid. You've captured the flavor it imparts; you now need to get rid of the greasiness.

**Get Rid of the Gristle**   Also—and this is finicky but will make a huge difference—quickly check every single piece of the meat for any lingering bits of gristle or fat and remove them. You may elect to do this with your favorite sharp knife, which you take everywhere, along with your trusty corkscrew.

Few things are worse in the dining context than absentmindedly taking a forkful of food and finding a piece of gristle or fat in your mouth. Guests and clients will notice and disapprove. Nobody will tell you what was wrong; you just won't get called again.

One 30-year-old bachelor bought a certain frozen meat pie twice a week for years, as a dependable, easily prepared dinner. One night he got a mouthful of gristle, and resulting disaffection was instantaneous, total, and eternal. Thus, a major food corporation lost the twice-weekly purchases of a consumer for a forecasted 55 years of life.

Having drained off the excess fat, you should now put the meat and the fried onions into a saucepan with some chopped vegetables. Anything goes, but obviously bay leaves, carrots, potatoes, peas, beans, tomatoes, mushrooms, the other half of the onion you chopped up earlier to put in the frying pan, perhaps a small can of tomato puree, and some chopped potatoes even if you're serving more on the side—whatever takes your fancy. Include some red wine if you wish to call it Boeuf Bourgignon, without fear of having the dish's authenticity challenged. Use your eye, experience, and common sense to decide how much of every vegetable you put in. A few drops of Worcestershire sauce, Accent (yes, monosodium glutemate), and ground pepper are further options.

But don't, whatever you do, put any salt into the mix because now, after a good stir, you must add the liquified beef stock cube, and that is salty enough. Put the pan covered with a lid on low and let it simmer. Check it every few minutes to make sure it isn't about to run dry and burn. Give the mixture a good stir at this time.

If the liquid starts to evaporate, as of course it may, although a well-fitting pan lid will keep this at a minimum, simply add hot water from any side vegetables you may have simmering, or just plain water, from time to time, and stir.

While the meat is simmering its way to perfection you can prepare the scheduled accompaniments—more potatoes, cooked in various ways, more vegetables, rice, salad, and so on. As little as 20 minutes of simmering will produce an edible mix, but an hour will yield better results. If you leave it much longer than that, the meat will start to break down to a level that is too mushy.

When the meat has achieved the level you require (taste small portions from time to time and see how easily it cuts), you should start thickening the liquid by slowly drizzling in some flour, mixing as you go with a wooden spoon. (A wooden spoon won't scratch the pan, which these days is almost certainly coated with a nonstick surface.)

You can cheat a bit here by putting some of the liquid into a mug or dish on the side and adding flour, mixing it well, crushing up those occasional little white blobs, and then adding it to the main pot and following with a general stir.

This should be the last thing you do to the stew. If you start thickening with flour too soon, glutinous little lumps will stick to the bottom of the pan and, although they are easily broken up, you may feel generally insecure about the process—and confidence is an important thing in cooking.

**SERVING**    It's now ready to serve, with crusty bread, mashed potatoes, rice, or just about anything. Also, you can let it cool, refrigerate it, and reheat it next day. If anything, the quality is likely to be improved by this delay.

You can even freeze it, transport it like that, and nuke it in a microwave oven at the function premises, and it will still taste good. When you practice cooking this dish at home, make more than you need for one meal, and refrigerate and/or freeze the remainder to check the results.

This simple stew, with its many available variations, is almost as easy to prepare for fifty as it is for two—it just takes longer and requires more work. Experiments at home are the key to easy production in catering.

## Chicken Stew

You can follow the above instructions with chicken and by simply exercising the red wine option, produce Coq au vin. In the unlikely event that you are asked to produce Chicken Curry, all you have to do is add curry powder and stir. Although even this two-dish repertoire would be enough to get you through life as a caterer, clearly you'll need to extend your range eventually because you're likely to get repeat business from clients madly impressed by the quality of the food you provide. Get into the habit of reading cookbooks for stimulation of ideas, but remember, none of them is the Bible. Mrs. Beeton's tome is an excellent basic store of information, which also includes useful household hints, details on how to carve every animal in the edible kingdom, and tips for folding napkins in decorative ways. The fact that some of the advice has been rendered redundant by advances in convenience foods and cooking methods is irrelevant, because you get some insight into the basics of cooking.

## A Quick Guide to Quantities

The following information is intended to stimulate your creativity with menus. At some time you must establish your own "Ideas File" and keep it handy. Also, you must have a rough idea at all times of what you can deliver for a certain price per head. If a potential client announces that she will be happy to spend $20 a head, or $100 a head (easy with a selection of wines), then you should have an idea of what sort of menu you can provide.

Sometimes a client will suggest the menu and ask you how much it would cost to provide it for a certain number of people. It's the same question put slightly differently, and if your answer is not encouraging you're immediately put on the spot to suggest alternatives.

It is of course important to have a formal notion of required quantities of food. A buffet for 20 featuring a version of Beef Stew requires at least five pounds of beef and at least five pounds of assorted vegetables, not including the potatoes or rice or salad to be served on the side. It's also essential, however, to develop what the French call *pifometre*, that is to say, an instinctive feeling for how much you need and how long it needs to cook. "Monsieur Pifo" is a French cartoon character with a long nose. If you ask French cooks for the secret of some dish you've just enjoyed, they'll often tap their noses, wink, and say "Pifometre . . ."

The accompanying table of quantities will point your thinking in the right direction. Even with this guide you must practice preparation and cooking on yourself, family, and friends. Preparing any dish at home and getting it absolutely right will boost your confidence enormously, and the stress and challenge of catering will be vastly reduced. Arriving at a function armed only with raw ingredients and a recipe is a good recipe for disaster.

Chefs and restaurateurs experiment all the time, and an amusing aspect of this constant experimentation occurs when chef and restaurant owner sample a dish, pronounce it triumphantly delicious, then solemnly shake their heads sadly as they agree that it's not suitable for a commercial menu.

Usually the reason is that it's too strong, too distinctive, too exotic, or too unusual. Even in Indian restaurants the advertising often contains phrases like "spicy—but not too spicy." On the whole, by the way, bland is good, or at least safe. After all, what are all those condiments for if not to add flavor to basically bland food? A plain steak can be enhanced by an individual diner with extra salt, pepper, mustard, horseradish, bearnaise sauce, A1, and half a dozen other standard sauces.

## A Traditional Menu

For academic interest, at mammoth feasts such as were typical in rarefied circles right up to World War II, the following sequence was traditional:

> *Hors d'oeuvre* or (starter, or appetizer)—pâté, melon etc.
>
> *Soup* (usually a clear (transparent) soup if served at dinner).
>
> A flour-based or "farinaceous" dish (usually only at luncheon).
>
> An egg dish.
>
> *Fish or shellfish.*

## GUIDE TO QUANTITIES

| ITEM | PORTION SIZE | QUANTITY REQUIRED FOR 50 GUESTS |
|---|---|---|
| Smoked salmon | 1 ounce | 3½ pounds, sliced |
| Shrimp, crab cocktails | Variable | 5 pounds frozen shrimp, crab, plus 3 pounds lettuce, 2½ pints sauce |
| Fruit salad, fresh | 4 ounces | 10 pints |
| Melon | Variable | 6–8 melons, depending on size |
| Fruit juice | 3 fluid ounces | 8 pints |
| Soup | 8 fluid ounces | 2½ gallons |
| Fish fillets (not main course) | 3–4 ounces | 10–12½ pounds, filleted |
| Shrimp or scampi (not main course) | 3–4 ounces | 10–12½ pounds |
| Steaks 6–8 ounces | 1 per person | 50 |
| Fish (main course) | 5–6 ounces | 15–18 pounds, filleted |
| Roast meats | 3 ounces | 18 pounds, raw, boneless |
| Chicken | 4 pieces each | 12 2½-pound birds |
| Turkey | 3 ounces | 18 pounds raw, boneless meat |
| Vegetables | 2–3 ounces | 6½–9 pounds prepared |
| Potatoes | 4 ounces | 12½ pounds prepared |
| Gravy or sauce | 1½ fluid ounces | 4 pints |
| Cream | 1 ounce | 2½ pints |
| Cheese | 2 ounces | 7 pounds |
| Crackers | 3 pieces | 3 pounds |
| Fresh strawberries | 3 ounces | 10 pounds |

Entrée—a garnished meat dish, often without vegetables. Sorbet (supposed to"cleanse the palate" and prepare it for further delights). In Normandy they would sometimes drink a shot of Calvados between courses, called "le trou Normande." A roasted bird, or game, often with salad.

Cold buffet—cold meats of various kinds.

A special vegetable dish—asparagus, artichokes, with a sauce. A sweet dish, or pie.

A savory—toasted cheese topped with anchovies, perhaps.

*Cheese*

*Dessert*—another sweet pudding or ice cream.

*Coffee*

*Various wines, beers* and *spirits* served throughout the meal.

If you live long enough you may see something approaching this scale, though it is frankly somewhat absurd for modern times, when gluttony is in general disrepute because we're all trying to keep our weight down.

## A Contemporary Menu

Nowadays, things are much simpler. A typical menu pattern might be:

*Soup*

$\left.\right\}$ Dry white wine

*Fish course*

*Main course* (entrée)—meat, fowl, or game      Red wine
*Dessert*
*Coffee*

OR

*Hors d'oeuvre*
*Fish*                        $\left.\right\}$ Dry white wine
*Main course*

*Cheese*
*Sweet or dessert*            Sweet white wine

OR

*Hors d'oeuvre*               Fino (dry) sherry
*Main course*                 $\left.\right\}$ Red wine
*Cheese*

*Dessert*                     Port, or sweet dessert
*Coffee*                      wine

## Convenience Foods

You should never use a convenience food unless you've tasted it yourself and found it satisfactory. Certain items offered by the food industry are utterly disgraceful, and it is extraordinary that the public should have tolerated them so long. Yet, there they are, prominently displayed on the supermarket shelves.

If you keep your eyes wide open at the supermarket, as every caterer should, you will observe that certain products dominate the shopping carts. You'll almost certainly note that the favorite products are huge bottles of diet cola, toilet tissue, and large jars of mayonnaise. Look for yourself—seek, and ye shall find.

"Pork 'n Beans" usually means a can of beans with a fingernail sized-blob of pig fat, which presumably just squeezes within federal food regulations. The result is by no means as hearty a campfire dish as the label would have you believe. Also, many pies, puddings, and ready-battered foods contain only a minimum of low-grade meat and lots of chemicals. So bad are some of these products that it is difficult to understand who or where the target market is, since pet food could not be less tasty or nutritious.

## Mayonnaise—A Good Convenience Food

Life for most people is a matter of compromise, and where convenience food is concerned, the news isn't entirely bad. Mayonnaise is a good example. Real mayonnaise—egg yolks and best-quality olive oil drizzled together and tenderly mixed (food processors make the process easier, it must be admitted)—is quite delicious and special. However, like most "real" food (and this is the fundamental problem with "real" food), it doesn't keep very well and takes time and concentration to make at home. You can't just make it, stick it in the refrigerator, and haul it out a month later.

But the reality is that 99 percent of consumers are happy with Hellmans and Kraft "Real Mayonnaise." They know no other. Many people would be somewhat taken aback by real mayonnaise . . . "looks funny, yellowy, what are those little black blobs? [pepper], tastes kinda strong . . ." etc.

The caterer's mission is not to challenge and educate but to deliver and satisfy. Bottled mayo is fine. Just make sure you have plenty of it available. The restaurants of America echo with the phrases "Heavy on the mayo." "Side o' mayo," and "Extra mayo." The requested product is bottled mayonnaise, not home made (which, for comparison, you might try for yourself sometime).

### How to Make Mayonnaise

½ pint milk or cream

¼ pint vinegar

3 egg yolks

1 tablespoon salad oil

1 tablespoon sugar

1 teaspoon salt

1 dessert spoon mustard.

Mix the oil, sugar, salt, and mustard well in a bowl, add the well-beaten yolks, next the vinegar, and lastly the cream or milk. Stand the bowl in a saucepan containing sufficient boiling water to surround it to half its depth, and stir the mixture over heat until it acquires the consistency of custard. Allow to cool.

## Combining the Real and the Convenient

Most cooks, especially in restaurants but also at home, learn to cheat a bit, sometimes with good results. One establishment featured homemade mashed potatoes in a small dish, browned under the grill before serving. It was discovered that far better visual and taste results were achieved by mixing powdered mashed potatoes with fresh.

At another place a crab and shrimp sandwich on black bread at $4.50 seemed like a steal. It was delicious—but it wasn't crab and shrimp—it couldn't be, at that price unless it was their featured "loss leader." It was, of course, Atlantic pollack, dressed and flavored—quite agreeably—to look and taste like crab and shrimp.

Here are a couple of simple menus including several items that can be bought ready to eat—convenience foods. Many are of high quality these days, though there are a few real dogs. Remember, catering is not a suitable arena for Luddites. Acceptable quality time savers should be embraced and welcomed.

Smoked salmon—bought ready-sliced in a packet, or frozen

Turtle soup—or any soup—from cans. Cheer it up with chopped parsley, croutons, or whatever

Fish (merely needs a few minutes in the microwave)

Steaks cut to size (can be quickly grilled)

Frozen peas or other vegetable

Frozen cooked potatoes

Frozen desserts

Coffee

Minestrone soup (from a can; grate Parmegiana cheese over it)

Fried fish, from frozen, served with Tartare Sauce from a bottle

Roast Turkey (frozen)

Sprouts (frozen)

Ready-roasted potatoes (frozen)

Plum or Christmas pudding with brandy sauce, or mince pies

Coffee

As a caterer, you are in the business of being practical and getting the job done to the maximum satisfaction of all concerned. It's good to establish a reputation for being able to "deliver the goods" without fuss or hesitation; thus, you should not disdain what some call the lowest common denominator (LCD) menu but if you serve it, make sure it's delicious. The LCD menu might be:

Mushroom soup

Roast chicken

Fruit salad and ice cream

Coffee

Huge bottles of inexpensive white wine

Common though it now is, roast chicken remains a favorite with those who merely eat to live and those who live to eat alike. Remember to keep your eyes open, as new convenience food items come along all the time. Some survive and become staples, but most don't. If you're friendly with your local supermarket people (as you should be, with your card on their bulletin board), you can ask them "Anything new?" from time to time.

Here's an idea- and memory-stimulating list of convenience foods that are easily transported and prepared. You can use it to jog your mind when you can't get it into gear. Lists such as this should be kept handy by the telephone, so that you can have instant menu discussions with potential clients and give an impression of professional efficiency. If a client says "I don't know what to serve" you should be prompt with your suggestions and not be afraid to take the initiative. Catering is an area, perhaps a bit like medicine, where people are often glad to have their thinking done for them.

### FOR APPETIZERS:

Canned or frozen fruit juice

Canned or frozen fruits of all kinds

Canned or frozen vegetables

Packet soups

Canned soups, especially the unusual ones such as vichysoisse, turtle, bisque d'homard (lobster), madrilene, etc.

Frozen or canned pâtés or terrines

Frozen shellfish

Smoked fish, smoked salmon, in packets, or frozen

### FOR A FISH COURSE:

Frozen shrimp, breaded fillets of various kinds of fish

### FOR A MAIN COURSE:

Ready-cut meats

Breaded meat items

Frozen boneless turkey

Frozen boneless chicken

Frozen vol-au-vents

Frozen vegetables and potatoes

Fresh, prepared vegetables—from a Korean store perhaps (likely to be somewhat expensive for large numbers)

Frozen pizza

## For dessert:

Canned and frozen fruit

Ice cream

Frozen gateaux, cakes, and flans

Frozen pastries

Remember, too, that food suppliers, given notice, can often take some of the prep work off your hands. A butcher will prepare meat ready for the oven such as crown of lamb or rack of lamb. A baker will prepare your pastries and breads, and perhaps deliver them, too. Never be afraid to ask advice from food shopkeepers, because everyone likes talking about food. As a subject of conversation, it threatens to replace sports, politics, television, and relationships.

# The Microwave

The microwave, which the catering and restaurant industry (and many a person who cooks at home) has clasped tenaciously to its bosom, is a controversial device. Some love it, others despise it. Probably many of its detractors either misuse it or simply expect too much of it. Its greatest glory is in the role of heating things up quickly and efficiently, without mess. Some of the convenience foods expressly designed to be prepared in the microwave are of excellent quality, and a boon to anyone who gets home from work or play, dying for something hot to eat but too tired to cook.

That all-American favorite, the baked potato, is now sometimes cooked in the microwave, and some swear that if this was *all* the microwave did it would be worth having. Even so, a food pundit recently quizzed on the microwave's place in the scheme of things observed, "There's no reason why you shouldn't bake a potato in the microwave—as long as it goes into a hot regular oven for twenty minutes before serving . . ." Baked potatoes are not an item high on the list of foods caterers lay on—they are an example of the kind of food that takes up oven space, takes time to cook and requires the extra lap of butter, chives, sour cream, and other toppings. However, if baked potatoes with all the fixin's is the proclaimed fare, then the microwave can work very well.

Focusing on this one food item among thousands makes an important point. The caterer may not have access to the premises until an hour before the function is scheduled to begin. This could be the case if it were being held in private, busy home, or on normally commercial premises open for business until a certain hour and then swiftly taken over and made ready by caterers. How would you like to arrive at a party venue at 5 P.M. to set up for drinks and buffet for 50 people arriving at 6 P.M.—with the near certainty of some guests strolling in no later than 5:45—and have to set about preparing something like baked potatoes? A host obsessed by this sort of item might make laborious arrangements to have them prepared off premises and delivered, but it's still a pain in the neck.

What the caterer *really* needs is a repertoire of easily and quickly prepared tasty, and engaging dishes, however prepared.

## Hints for Caterers

Here are some miscellaneous tips that many a professional chef doesn't know.

- All meats benefit from slow cooking. Big birds such as turkeys sometimes require several hours of cooking and regular basting, so if you are serving something along these lines you must factor in the cooking time. Restaurant chefs have been known to drop ducks into the deep-fry and serve it as "Roast Duckling." Even if he wished to exercise it, which is unlikely as the result is dreadful, the caterer will not usually have this option available.
- "Hot" means piping hot, but not so hot as to burn the lips. A famous hamburger chain recently lost a case in which a customer was burned by coffee. It sounds tacky, but remember, you can always warm things up fast, if there's a complaint, by resorting to the microwave. Amazingly, even at expensive restaurants, where the food may have to be delivered from a basement kitchen along drafty corridors and up windy stairs, it's not uncommon for a diner to request that a dish be warmed up. Sometimes a microwave oven is installed for this precise purpose just inside the server's area. If you or one of your staff receives such a request, there's no need to die of embarrassment. Just warm the dish up. And smile.
- Cold, if we're talking food as opposed to cocktails or beer, means cold but not refrigerator cold. Just as white wine often tastes better a few minutes after it's taken from the refrigerator, cold foods benefit from warming up just a little—but not to the point where they start to wilt or sag, as many foods, particularly salad items, can and do.
- Hardboiled eggs will not acquire a black line (harmless but unsightly) around the yolks if they're cracked and allowed to cool in cold water until it's time to serve them.
- Creme fraiche. A simple recipe for this very popular and fashionable mixture—suitable for use in either sweet or savory dishes, is as follows. You need

a cup of heavy cream at room temperature and a tablespoon of yogurt or buttermilk, also at room temperature. Put the cream and yogurt (or buttermilk) in a screw-top jar. Cover the jar and shake it well. Store the jar in a warm place until the cream thickens. This could take four hours on a hot day or two or three days in winter. Once it's thickened, it will keep for two or three weeks in the refrigerator. For larger quantities, simply increase the amount of the ingredients and, of course, the size of the container.

- Tomatoes can be peeled easily if they are briefly immersed in boiling water.
- Raw onions should be an option, "on the side" where possible, and not automatically included in dishes, since many people won't eat them. They may like them, but don't wish to risk breathing joy on their companions. Cooked onions won't make your breath smell, but raw ones consumed in quantity will.
- The best remedy for "food breath" of any kind is to drink lots of water and gargle with antiseptic or mouthwash. Some advocate the chewing of parsley, especially after eating garlic, the smell of which emerges on the skin as well as on the breath, often disrupting the effect of highly expensive scent, perfume, or cologne.
- The worst bad breath comes from the stomach—hydrochloric acid with added odors can produce malodorous horror. Not eating, but downing a glass of white wine or two at the end of the working day will produce the breath from hell as the chemistry kicks in. A regular diet of garlic-laced coleslaw—eaten for breakfast by some—will result in the kind of breath that aboriginal trackers can detect easily from a distance of a mile, a facility put to good use by the American army in certain theatres of war. People on some weight-reducing diets are advised to drink lots of water—lots means a minimum of 8 pints a day—to avoid offending friends, family, colleagues, fellow-travelers, lovers, and corporate superiors.
- Roast potatoes and French fries will develop an engaging crispness if their surfaces are scraped with a serrated knife before cooking.
- Hungry party goers will be delighted by the production of such banal dishes as microwaved pizza and fresh pineapple. Often, especially where alcohol flows, the appetite strikes suddenly and wildly—just about anything is acceptable. The efficient caterer should know and be prepared for this.
- Perfect mashed potatoes can be made quite simply by the following method. Choose floury soft potatoes. Cut them into equal-size chunks to ensure they cook at the same rate in salted water, brought to the boil and then allowed to simmer. Rapid boiling cooks the surface faster than the interior. After draining, allow excess moisture to drain away. For the mashing process, a food mill or a potato masher is the best tool. Don't use a food processor as this makes the starch go out of control and results in gluey potatoes. Butter and milk should be preheated together before mixing, as cold milk will cool the starch, again producing a gluey effect. Salt and pepper can be added, as well as grated nutmeg. Experiment by adding anything from saffron to basil. When serving with fish you can add parsley, lemon zest, and fish stock.

# Chapter Fourteen

# Canapés

PROBABLY one of the most common functions you'll be required to organize is one where only cocktails and canapés are served. From this to the full-blown buffet lunch or dinner is but a step, of course, but often clients and hosts will feel that offering a decent selection of fairly substantial canapés is a sufficient gesture of hospitality. In the restaurant business, where canapes such as tiny pizzas or meat balls are sometimes offered free at the cocktail hour, there is often a small clique of customers who will provide themselves with their evening meal for the price of one drink—much to the ire of the owner.

If a sit-down luncheon or dinner is offered, you needn't offer elaborate canapés during the preprandial reception when drinks and cocktails are offered. Dishes of nuts, potato chips, olives, cocktail onions, and "nibbles" that come in packets are sufficient. There's unlikely to be a great demand, so it's only necessary to make a gesture, not the full production. Often, hosts don't offer any canapés at all at this stage.

You should be careful in your choice if you decide to use oven-ready canapés from a shop—things like shrimp already battered, floured, or dipped. Such items, indeed many of the ready-made meat and fish dishes that abound in the food industry, can be very hit-or-miss. They tend to have very little meat, and then only of the cheapest variety, but lots of batter or pastry. The list of ingredients on the label hardly makes for a "just like mom used to make" image, and they are heavily laced with preservative chemicals to ensure near-eternal shelf life. Several items on the market are really a joke—nobody will ever buy them twice, and one wonders what their marketing departments are up to, since brand loyalty is a fundamental aspect of selling any product.

Some purists find the whole concept of canapés rather tacky, taking the view that a bowl or two of peanuts—unsalted to obviate the necessity to smack the hands together and then rub them surreptitiously on the seat of the pants or a napkin to get rid of the sticky salt—is quite sufficient. But most people like a nibble with their drink. Apart from anything else, if some guests had a sparse lunch they may welcome some "blotting paper" to enable them to enjoy their cocktails more. In this chapter we will look at some ideas for tidbits to serve with cocktails.

## Tapas

In Spain a great fuss is made of small dishes that accompany drinks, called *tapas*. These can range from *Gambas al Ajillo* (shrimps cooked in individual little dishes with oil and garlic) to *Rinones a la Jerez* (kidneys, again in individual little dishes, cooked in sherry, with garlic), to cubes of cheese. Many American cities now feature tapas restaurants that offer nothing else, and some do very well. Eyebrows are sometimes raised when the bill for a few drinks and nibbles is received. Those low prices soon mount up when you're having a selection of foods.

## Caviar

Caviar is the ultimate thing to serve on these occasions with or without hot blinies, which can be bought frozen and prepared in the oven. Sour cream and chopped onions are further options. Beluga and Sevruga are the greatest caviars, the Iranian kind from the Caspian Sea being difficult to find these days.

Caviar is the eggs, or roe, of the sturgeon, a fish without scales (which means certain religions forbid its consumption) that can reach 17 feet in length and weigh more than a thousand pounds. It inhabits the Black Sea off Russia and the inland Caspian Sea, which are now severely over-fished. This has led to a huge price increase, making caviar without doubt a super-luxury item. It was never exactly cheap, but was usually an affordable occasional treat. For a time it was available on the black market in Russia, and people on Baltic cruises often bought it in large quantities to bring back to America.

It is unlikely that you'll be required to supply caviar often. Sturgeon are now being farmed, but this is in the early stages, and if caviar from this source proves feasible, it's still six years down the line. As we regularly read, fish farming is not without its problems. A much cheaper version of caviar is red or black lumpfish. Caterers and consumers will have to make up their own minds about this food item. It is very salty and heavily dyed to red or black. A grain or three on other canapés is decorative and will not offend.

A happy compromise exists in America in the shape of the reddish colored eggs of the American salmon. This caviar is of excellent quality and affordable.

An eight-ounce jar will produce at least 30 canapés in the shape of teaspoonfuls of caviar simply placed on small crackers. A lemon wedge will add zest.

Oddly, not everyone likes caviar, which is in a way a godsend as not everyone will make a dive for it at a party. An army caterer in the Middle East years ago discovered that the local caviar was cheap and bought some to put on the soldiers' menu. As he strolled around the mess hall, beaming with triumph and awaiting praise, one of the soldiers said he had a complaint. "Excuse me, sir, but the blackberry jam tastes of fish."

A passenger traveling first-class on an international flight was offered an unexpected bonus when the cabin crew opened a large jar of Beluga and offered it around. There were only six first-class passengers, and five of them declined. Toward the end of the flight, the cabin attendant offered the jar, which was still nearly full, to the caviar loving passenger. Regulations required it to be either consumed or thrown out. The crew weren't allowed to take food home, and none of them liked caviar, anyway. "One man's meat . . ." Caviar lovers should not get worked up as they contemplate the amount of caviar that may be getting thrown away on the airlines of the world .

Caviar is best simply spread on crackers. A little cream cheese can be spread first if desired. Don't overload the crackers or they may become unwieldy (but don't be too mean, either). The object of all canapés is to be easily popped into the mouth and swiftly consumed.

In a rich house the Beluga may be left in the pot and guests invited to serve themselves on little plates with traditional horn spoons.

# Shrimp

Shrimp is probably the favorite all-purpose canapé. Some hosts simply provide a large quantity of shrimp in a bowl, napkins, small plates, and seafood sauce (ketchup, salt, pepper, and horseradish is a standard mix). Shrimp can be bought frozen, of course, but it's best to check and experiment since if you get the wrong kind they will taste of nothing but wool.

A more ambitious alternative is to dip the shrimps in a batter of flour, water, and egg, cook them in boiling oil, and serve them with toothpicks. At some elaborate parties, a curry sauce is laid on. A waiter (perhaps in a turban) takes around the plate of hot shrimp, straight from the kitchen, and is followed by another waiter who carries the hot curry dip. Then follows another waiter with a pile of napkins on a tray.

To make shrimp go a little further you can spice them up and spread them on crackers. You'll need:

8 ounces shrimp, chopped

10 stuffed olives (from a can)

1 bunch scallions, finely chopped

2 ounces flaked, toasted almonds

juice of half a lemon

1 tablespoon olive oil

1 tablespoon tomato puree

Dash Worcestershire sauce

salt and pepper

Mix all the ingredients well in a bowl, and chill. This makes about 12 ounces.

# Angels (or Devils) on Horseback

This concept covers a multitude of canapé ideas, and the title is accorded to several small, savory dishes. Here we are talking about strips of bacon wrapped around various tasty morsels.

You can wrap bacon around prunes, oysters, or pieces of chicken liver. Other inspirations may come to you. Having wrapped up the canapés and secured them with cocktail sticks, as toothpicks are sometimes more politely called, you can either grill them or bake them in the oven.

# Bacon and Tomato Canapés

Tasty and easy to prepare, bacon and tomato canapés are always popular. You'll need:

4 small tomatoes

4 strips bacon

salt

paprika

1 tablespoon brown sugar

4 slices buttered toast

Peel and slice the tomatoes. Lay the slices on the buttered toast, and cover with the bacon. Season with salt, paprika and brown sugar, and cook under a hot broiler until the bacon is crisp.

This is a good example of a dish you can prepare in quite large quantities—in a sort of production line almost. You can have several trays (stacked up and

put one in the oven every few minutes, since they take very little time to cook).
Fresh-from-the-oven dishes are always zesty.

## Sardines

Sardines can be used in various delicious ways. If you thoroughly mix 1 small can
of skinned and boneless sardines with:

½ teaspoon Worcestershire sauce
½ teaspoon tomato ketchup
1 tablespoon chopped onion
4 green olives, stoned and chopped
1 tablespoon French Dressing
paprika
salt

you will have a basic sort of pâté that you can spread on crackers or on small slices
of bread. You could grill it, too. This is an amusing area in which to experiment.

## Chicken Liver Pâté

This pâté can be served on crackers, in small cocktail tartlets, or stuffed in small
button mushrooms. You'll need:

12 ounces butter
2 small onions, finely chopped
1 pound chicken livers
2 tablespoons brandy, Southern Comfort, or sherry
5–6 drops Tabasco
½ teaspoon dried thyme
salt and pepper

Melt 4 ounces of the butter and fry the onions in it for 2–3 minutes. Add the
chicken livers and cook for 3–4 minutes, stirring all the time. Add the remaining
butter and the other ingredients. Stir until the butter melts. Chop the mixture in
a food processor, or puree it in a blender. Leave it to cool, then spread it on crackers or small pieces of bread. You can decorate it with parsley or perhaps put some

cherry tomatoes alongside. These quantities will produce about 1½ pounds, comfortable enough for about 40 people.

# Guacamole

This dip is a great American favorite. You can serve it with nachos or with vegetable slices such as cauliflower or celery. You'll need:

2 tablespoons lemon juice

2 ripe tomatoes, finely chopped

2 tablespoonfuls finely chopped onion

Salt and pepper

2 ripe avocados

Mix all the ingredients except the avocados—chill them until required. Mash the avocado flesh with a fork, or puree in a blender, and stir into the tomato and onion mixture. This will provide about 12 ounces. If you need more, simply increase the ingredients accordingly.

# Cocktail Kebabs on Sticks

The sticks here are really toothpicks. Here are some combinations to try:

| | |
|---|---|
| Sliced cocktail frankfurters | Salami cubes |
| Cubed pineapple | Cocktail gherkins |
| Smoked cheese or cheddar cheese cubes | Diced pears |
| Cocktail onions | Smoked ham cubes |
| Diced apples | Canned peach cubes |
| Halved strawberries | Diced cucumber |
| Brie cubes | Halved cherry tomatoes |
| Button mushrooms | Smoked turkey cubes |
| Chunks of baby corn | Diced kiwi |

Remember to supply places where people can discard their cocktail sticks, and lots of napkins. If these are not provided, guests may be reluctant to indulge for fear of making a mess.

Also, tidy and clear automatically as you go—as all your staff should—in order not to allow debris to accumulate.

Now for a hot, favorite canapé on a stick.

# Spicy Meatballs

These meatballs make delicious *bonne bouches*, served on a stick. They can be presented on a bed of watercress or alfalfa sprouts, with a small bowl of mustard or ketchup alongside as a dip. You'll need:

8 tablespoons cooking oil

3 teaspoons ground cumin

2 tablespoons curry

3 cloves crushed garlic

1 onion, finely chopped

2 tablespoons grated fresh ginger

1½ pounds minced beef or lamb

salt and pepper

Fry the spices in 5 tablespoons of cooking oil with the garlic, onion, and ginger for 2–3 minutes. Place the meat in a bowl and add the fried spices and vegetables. Mix everything together and shape and press into 50 small balls. Fry the balls in the remaining oil for about 7 minutes in batches of 15–20. Keep them on the move while they're frying, so they don't stick. When they're thoroughly cooked, keep them warm and serve with ketchup. This recipe provides enough for about 50 people.

Simple slices of various cheeses and fruit such as apples or pineapples will bolster your selection. Sausages on a stick are usually popular, especially if accompanied by fresh mustard or some other kind of dip. Microwaved pizzas cut into small portions are also a favorite.

# Fifteen

# Food Safety, Hygiene, and Health

## Food Poisoning

When a food poisoning incident occurs at a catered affair (and, sadly, it does regularly) the word-of-mouth effect can be widespread and devastating to the caterer's reputation. Often it isn't just one person who becomes sick but several—the whole office, the whole family, the whole club. People may compare notes and discover that they all ate or drank the same thing.

Poisoning your clients is hardly the best way to promote business, and it is easily avoided. You may find yourself being sued, and court annals are full of cases successfully brought against caterers and restaurants. The late Yul Brynner successfully sued a famous New York restaurant that had poisoned him and his family with spare ribs. A woman who was bitten by a rat enmeshed in a glue trap, which the exterminator had thoughtlessly failed to remove from beneath a restaurant table, enjoyed similar success. The law often displays a peculiar wrath towards those who betray public trust—and who can argue the wisdom of this?

In some states, if you register as a business you, or at least one employee, will be required to attend a hygiene course and obtain a certificate, as in the restaurant industry. This ensures that at least someone knows how food and drink should be handled to protect people from poisoning. The laws in this area are strict but entirely reasonable. Inspectors are trained to concentrate on health threatening infringements, and will usually not split hairs unless tempted to look for trouble, perhaps goaded by an uncooperative attitude.

# How to Avoid Food Poisoning

## Cleanliness

Basic personal cleanliness and ordinary good housekeeping are the commonsense factors that protect most of us from each other. It's a century or more since Doctor Lister insisted that hospital doctors should start washing their hands after examining a patient and before examining another. Undoubtedly, millions of lives have been saved by this now common discipline. The recent discovery that coughs, colds, and flu are spread more by hand contact than by other people's coughs and sneezes has encouraged many people to wash their hands regularly throughout the day but particularly after any kind of public contact such as a ride on a bus or subway.

The most common form of food poisoning, Salmonella, is often transmitted by urine from people's unwashed hands. Now you know the reason for the sign hung, by law, in restaurant bathrooms—"Staff must wash hands before leaving this room." As to whether all employees can read and understand this instruction is, of course, a moot point.

Correct washing of dishes and utensils is important, too. Useful though dishwashing machines undoubtedly are, they cannot be entirely trusted. They often won't remove lipstick from cups and glasses, for instance. A visual check of all items displayed at any function is essential. The client or host will always get the glass with the lipstick if you don't eliminate it from the proceedings, and possibly wonder how many guests have been similarly blessed.

Dishes and glasses that have been handwashed must also be rinsed—a small fact of life that escapes an extraordinary number of people. Though the soapy residue may not be visible, it may impart an exotic, but on the whole unwelcome, flavor to the food placed on the plate. As for unrinsed glasses—they can ruin a glass of wine, and beer poured into such a glass will flatten instantly.

Remember, one bacterium can multiply into a million in less than seven hours. Viewed through a powerful microscope, a swab taken from a dishcloth or bar mop, after only a short period of use, is alarming. The germs swarm busily about. In general, dishes which are washed, rinsed and left to dry in the air will be cleanest and safest.

However, there is sometimes a need to polish both glassware and silverware. When this has been done, the dishes, utensils, and glassware should be washed again. The shine will not be dimmed if they are finally rinsed in very hot, then cold, water, and allowed to drain dry.

## Proper Food Handling and Storage

A favorite scapegoat for outbreaks of poisoning is mayonnaise. Especially when left out in the sun, it will start to break down into its various ingredients as soon as it leaves the refrigerator and will breed offensive bacteria. There are those who staunchly defend mayonnaise in this respect, but any food long exposed to warmth and the elements is hardly an appetizing prospect. Apart from anything else, insects may visit and deposit eggs or germs. Smell and taste are one's best protection, of course, and the old adage "When in doubt throw it out" is a sound one.

Overzealous promptness of preparation is sometimes a problem. While it's always a good idea to be set up for a function in good time (bearing in mind the penchant so many guests have for arriving early), exposing food too soon can be disastrous. A recent investigation into a mass poisoning in which, fortunately, no one died but several were quite sick, revealed that a quiche had been exposed for eight hours before being consumed—a recipe for disaster.

Some caterers are particularly unscrupulous in the area of health and hygiene. One caterer at a smart fashion show discovered to his horror that a large container of Chicken a la King had gone bad probably as a result of incorrect refrigeration or the unnoticed breakdown thereof. A scum had formed on the top of the food and it smelled horrible. Jettisoning this dish would have left the caterer seriously short of food to feed the guests, but the wily French cook knew how to deal with it. "Add bicarbonate of soda and bring it swiftly to the boil" he advised. This was done.

The dish was served—and pronounced delicious. Although this may strike some as a rather hardnosed decision, it should be noted that by boiling the food, any danger of infection was removed—credit where credit's due. However, no responsible caterer would dream of taking such an action.

Very few caterers or restaurateurs will deliberately serve food that they know to be of dubious quality, though many will. However, the majority of food poisonings are simply accidents. Most people will have been poisoned, or at least will have suffered an upset stomach, on some occasion in their lives.

It's more common to be poisoned away from home. Unfortunately, some workers will not bring the same standards of consideration to bear when they're servicing the anonymous public as they would when at home, feeding their family. It's interesting to note the comparative rareness of food poisoning outbreaks in intensive and large scale areas such as hospitals and the armed services. The explanation is obvious—lots of training and strict supervision and authority.

If one is abroad, the simple explanation may be attack from new and different organisms that can penetrate the immune system. We all know that in foreign climes bottled drinks are supposed to be safer than tap water, but suppose the ice is made from the local tap water? A story is told of the traveler in Africa who came across a man filling bottles from a well. "These crazy tourists . . . " he said, shaking his head in wonderment, "They won't drink water unless it's served in these little green bottles . . . " Incorrect storage accounts for a large number of food poisoning cases. Refrigerated space is often in short supply, and in hot weather there is clearly more demand for it.

Cooked food should never be stored alongside or underneath raw or uncooked food. This particularly applies to the positioning of cooked and uncooked meats. Ideally, everything will be individually wrapped, cooked foods at the top, the raw below, in order to prevent cross-contamination.

In general, food should be served either piping hot or quite cold. It is the middle temperatures that create the most dangerous climate for the breeding of dangerous bacteria, which puts dishes like the recently fashionable Salade de Canard Tiede (a tepid salad of medium rare duck breasts and vegetables) rather in the shade, but there we are. Many gourmets are happy to take a chance with certain dishes, if they have confidence in the cook.

A well-know culprit in this unappetizing area is the sausage or hotdog. Sausages are sometimes cooked but not eaten right away. If they are at some point eaten cold, this is usually safe, but if they are reheated, then they must be thoroughly heated, or they may make someone quite ill. Indeed, the cooking process is what protects society from regular epidemics of food poisoning.

**Refrigeration**    A lurking danger in food storage is refrigeration that "goes down," or is accidentally switched off unbeknownst to the cook or caterer. Food may be stored correctly in a refrigerator then during the night, perhaps as a result of a power failure or the sort of temperamental breakdown that old equipment sometimes suffers, the refrigerator becomes warm. Next morning, power having been restored, nothing seems to be amiss but the damage has been done.

An experienced food-handler will cast a suspicious eye on the refrigerator's contents for signs of warming. In restaurants one has to be particularly alert to this danger. To a small operator the prospect of losing several hundred dollars worth of frozen shrimp and steak is daunting.

Despite the horror stories involving cockroaches and vermin, the usual culprit in food poisoning cases is carelessness. Food handlers sometimes work under great pressure. The amount of prep work to be done in restaurants and before catered events is enormous, and it's difficult for some to avoid the temptation to cut a few corners. Incorrectly washed salad items can be dangerous because of lurking amounts of soil. Staphylacoccus love anything creamy and warm.

Although home is generally safer than elsewhere, the popularity of the barbecue has added a number of risks. Food is exposed to the elements, especially the hot sun. The same utensils used to put raw meat on the grill may be used to remove the cooked. Not uncommonly, meat quite burned on the outside will not be thoroughly cooked on the inside.

Also, new bugs are coming along all the time. *Campylobacter*, for instance, didn't figure in the statistics 15 years ago, but is now high on the list of public enemies. A recent scare was *Salmonella* in chickens. This severe form of poisoning can be deadly to the elderly, young, or infirm.

# Monosodium Glutamate Reaction

A "fashionable" form of food poisoning these days is so-called reaction to monosodium glutemate. About .3 percent of the population may be genuinely allergic to this chemical which is widely used in cooking. Chinese restaurants lean heavily on its flavor enhancing qualities, which is why some strenuously and stridently insist that they don't use it at all. A brand-name product Accent, is the most well-known form of MSG and is by no means disdained by even the most refined chefs. Indeed, it's a standard item.

Unlike salt, which has an effect on the taste buds and the way they perceive food, MSG actually changes the flavor of foods. Clearly it is attractive to people on a low-sodium diet. The main reason for its occasional unpleasant effects seems to be that it is widely used in soup.

There is nothing quite like a bowl of soup on a cold day when one is hungry. But if one drinks soup on an empty stomach, all the chemicals in it, including the MSG, will be swiftly absorbed through the stomach wall. The effect can be compared with the results of drinking a refreshing Gin and Tonic on returning from a long run or a game of squash—don't try it, it will go straight to your head.

This is the whole attraction of a quick "food fix" of course. But if there is any degree of allergy to MSG, the drinker may feel distinctly queasy. Used judiciously and sparingly, there should never be problems with this useful additive.

## Botulism

This cheerful section would not be complete without a reference to botulism, which is produced by the organism *Clostridium Botulinus*, a charmer that grows without oxygen at low temperatures and is resistant to boiling and canning. Chemical warfare experts have long embraced its possibilities. It has killed a few Americans in recent years.

Food from a seriously dented can is never safe because it may harbor the botulism toxin. Any cans that show signs of rust that cannot easily be brushed off, or that bulge or are swollen, or have missing labels, or are out of date, should be discarded. Safe cans may be stored for years before distribution. In test cases, food from cans 80 years old and more have been shown to be edible. Indeed, old sardines are much prized by connoisseurs. The caterer isn't trying to defend food industry practices. The general idea is to feed customers safely and satisfactorily. If a can has a bulge, it means that fermentation has occurred and that the contents are under pressure.

# Illness Is Not Drunkenness

There are few events more embarrassing than being taken ill, perhaps through taking a wrong dosage of prescribed medication or forgetting to take it. In addition to enduring pain and discomfort, you somehow have to get across the message that alcohol isn't the problem. In such cases the police are sometimes unsympathetic. They've heard it all before. When the paramedics arrive, the picture usually clarifies. They've seen it all before, too, but they tend to keep a more open mind. The wisdom of this is clear, given the numbers of casualties seemingly dead at the scene but dramatically resuscitated by diligent paramedics.

# Food Safety Rules to Remember:

You would do well to memorize the following safety rules for the safety of your clients and their guests and the health of your business.

- Get into the habit of checking the refrigerator thermometer. The freezer compartment should never be higher than 0° F., and the main compartment should never be above 40° F.
- When shopping for high-risk items such as raw meat and poultry, take along a cool bag—the ones made of double plastic with snap fasteners—possibly containing small freezer blocks taken from your own deep freeze, and refrigerate the food as soon as possible.
- Make sure that egg dishes, pork, and chicken are well cooked. Follow use-by dates rigidly.
- Store and prepare raw and cooked food separately.
- No matter how eager you are to get set up, don't display foods too soon. Too-soon displayed salads soon go limp and soggy and can be dangerous.

Just for reference, here's a list of the seven most infamous bugs and the places where they love to lurk.

- *Salmonella*: meat and poultry left in warm, moist conditions and then not cooked properly, raw eggs used in mayonnaise, mousse, and homemade ice cream.
- *Campylobacter*: poultry; unpasteurized milk.
- *Listeria*: chilled, processed food stored warm, then not thoroughly heated; soft cheese and pâté left in warm, moist conditions; chicken insufficiently cooked; salads prepared carelessly and exposed to the risk of cross-contamination.
- *Bacillus cereus*: cooked rice. Rice should be cooked, cooled quickly, and refrigerated.
- *Clostridium perfringens*: meat dishes. The bacteria can multiply in slow cooking, warming up, or long cooling periods. It's particularly fond of gravies, cooked meat dishes, stews, and pies. Poorly washed salad and vegetables may carry tiny soil particles.
- *Clostridium Botulinus*: from damaged cans.
- *Staphylococcus aureus*: any food, but particularly that handled by humans.
- *E Coli*: meat, particularly minced beef. Proper cooking eliminates the risk.

The good news is that typhoid is no longer the danger it was in the days when an itinerant dishwasher called Typhoid Mary caused several epidemics before being discovered.

# Choking

Poisoning isn't the only risk that attends people and food. Choking can kill people, too. The "worst case scenario" in this area is the person who has had a bit too much to drink and then, perhaps careless or overcome by hunger, bites off too much steak. (It's almost invariably an unchewable mouthful of steak or, occasionally, a fish bone.) Seconds later they're choking, excusing themselves, blue in the face, and clearly in danger of dying.

Once it becomes clear that someone is in serious trouble, one thing which may save the situation is the Heimlich Maneuver, which you and your staff would do well to learn how to perform properly. Pretty it ain't, but lives have been saved this way.

Much publicity was given to a recent incident in which a man attending a formal dinner suddenly excused himself politely and left the table. A woman diner sensed something was wrong and asked someone to go to the men's room to see if everything was all right. The man was found in great distress, politely choking to death. A very lucky man, he was saved by the Heimlich Maneuver. In some states the law requires instruction in this technique to be prominently posted in restaurants. A graphic poster with precise instructions is supplied, and it shouldn't be hard for a caterer to obtain one for reference and to show assistants.

# Other Medical Crises

There are other casualties of overindulgence. When somebody collapses, however, there's no time for sermons. Accidents happen. Irresponsible people play games with alcohol such as spiking other people's drinks. Youngsters, carried away with the excitement of their first grown up party, may accidentally overindulge.

Causes and reasons are irrelevant against the immediate necessity of saving a life. Collapse or other medical indicents may, after all, have nothing to do with the social occasion or alcohol. They might have happened anyway, anywhere. It should never be assumed because someone collapses at a function where alcohol is being served, that they've simply had too much to drink. Although this is clearly a possibility, it's important to keep an open mind. People sometimes collapse because of poor ventilation, for instance. All they need is air.

The caterer, sober, responsible, and detached, can save such situations. People will often look to a caterer, or a staff member, as a sort of authority figure to whom they turn when in difficulty whether it's the small matter of finding out where the bathroom is or taking charge when someone becomes taken ill.

If someone collapses, possibly having consumed too much alcohol, or overcome by hot air from one source or another, the single most important thing is to ensure that they can breathe properly. Undo tie, shirt, blouse, whatever, and make sure the head is higher than the chest. Modesty must take a back seat on these occasions—belts, bras, and corsetry must be removed immediately if they constrain circulation or breathing. The danger of swallowing false teeth or tongue must be averted. Since when was there any dignity in sickness?

Unsupervised victims of alcohol often "drown" by choking on their own vomit after they've become unconscious. It's sometimes more technical than that. There's acid in vomit, and when this hits a victim's lungs, a crucial spasm can occur that causes more or less instant death.

# Guests Who Overindulge

If a guest at a function becomes the worse for wear as the result of drinking too much, he (or she) must be restrained, or at least controlled, to protect others and himself. If he (or she) straightens up enough to be allowed to go home, he shouldn't be allowed to drive or to leave unaccompanied.

## The Dangers to Servers

Alcohol servers have been successfully sued after traffic accidents. This is a change in the law's general attitude, which had traditionally been that no one is forced to drink alcohol. It clearly hinges on the fact that, in law, drink may be refused if a server feels there is good reason. As to how much account lawyers will take of a scenario in which a young bartender is confronted by a group of older and possibly menacing would-be drinkers is a matter for our courts. Further, a question that would tax the wisdom of Solomon, and certainly any court, is did the drinker imbibe elsewhere, before or after taking drink from the accused server?

Regular bartenders soon learn that the quiet new arrival who politely orders a drink may suddenly erupt into a noisy, violent person as a result of the latest cocktail being added to previous drinks. Who can ever tell which drink will escalate the consumer to a state of drunkenness?

## The Dangers to the Guest

A further danger to unsupervised drunks is that they may be attacked and mugged. Criminals will target and observe bars, restaurants, and party venues in the hope of spying someone staggering home, whom they'll follow in order to attack and rob. By the way, you don't have to be absolutely "sloshed" in order to incur this risk. Just being relaxed, less aware than usual, savoring the witty remark that has just sprung to mind but that you failed to make at the propitious moment, or being engrossed in conversation with a companion, may invite criminal interest. Leisurely strolling, especially at night, is now a forgotten luxury in some cities.

## Curing, and Avoiding, Hangovers

Strong black coffee will help drunks sober up, but not much, and not very quickly. Time is the great remedy—the liver takes an hour to excrete one ounce of alcohol. The best hangover remedy is plenty of water, aspirin, and fresh air.

**Hair of the Dog**   The notion of "a hair of the dog" is a sound one. One traditional theory is that. . . when too much alcohol is consumed, the liver goes into overdrive, producing enzymes to help the overloaded digestive process. Even when the alcohol has been excreted, this imbalance will remain for a while and the discomfiture it causes is part of the hangover effect. Therefore, a small intake of alcohol, such as a beer, a beer mixed with tomato juice, a glass of sherry, or various concoctions and cocktails such as the Prairie Oyster (there are many versions but it's basically vodka, tomato juice, an egg, and lots of hot spices), may actually make the patient feel better.

**Clean Drinks**   The cleaner the drink, the less likely is it to cause a hangover. "Clean" in this context means containing fewer congeners, or chemicals other than water and alcohol. Thus, the cleanest drink of all is vodka, followed by gin, Scotch, and so on down the line through wine to dubious Pastis. Many think that, because of its appearance, white wine must be a "clean" drink. But since white wine became the single most-consumed alcoholic beverage after beer, many a drinker has found himself nursing a headache that, considering the small amount of white wine consumed, seems thoroughly undeserved. Despite its innocent looks, white wine is loaded with chemicals, including sulphites, a fact which, by law, must now be stated on the label.

Some drinks simply don't agree with some people. Red wine is a notorious example. It may taste wonderful, but its effect isn't worth the candle. However, the crucial hangover-creating factor is almost invariably the quantity of alcohol consumed, not the type.

**No Alcohol**   Of course, the best way to cure a hangover is never to have one. By avoiding drinking on an empty stomach (even to the extent of drinking milk or olive oil before imbibing alcohol), by drinking plenty of water, by making it a rule never to drink alcohol to quench thirst (one should have a glass of water before a cocktail), and simply not drinking too much, the threat can be easily averted.

# Safety for Caterers

The health dangers to the busy caterer are mundane and easily dealt with. At peak holiday time, when it may not be unusual to work for ten days straight, obviously fatigue will be an accumulating problem.

## Keep Fit

You need to be reasonably fit to perform in this business, so it's unlikely that you have any threateningly bad habits. However, some people under pressure fall into the trap of deriving false energy, or a second wind, from alcohol or coffee. Many of us need a cup or two of coffee to get going, and a small drink may pep us up. But these stimulants must be strictly rationed; otherwise, an unhealthy dependence starts to build up.

If overindulgence creeps up—as it can over months and years—normally healthy people will start drinking coffee nonstop, and often get withdrawal symptom headaches if their supply is threatened or if someone gives them decaffeinated coffee by mistake.

A well-known figure in the hospitality industries is the person who takes a sip of wine every ten minutes throughout the working shift in order to maintain a gentle buzz at all times. This is bad for the health and also irresponsible. A caterer is supposed to be in charge of an event.

## Wear Sensible Shoes

On a more mundane level, a lot of standing is involved in catering, as well as walking, sometimes on quite hard surfaces. In order to avoid varicose veins, hemorrhoids, backache, sore feet and other medical delights, it's important to wear sensible shoes. Fortunately, they don't need to be too orthopedic-looking these days, and they are certainly at least as attractive as current sneaker styles. Gel insert soles and elastic support stockings should not be disdained either. If you think this fuddy-duddy or just plain *old*, remember, no one can see these comforting items, and they make a huge difference. Unglamorous they may be, but what's so cool about hemorrhoids?

Another tip for avoiding the perils of standing for long periods—behind a bar, in a kitchen, or when everything's been served at a table and you have nothing to do for several minutes but must be on hand—is to discreetly raise one foot and support it on something a few inches off the ground.

## Watch the Lifting

Occasionally some moderately heavy lifting will be required. Bags of ice, food containers, and cases of wine or liquor can be quite heavy. It's important to establish strict disciplines. Know how to lift propertly—with your legs, not your back—and always seek assistance if it looks like more than a one-person load. Try not to be in a tearing hurry so that you can enjoy the luxury of making more trips with lighter loads. Never be afraid to make two journeys, or of being thought a sissy because you can only carry one crate of beer at a time.

Remember, back incidents are often the result of cumulative effect. The seeds of the pain that puts you in bed or on the chiropractor's table may have been sown months before, especially if there is some repetitive heavy task that you've gotten into the habit of performing. Even sitting in a draft can trigger back problems.

If you know in advance that there's lifting to be done, it's not a bad idea to invest in a support belt such as beer delivery people always wear. But only wear it for a specific purpose, not as a regular item, or you may build a muscular dependency that will throw your body out of kilter.

The secret of avoiding back problems is eternal vigilance and good habits. Almost everyone who ever has such problems will be instantly converted to good habits, but membership in the Bad Back Club is to be strenuously resisted. Once you've had an incident, you'll be back-aware for the rest of your life. Even young and very fit people are not immune to these problems because it's more a question of mechanics than physical condition and health. Maintaining good stomach muscle tone affords some protection.

## Consider Health Insurance

If you get to the stage where you're working regularly and have put together a more or less steady crew—even if they're all part-timers, as is likely—you might give some thought to setting up a health or dental plan. Sometimes insurance companies will accept a fairly informal grouping of people in their plans.

# Final Words

H AVING discussed the grand scope of catering, it is time to review what it's all about.

## Starting Out

Clearly the scope and extent of operations is limitless. You could already be working in one of the hospitality industries such as hotel, restaurant, or catering. In this case, you may wish to supplement your income by occasionally catering for parties of various sizes. Experience shows that these will most often be for no more than a hundred guests, and more likely for about fifty, and that cocktails and canapés, perhaps expanding to a buffet, will be the usual scope. At the top end of this scale you'll need up to three assistants. Your general experience will enable you to cope with stress, and as you begin to feel your strength, you may well become more ambitious.

## Defining Your Strengths

If cooking is your forte, you may wish to limit yourself to going to people's houses to cook for them. Many a host with a pleasant apartment or house, particularly if it boasts a nice dining room, will want to utilize the assets of, yet not wish to employ, a cook.

"Why wouldn't they just go to a restaurant?" some may ask. The answer, believe it or not, is that a lot of people don't like restaurants. Unlike restaurant buffs, they actually resent the imposed theater and ritual and having to share space with people who may be noisy or unattractive to look at. They consider restaurants remarkably poor value. You could feed six people lobster and champagne, by paying a cook perhaps as little as $60. That may be far less than they would pay taxiing across town to the delights of Coup de Fusil, as one New York restaurant used to be called (it's French for "rip-off").

If bar work is your main strength, you can upgrade yourself by filling the role of butler at the same time. Without being too gimmicky or so characterful that you look like a sort of cabaret turn, detracting from the purpose of the occasion or the charms of the host, it's a good idea to demonstrate a pleasant, capable personality that fills clients with confidence that they're in good hands.

## Drumming up Business

As regards obtaining business, the methods are simple and tried and true:

- *Word of mouth.* Tell the world you're a caterer, and spread your business cards and flyers everywhere.
- *Advertising.* Place small advertisements in the local press. Some newspapers have a special section for such ads, but don't feel that yours will be lost among the others. Think positive—potential customers want to know where to look. Try to develop an advertisement that is punchy but not too cute—for example, "Why not relax and enjoy your own party for a change? Suzie and her experienced staff take the effort out of entertaining."
- *The direct approach.* Approach stores and companies directly—in person so that they can see what you look like. Leave a card and a flyer or two.
- *Selling yourself.* Talk to other, bigger caterers. Not just a couple, but every one in town. They may well call you in from time to time. Once you've proved yourself reliable, you may be agreeably surprised by the frequency of calls. Many a dedicated worker is so well connected that he or she can put together enough work to make it a full-time job and even turn down work at busy seasons.

In the catering business, almost everyone starts small. It is a major joy of the service industry that you don't have to take out huge loans, borrow from friends and family, or risk your life savings to put the show on the road. Your service is the product, and that's what you sell.

## What Sort of Person Will Succeed in Catering?

Cheerful people who ooze competence and know-how will succeed. Good looks don't hurt, but are not essential. They can even be a negative if a client fears that the catering crew will attract too much attention and perhaps detract from the function's focus. Conservative dress is important—make sure that white shirt or blouse is aggressively, sparkling white and well ironed, not just able to pass muster.

## A Success Story

A California woman was originally a successful accountant. She made a good living, but felt her work lacked emotional reward and became restless.

Cooking was her absolute passion. One Christmas she decided to create a gift of a small gourmet food item and settled on baked apple breads, each one of which she stuck to an apple-shaped wooden cutting board. It caught people's imagination because it was a little different and inexpensive.

For a while she operated from home with a full-time assistant. Then she rented a larger kitchen facility with an office. The business simply grew and grew, such was her diligence and application. "Quality and consistency" were her watchwords, and she is proud of the large number of repeat clients she's amassed. None of her philosophy is particularly arcane or obscure. "Good business sense is as important as creativity and quality," she says, adding that "good organization is essential."

Her single most important marketing tool is personal referral, which apparently, although clearly no guarantee of a perfect party, people have more confidence in than in the Yellow Pages.

This is not to suggest that a caterer should disdain the Yellow Pages by any means. People who are not blessed with personal references regarding caterers will have to start somewhere. Besides, if you're in a service industry, you should be there—there's no point in waiting for the world to seek you out and beat a path to your door.

## God Is in the Details

Successful caterers don't ignore what some may find the "boring bits" of putting a business together. You should obtain a license from whoever dishes them out in your area—the Board of Health is the most common authority. Once in a while, especially if you're being hired by, say, a school, the clients may ask to see a license to cover themselves against liability. Also, if you find yourself employing people, even on an occasional part-time basis, you should check out the insurance situation. It may well be that accidents to persons or properties are simply covered by the insurance on the premises at which you perform, which would seem reasonable, but it's as well to be informed. In some states there is a thing called a sales tax deferral, or seller's permit, which will enable you to buy certain items free of sales tax as a member of the trade.

Finally, the fewer headaches a client has, the greater the likelihood of repeat business. And, on a mundane note, if the premises are left cleaner than they were before the caterers arrived, this may be just about the best referral imaginable.

# Index